MW01626252

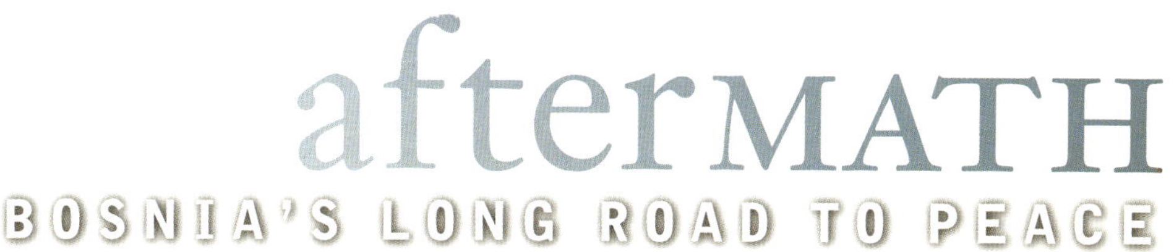

afterMATH

BOSNIA'S LONG ROAD TO PEACE

SARA TERRY

afterword by Lawrence Weschler

CHANNEL PHOTOGRAPHICS NEW YORK

The first edition of
Aftermath: Bosnia's Long Road to Peace
is published by

CHANNEL PHOTOGRAPHICS
116 EAST 16TH STREET, 12TH FLOOR
NEW YORK, NY 10003
P: 212-254-5240
F: 212-254-5246
E: info@channelphotographics.com
W: www.channelphotographics.com

Distributed by SCB DISTRIBUTORS
15608 South New Century Drive
Gardena, CA 90248
P: 310-532-9400
F: 310-532-7001

Book Design by Annette Prapasiri and Linda Johnson, Swell Design, Santa Fe, New Mexico

Printed in China by Global PSD

First edition 2005

ISBN: 0-9744029-6-6

My thanks go to my friend, the poet Richard Hoffman,

for his poem “Bosnia Aftermath.”

I borrow his words to dedicate this book

to all those individuals whose hearts persuade them

“that no one who has known goodness even once is ever wholly lost.”

sadržaj
TABLE OF CONTENTS

predgovor
FOREWORD

> SARA TERRY

I should say, from the beginning, that I never flew into Sarajevo on a military cargo plane, listening anxiously for the sound of artillery fire. I never saw anyone killed in the infamous Sniper Alley that was a death trap during the three-and-a-half-year siege of Sarajevo by Serb forces. I never had a gun pointed in my face. I never feared for my life; I never interviewed a man who would die the next day, a woman who had been gang-raped, a parent who had just buried a child, or a family that had fled the blood-soaked soil of a village burned to the ground in the name of "ethnic cleansing."

No, for me, the 1992-1995 war in Bosnia and Hercegovina was something that happened far off, in a place I'd never been. It was something I ignored when the news was too depressing or struggled to understand from my home in Boston where I wrote of other things. I did not come to Bosnia until the fall of 2000, in the midst of changes in my own life. I found myself drawn at last by a newspaper article that said that just as Bosnians were finally feeling secure enough to start returning in large numbers to homes they had fled during the war, the international community was becoming "fatigued" with the Balkans tragedy and was starting to move its aid and attention elsewhere. The result was that few Bosnians would receive help in what seemed to me to be a Herculean task of returning to homes haunted by tragedy and lingering hostilities. I was dismayed by the quick-fix shortsightedness of it all, concerned that the West was turning its back on Bosnia once again, just as it had during a war that was marked by the worst genocide in Europe since the end of World War II.

I felt compelled to go, to do whatever I could as a journalist to be a witness to the country's ongoing struggle to rebuild a civil society. Although I began my career as a print journalist, working first for *The Christian Science Monitor* as a staff writer and later as a freelancer for *The New York Times*, *Rolling Stone*, *Fast Company*, and others, by the year 2000 I was well into a career transition into photography and had been ready for some time to take on a long-term documentary project.

So I went to Bosnia to cover the aftermath of war – to try to capture the images that are the all too often forgotten companions of the vivid pictures of war itself. I came with the conviction that war is only half the story. I believed, and still believe, that what happens in the aftermath of war is as newsworthy, if not more so, than the destruction and horror of war. I went to Bosnia with a desire to document that incredibly difficult period when humans move out of war's desperate struggle to survive and begin another equally mighty struggle – that of learning to live again. In the four years I spent making the images that would ultimately become this book, I became convinced that we need post-conflict images to remind us of our humanity – to testify that war is not the final word on who we are as human beings, nor the final image of our spirit.

My experience of Bosnia has been marked not by war, but by the echoes of war, by the scars it has left behind. My work and travels have been charged with the struggle of rebirth, not the horror of destruction. I have spent long hours with widows of Srebrenica – the Muslim women who lost some 7,000 to 8,000 men and boys in a 1995 massacre by Serb forces. I have been with them as they returned to visit homes they fled in terror. I have been with them when they have laughed, cried, and prayed for their dead.

I spent a rainy afternoon with a man as he exhumed a shallow grave containing his father, killed eight years earlier by Serb neighbors. I have spent days in a warehouse lined with body bags, filled with the remains of recently-exhumed victims of the Serbs' 1992 "ethnic cleansing" campaign – while family members, mostly women, walked the aisles of skeletons, sobbing quietly, looking for loved ones, and as one woman picked up skull after skull with her bare hands, searching for signs of a son. I have stood on the freshly laid concrete floors of homes being rebuilt by returning refugees, determined to reclaim their land and their lives.

I was in the crush of a group of young people, crowded in the square outside the National Theatre in Sarajevo, cheering wildly as they greeted Danis Tanovic, fresh from his Oscar victory for his film about the war, "No Man's Land" – a victory he celebrated in his homeland on April 5, 2002, just one day short of the tenth anniversary of the beginning of the siege of Sarajevo.

I have spent afternoons in Sarajevo with the 3K Sarajevo wheelchair basketball team, made up of young men who were wounded by snipers as civilians or while serving on the frontline as soldiers. I have watched them sweat and spin on a dime and flirt with girls when practice was over, and I have come away determined that the world's final image of them be their strength and grace and not the moment when they lay sprawled on a city sidewalk, another tragic victim of war, another image of despair. I want to tell the story of their aftermath. I want to tell it all.

The end of war does not mean peace. It is simply the end of war, the end of death and destruction. Every story of war includes a chapter that almost always goes untold – the story of the aftermath, which day by day becomes the prologue of the future.

And finally, a note about the war. This book does not attempt to re-tell that story; there are many, many fine books, which detail the conflict and why it happened. But it is important, I think, to know a few things – to understand that the war in Bosnia, which occurred during the break-up of the former Yugoslavia, was fueled by nationalist aggression and propaganda from its neighbors, Serbia and Croatia, whose leaders wanted to split the country in two.

It is important to know that politicians in the West and the United Nations did everything they could to avoid being drawn into this war – repeatedly appeasing aggressors like Serbia's Slobodan Milosevic and urging Bosnia's leaders to allow the country to be carved into pieces. And while, unfortunately, many Bosnian Serbs continue to deny what was done by them, or in their name, it is crucial to know that the biggest victims in this war, by far, were Bosnian Muslims, who were targeted for expulsion, rape, torture, and death simply because of their identity.

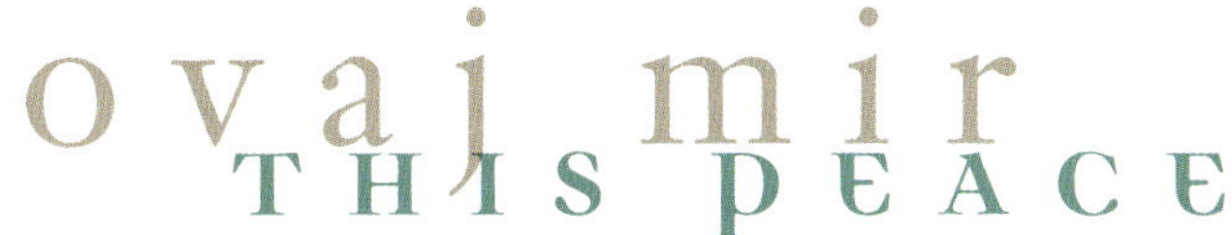

"Everyone thinks it's great that the war is over. But we Bosnians often say we have yet to survive the peace. This peace."

> **edib palalic,** university student, sarajevo

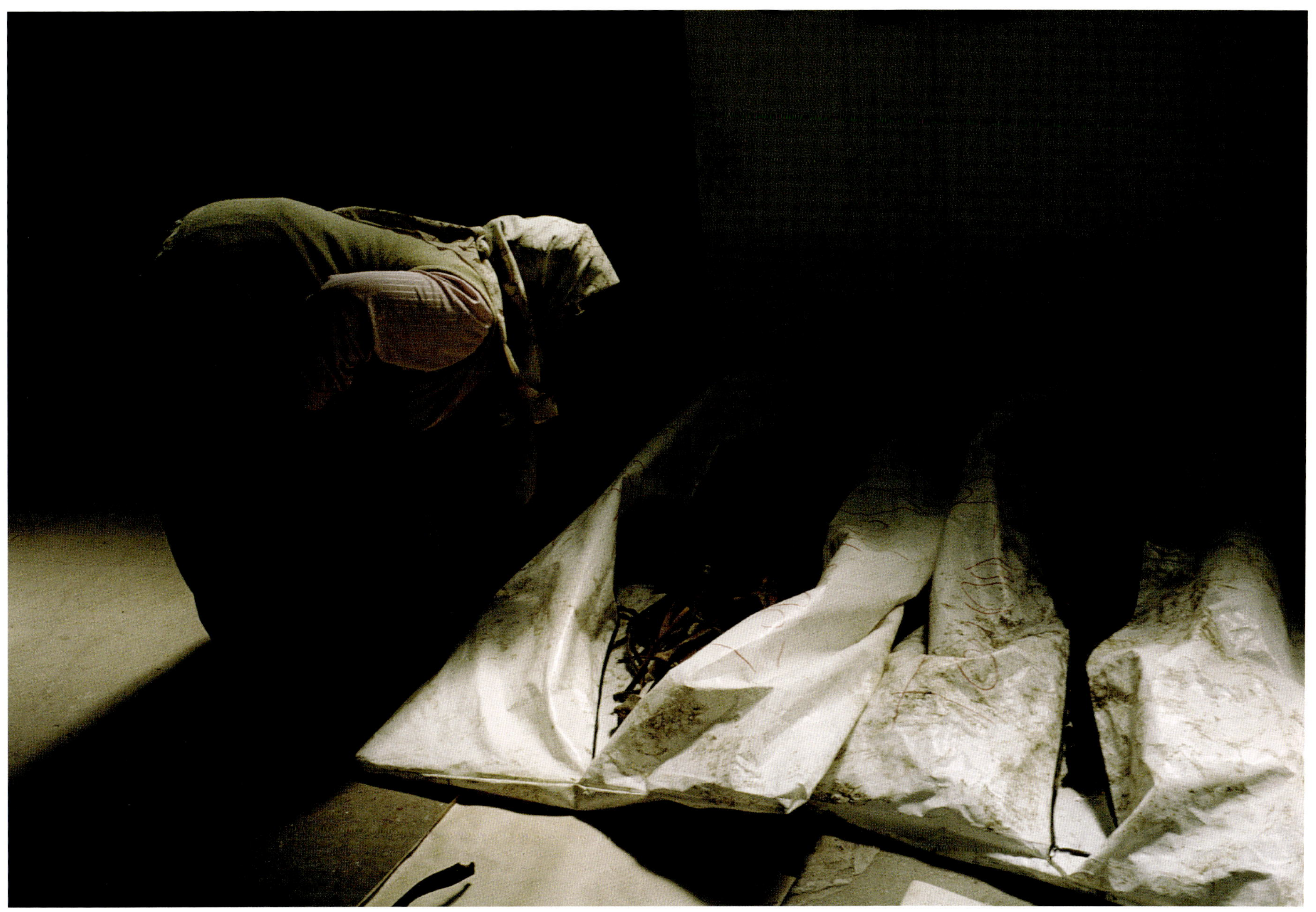

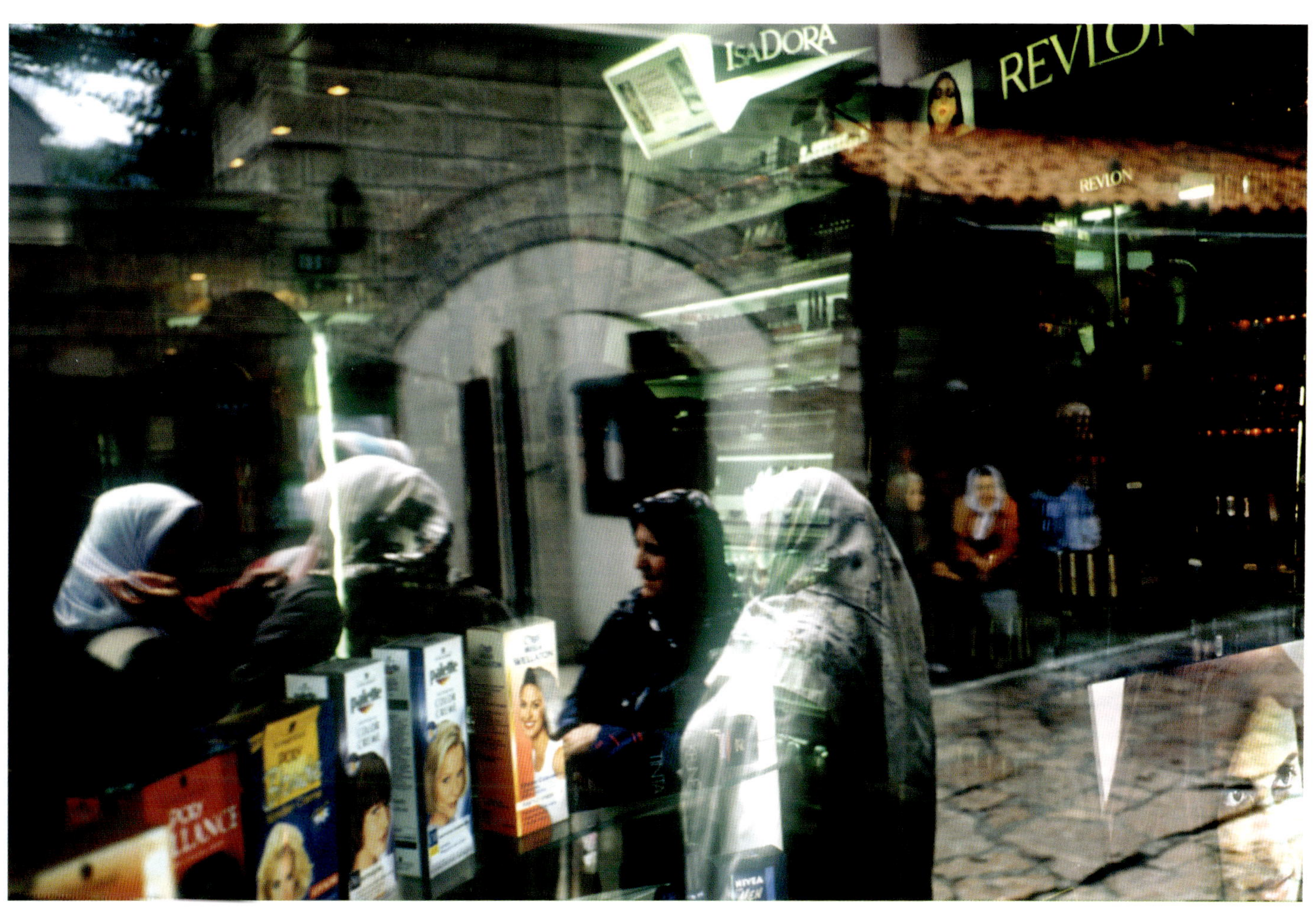
IsaDORA
REVLON
REVLON

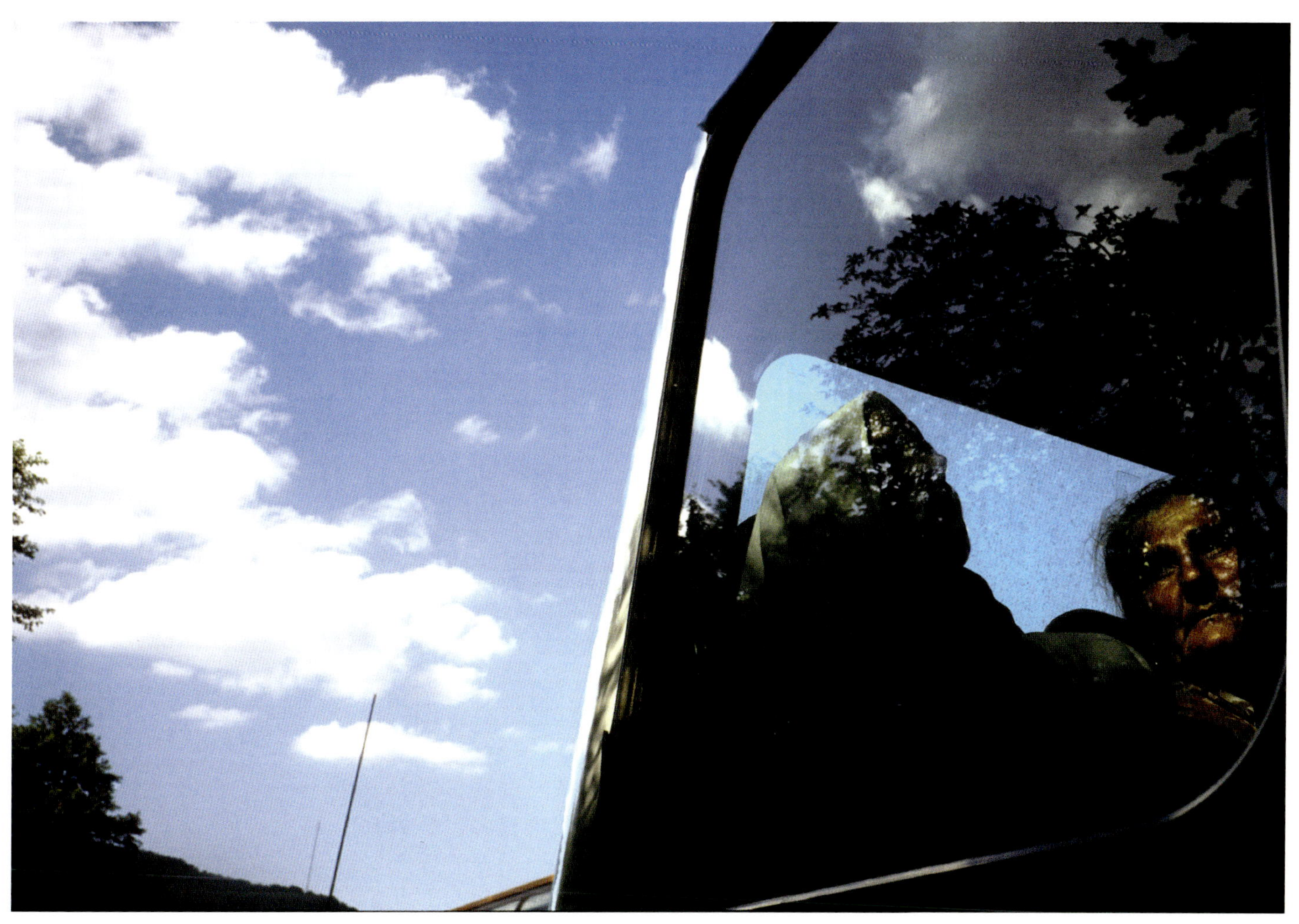

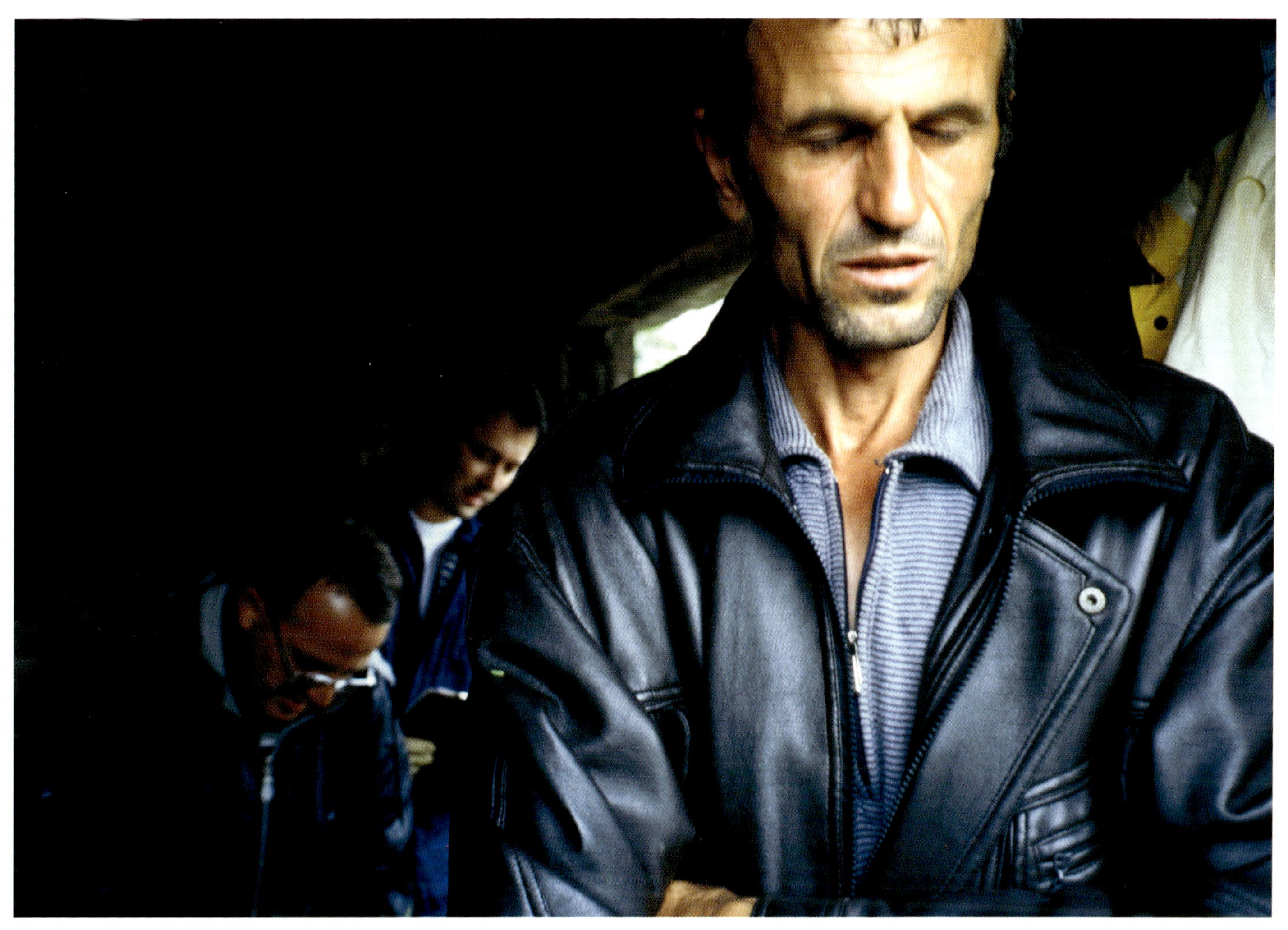

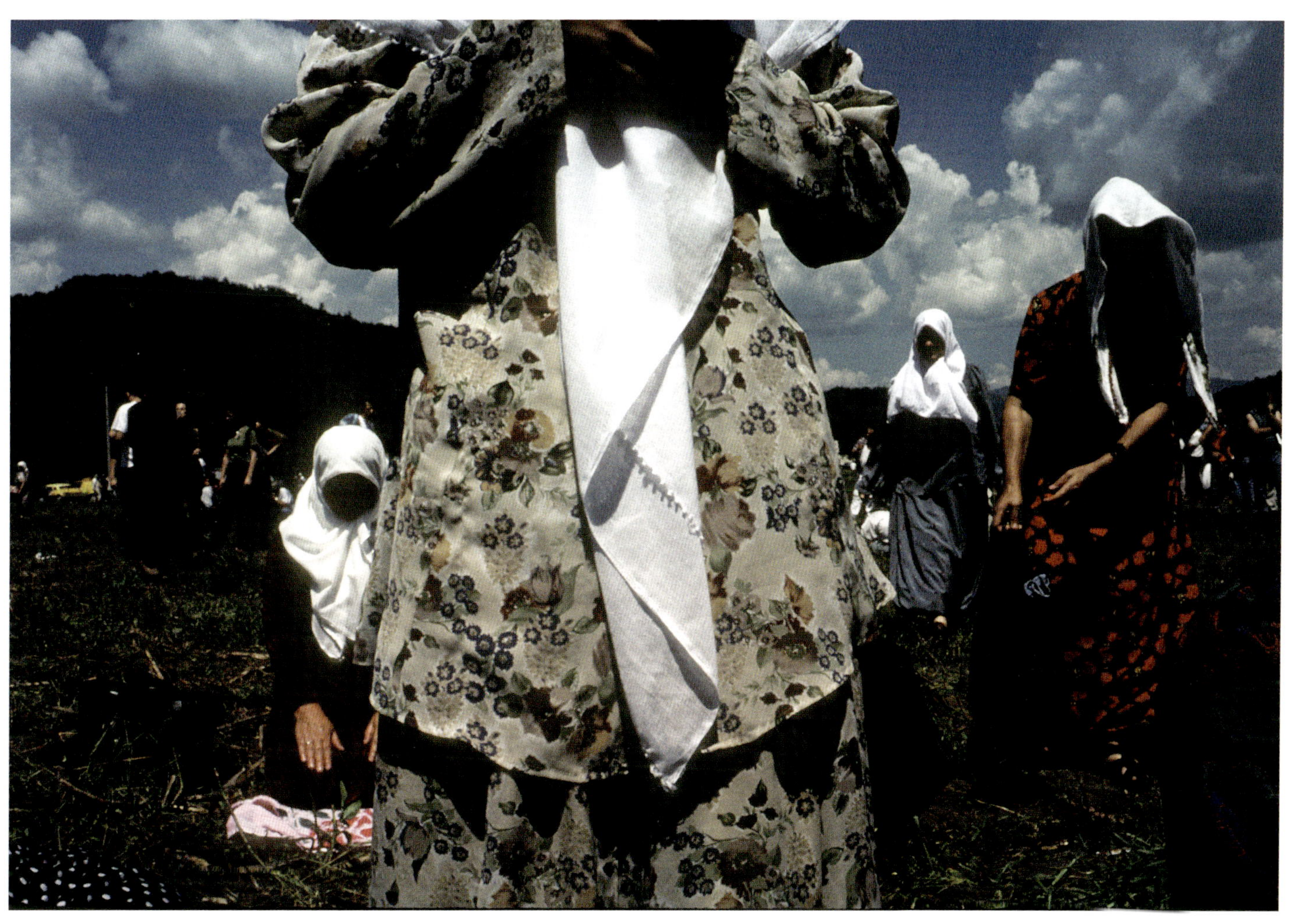

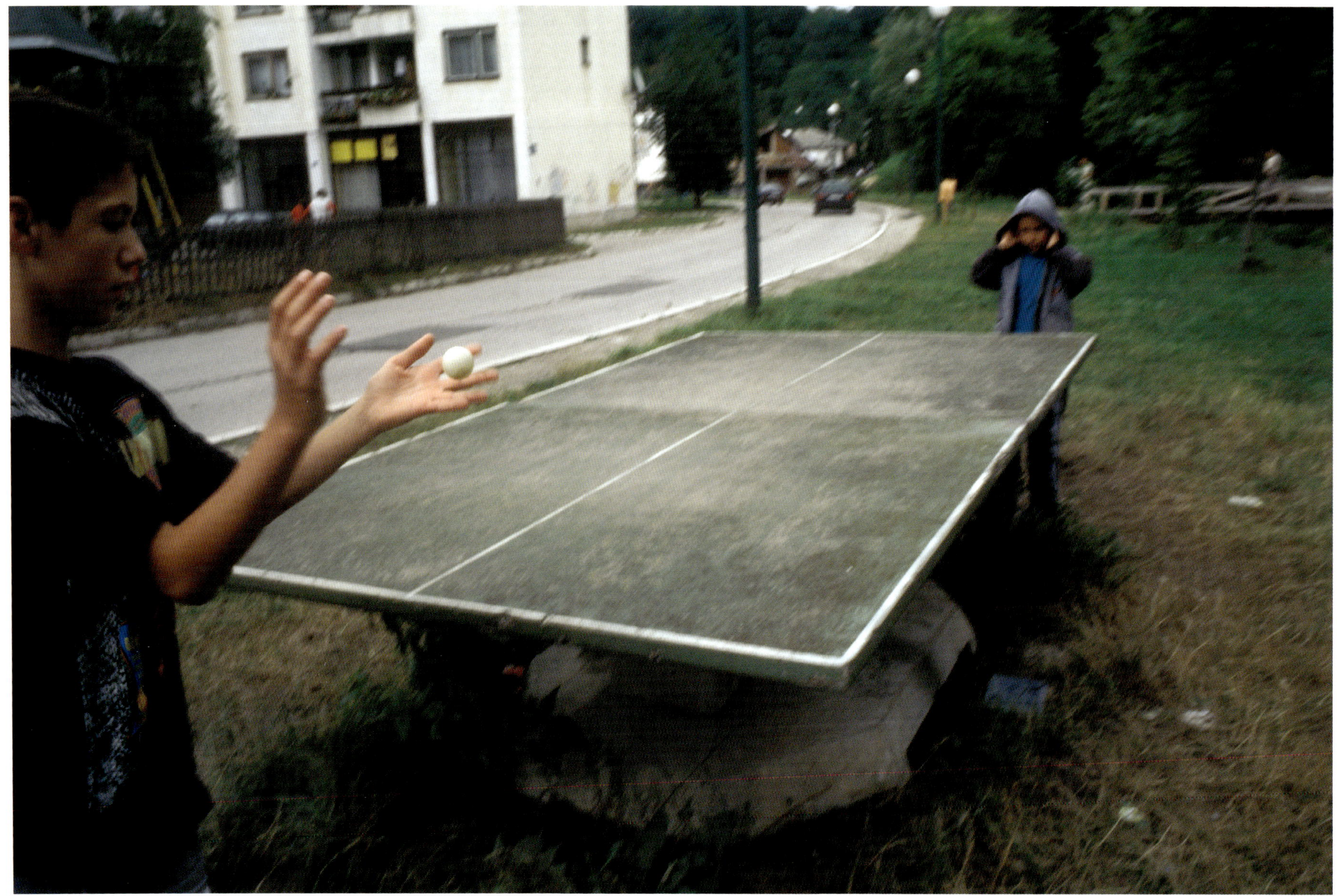

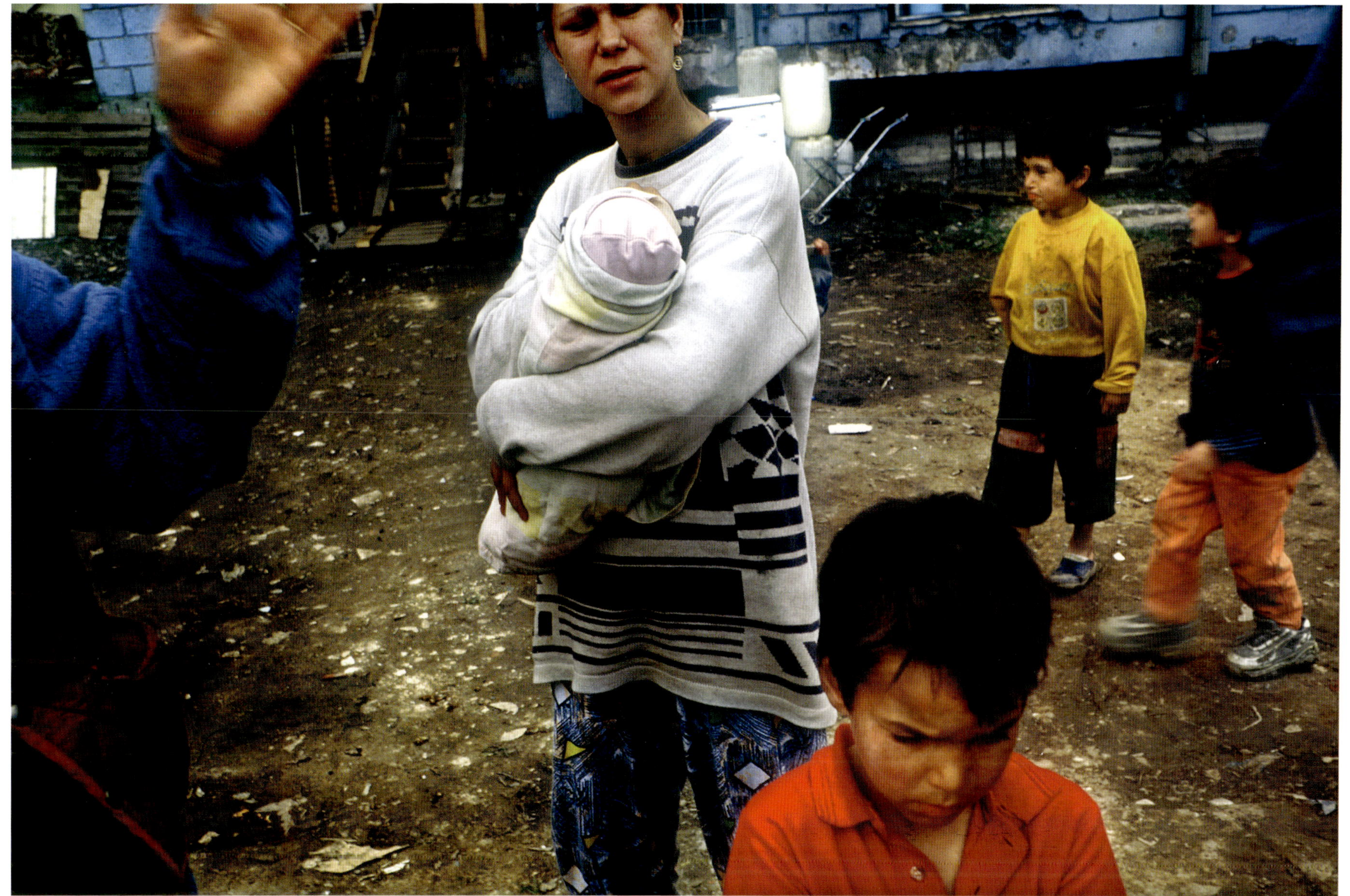

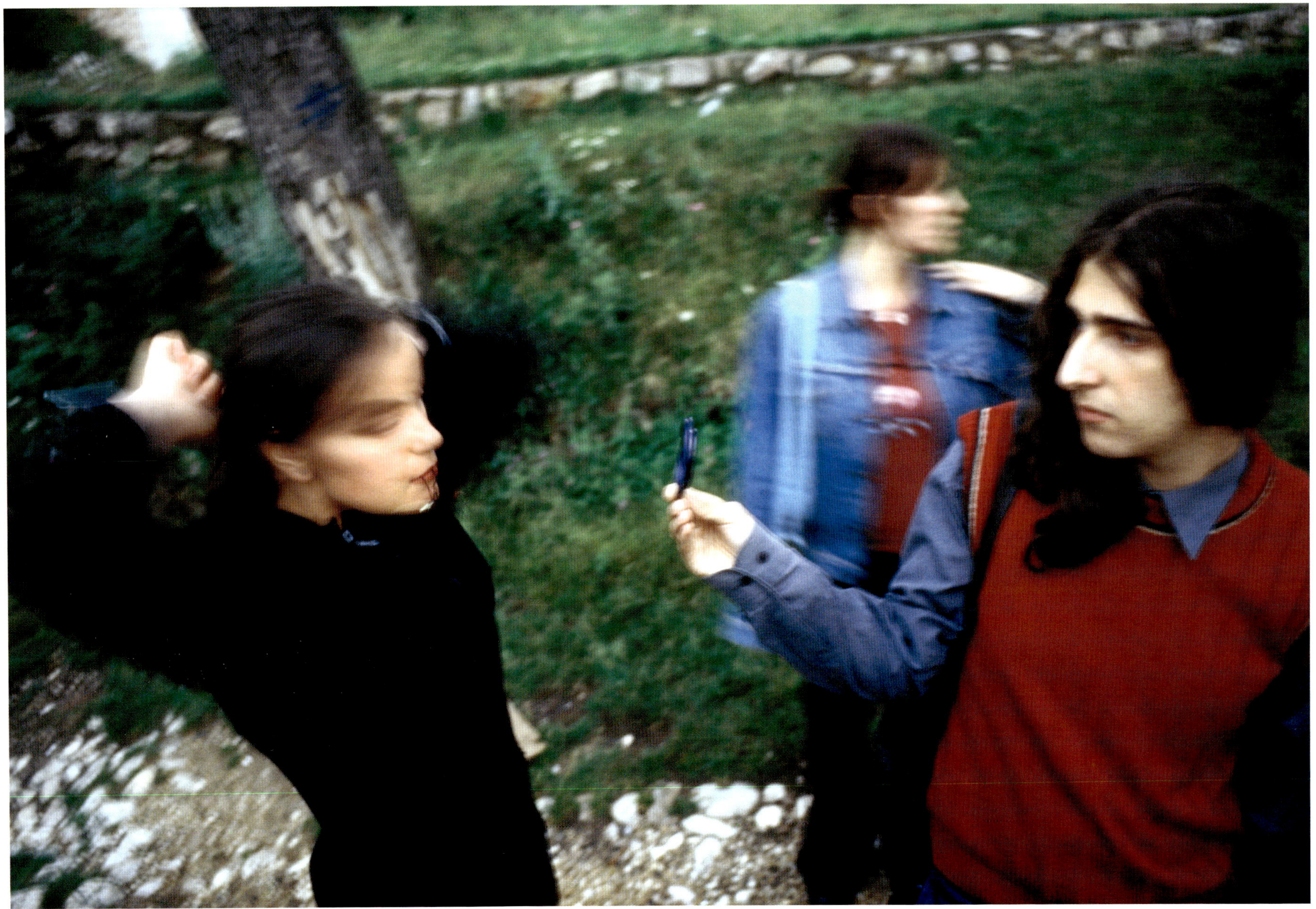

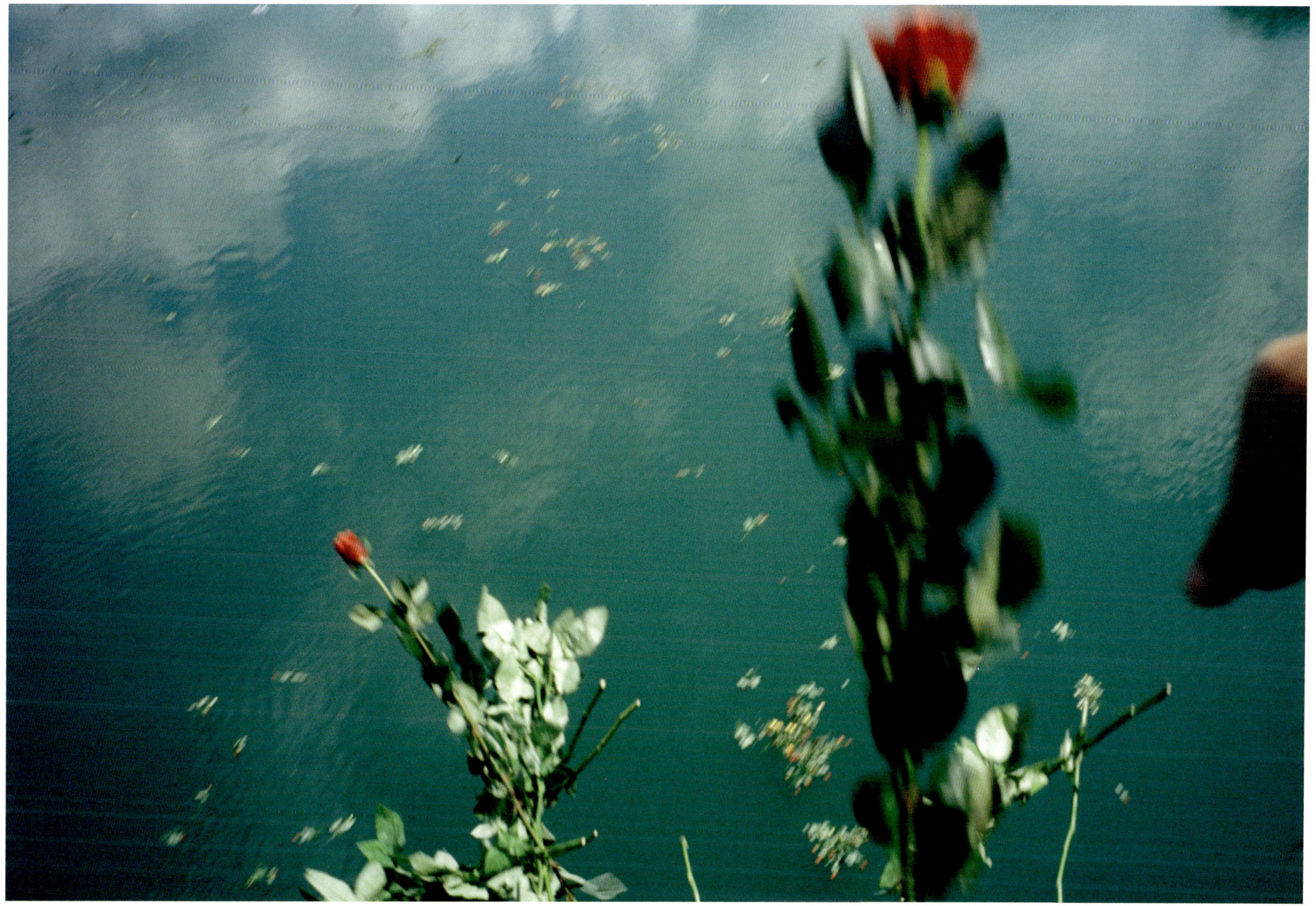

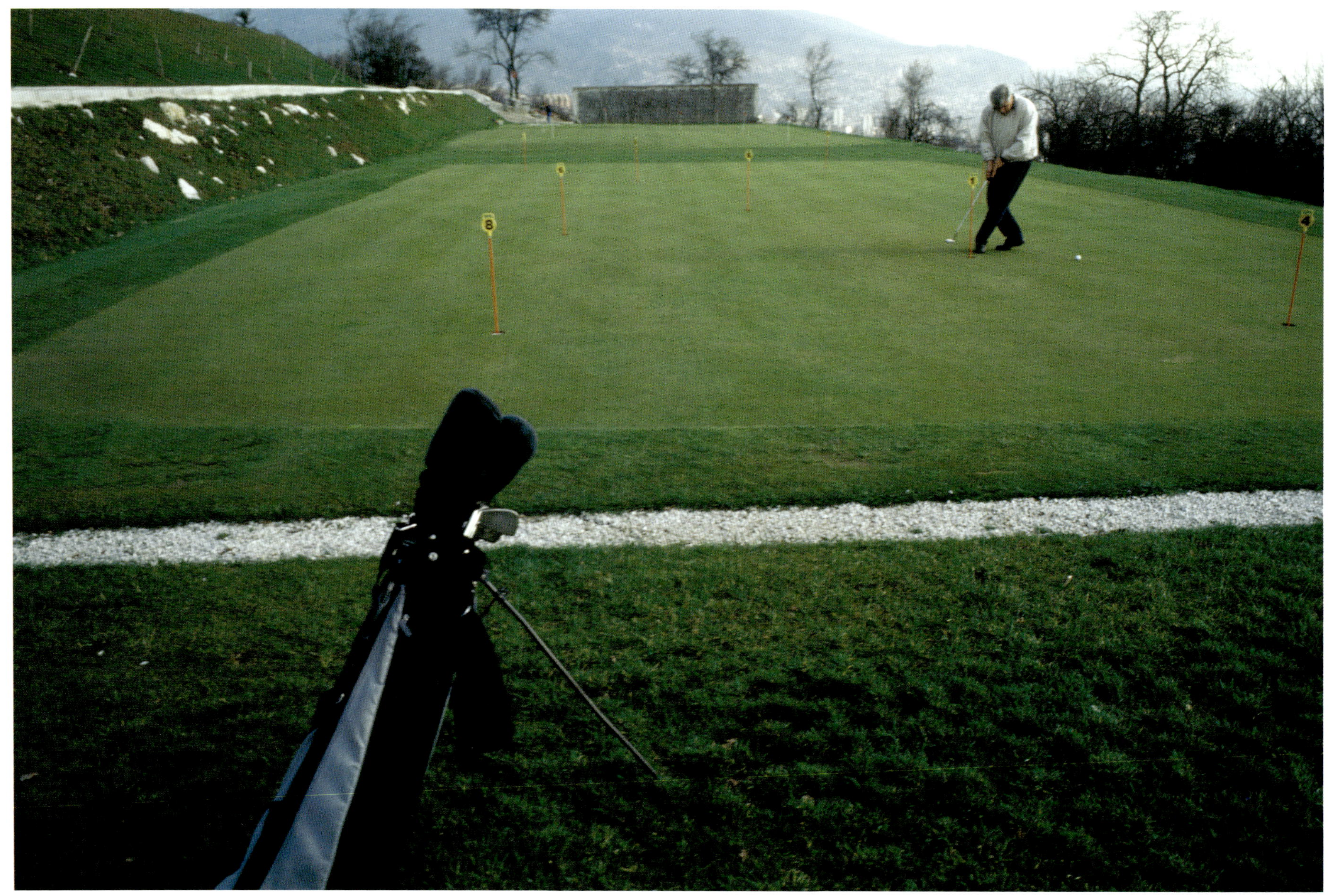

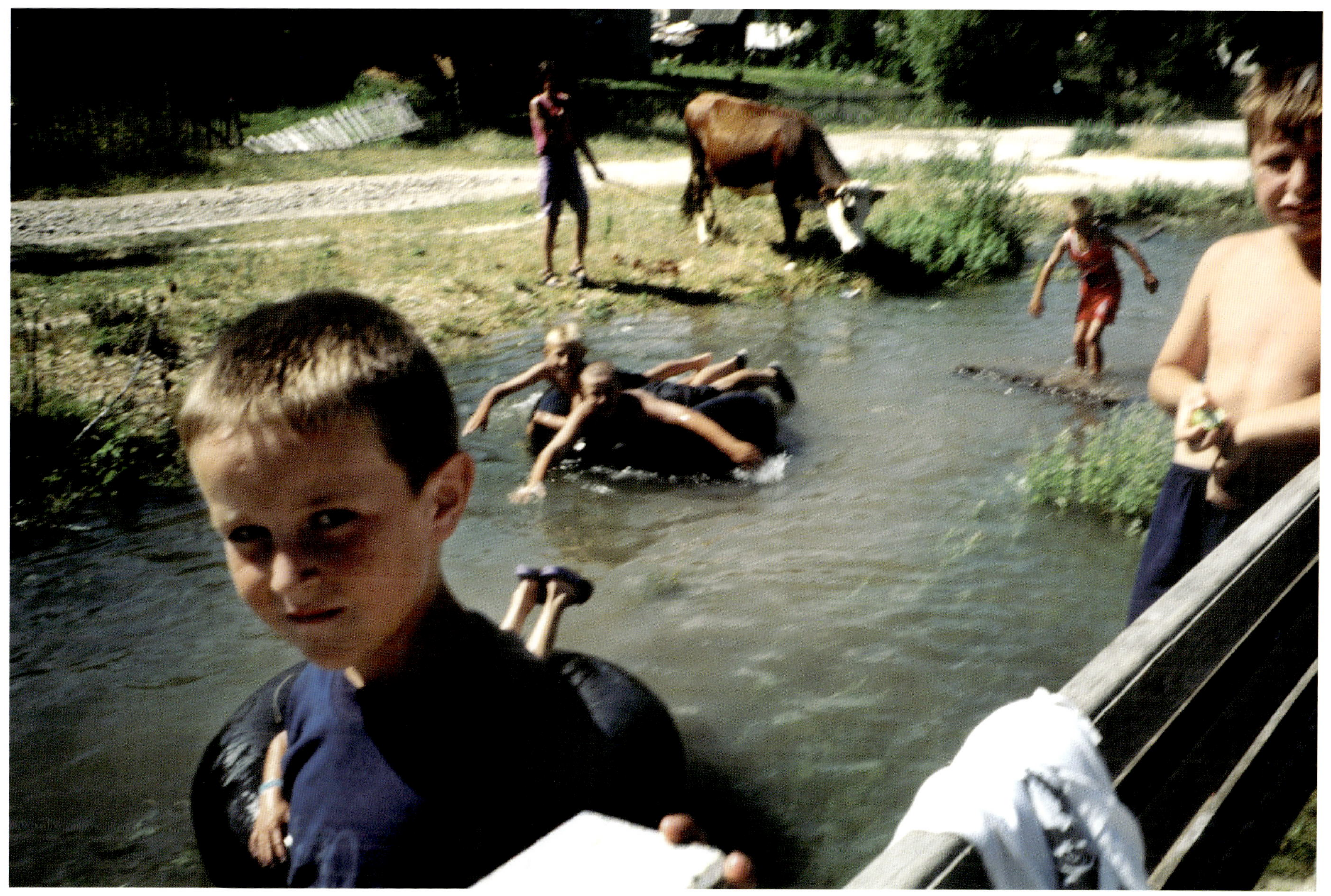

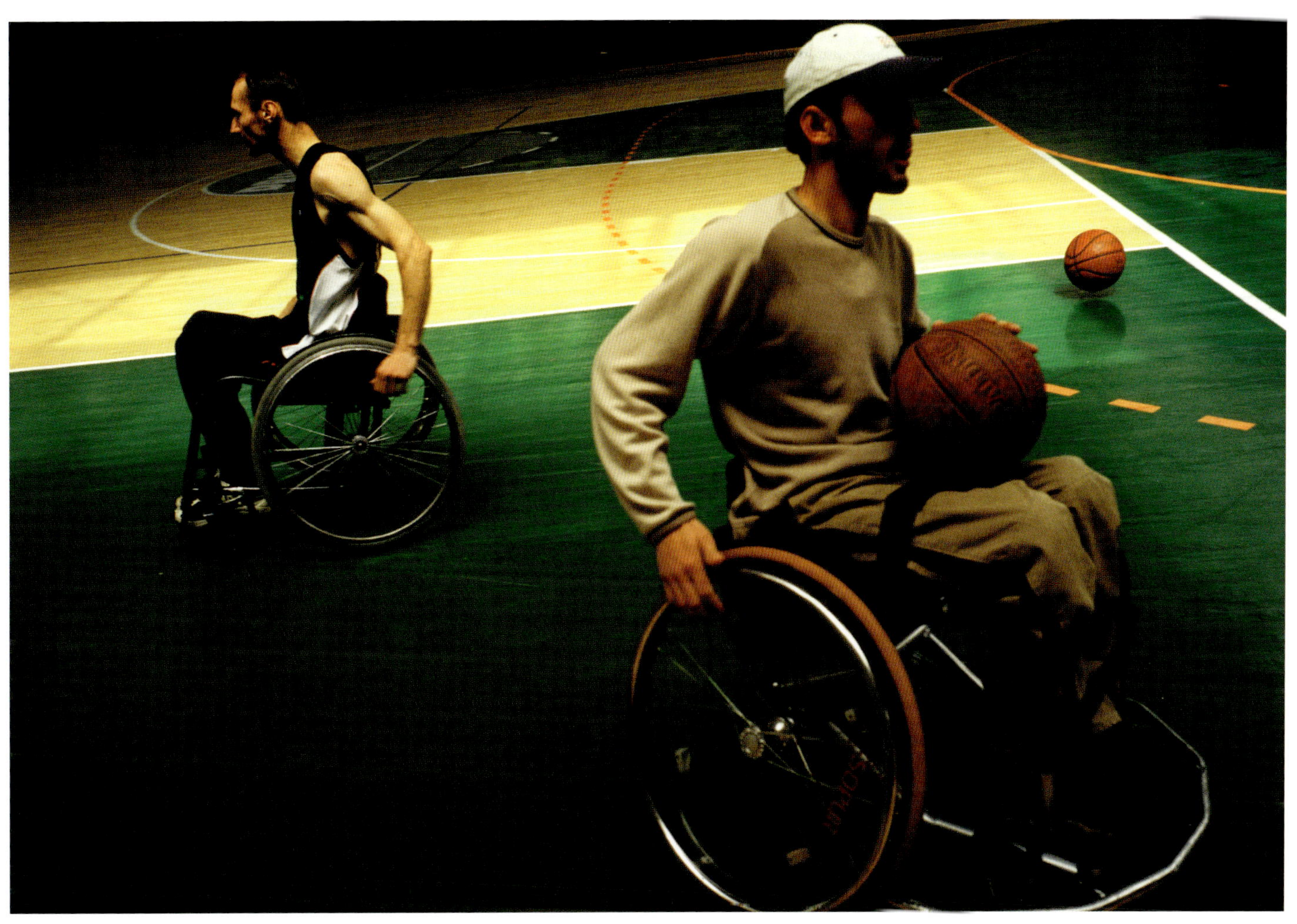

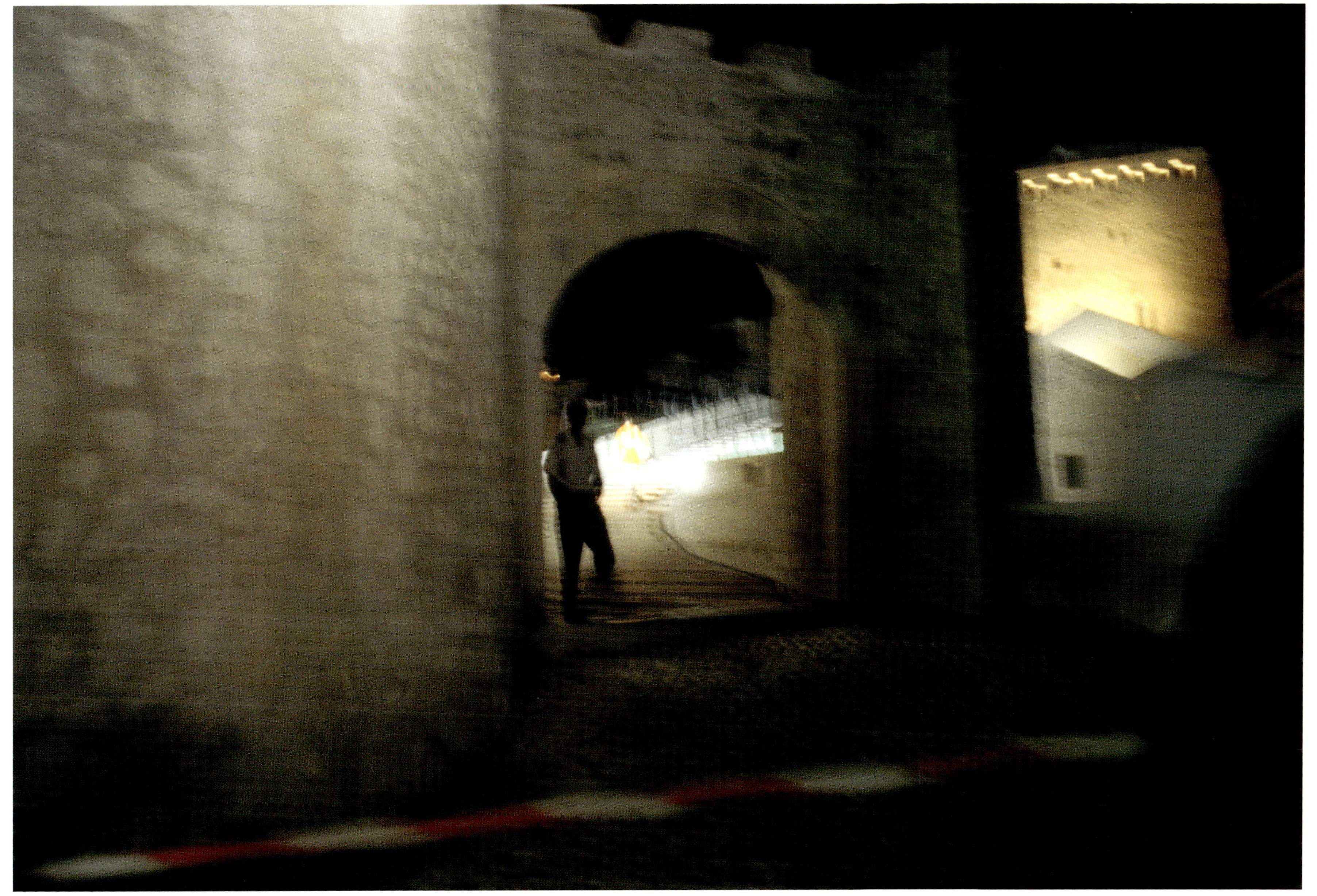

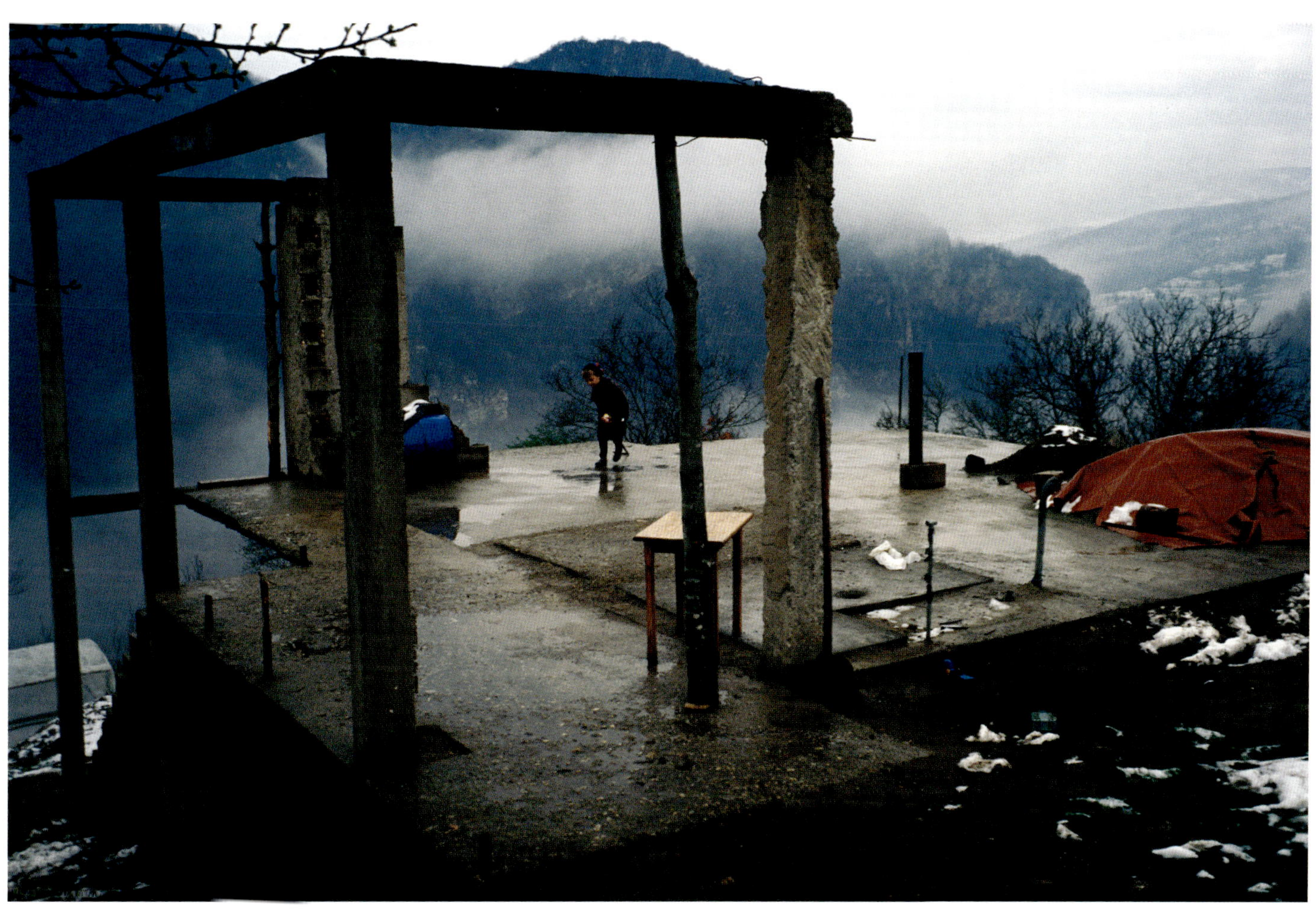

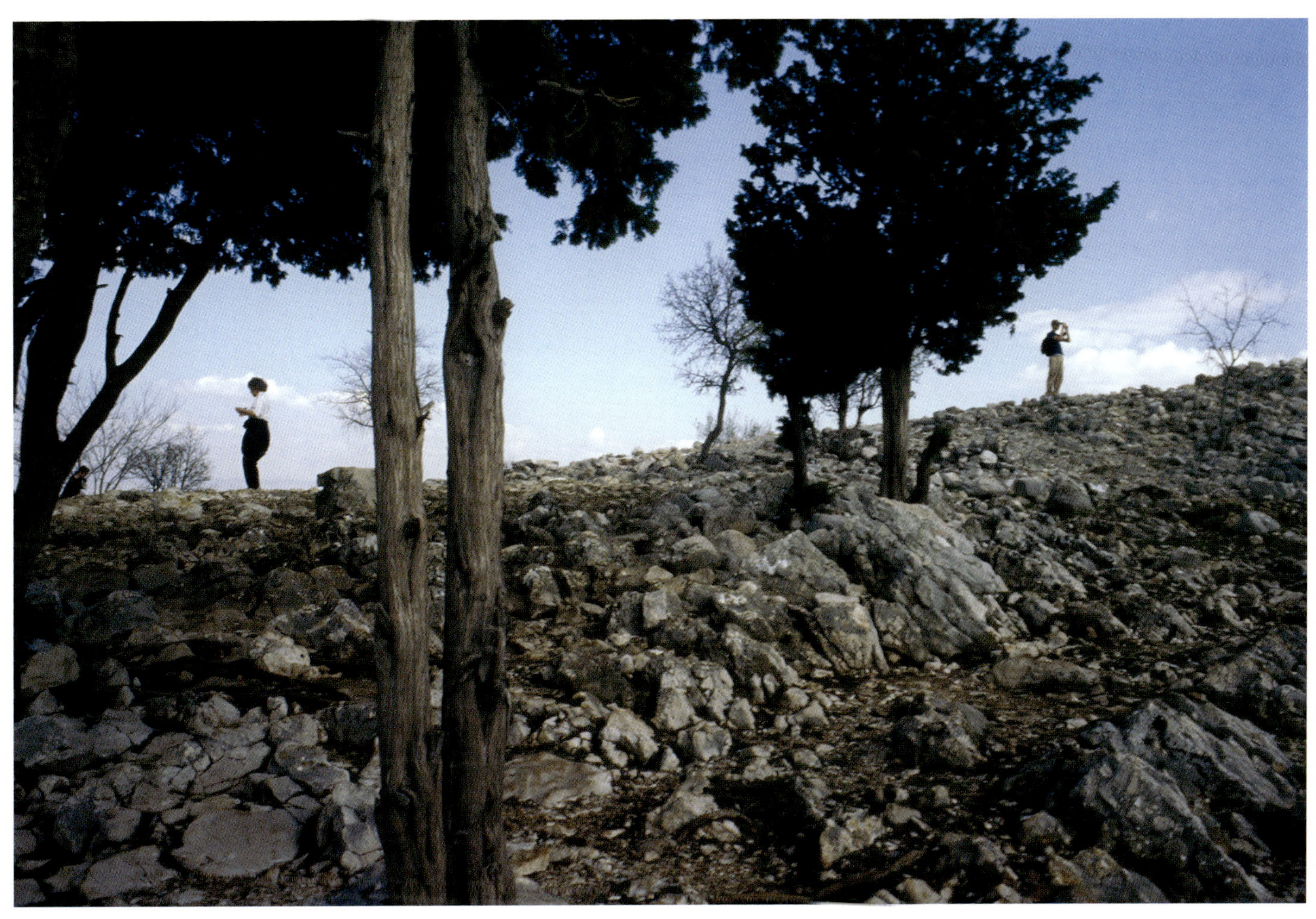

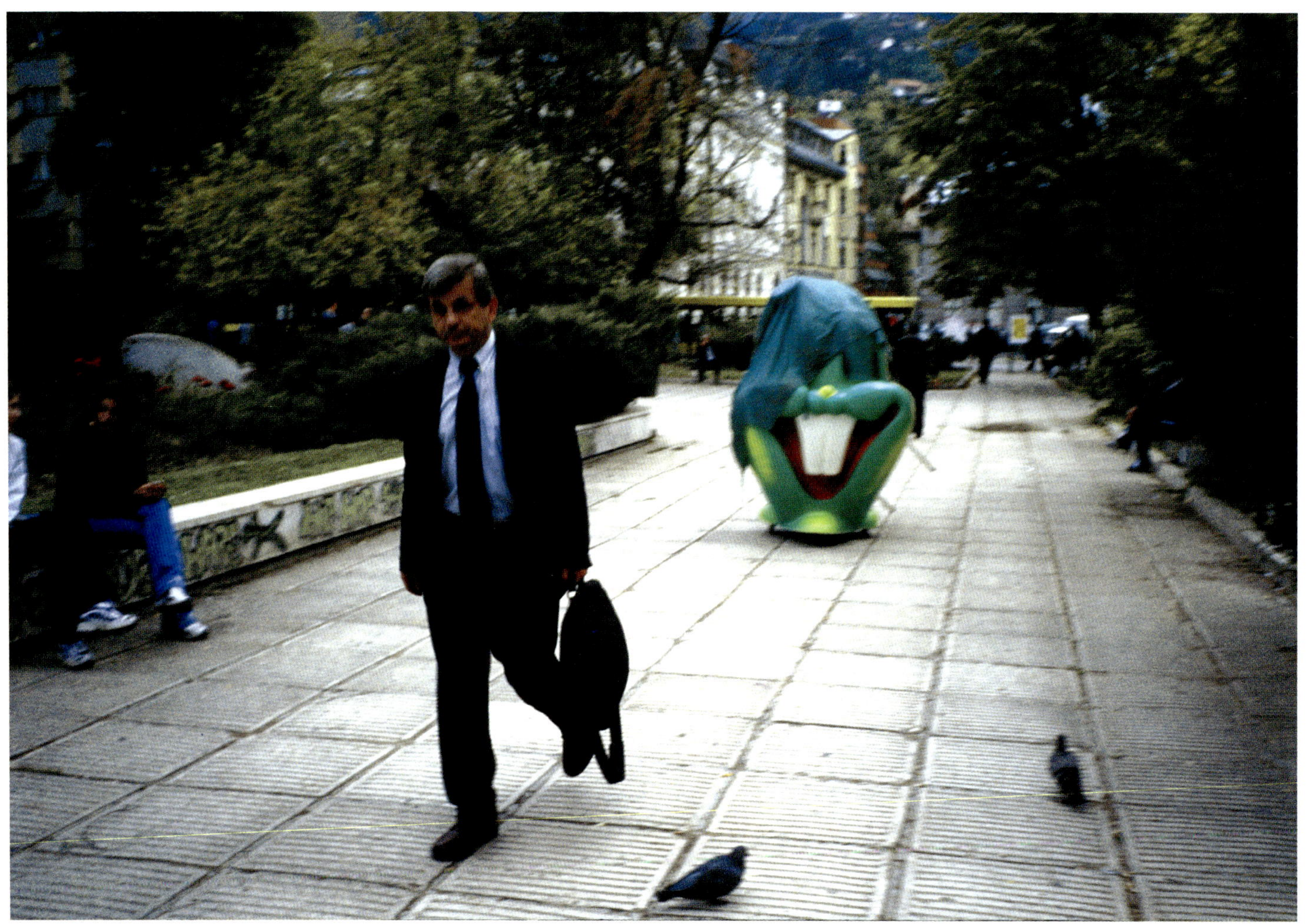

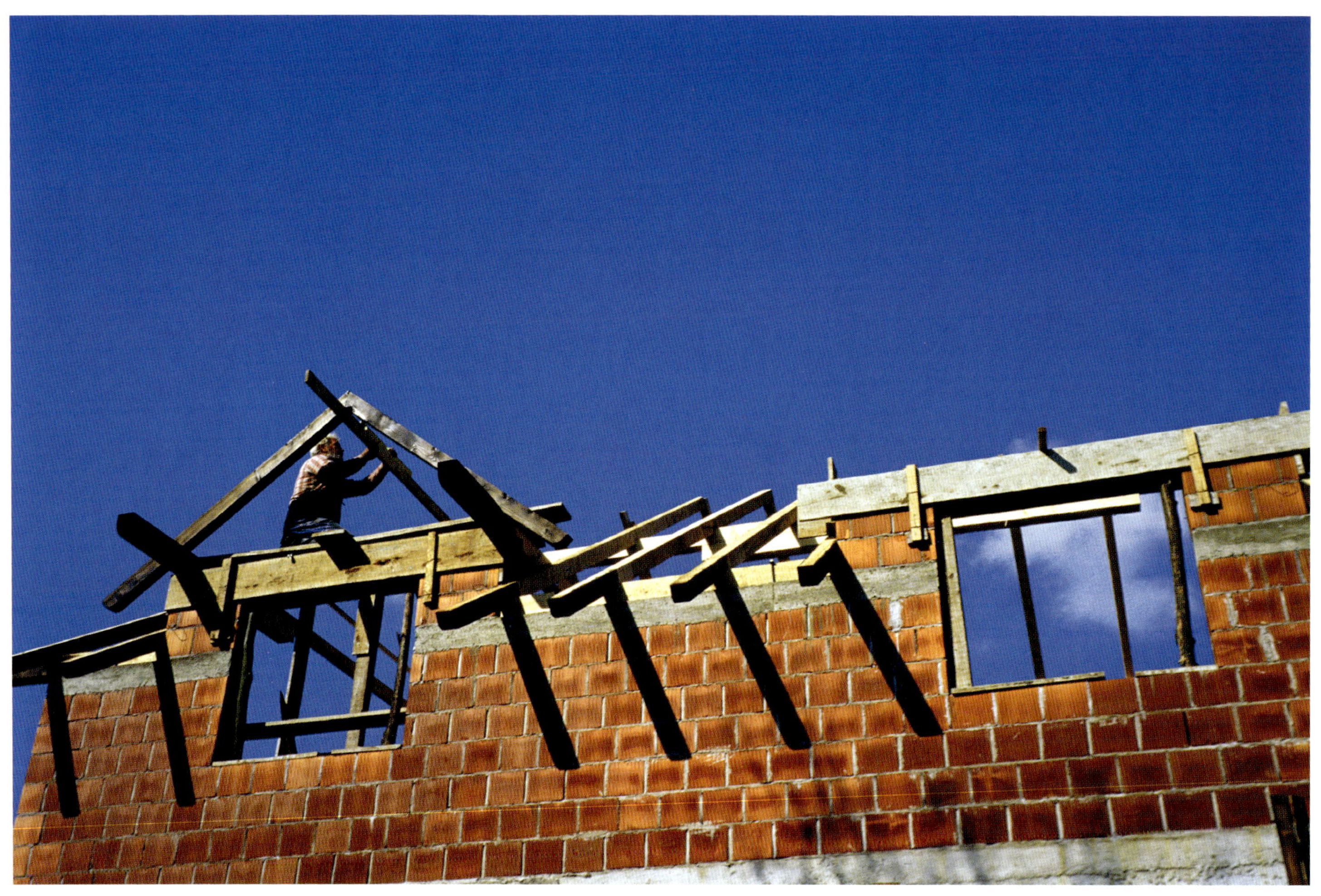

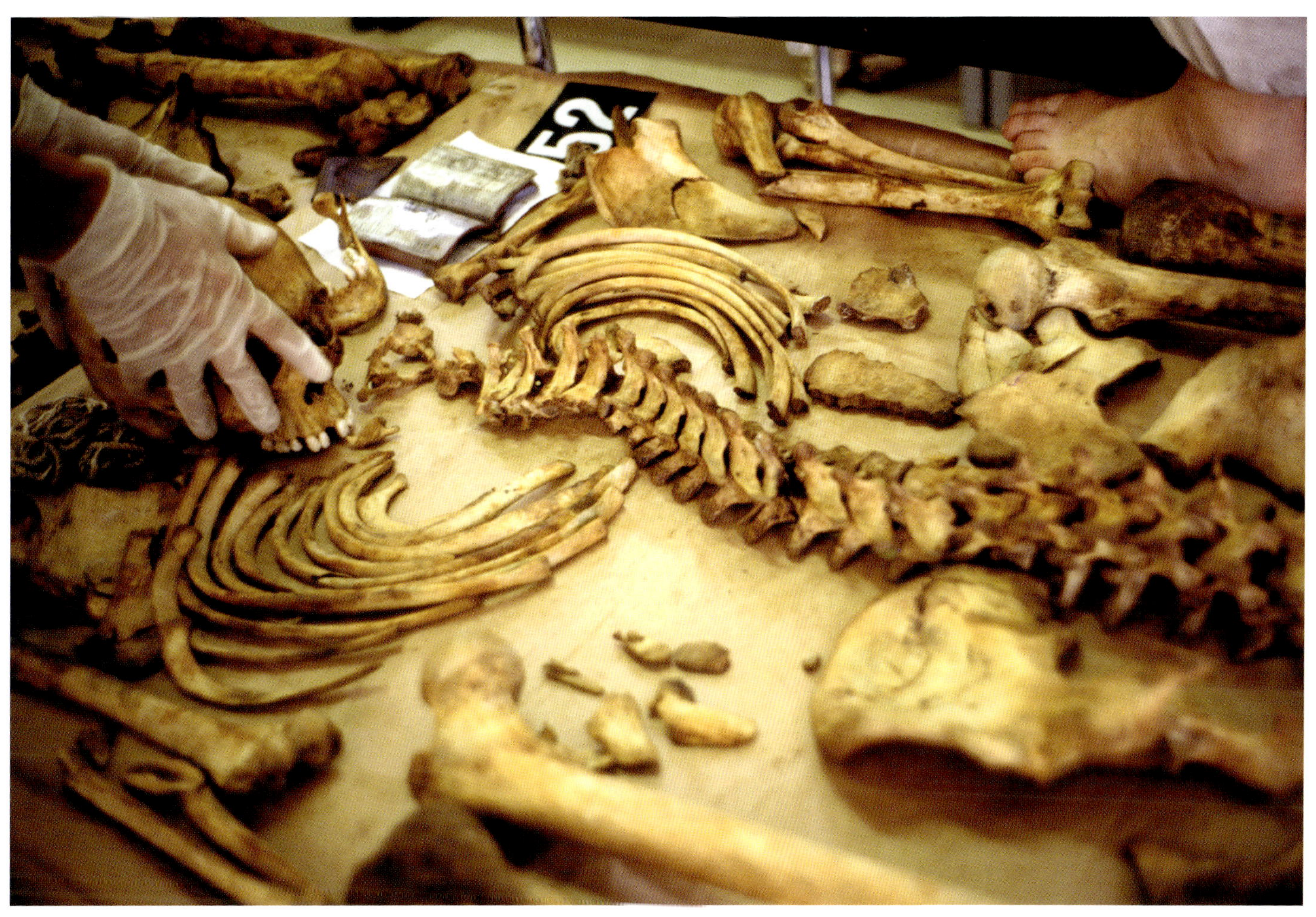

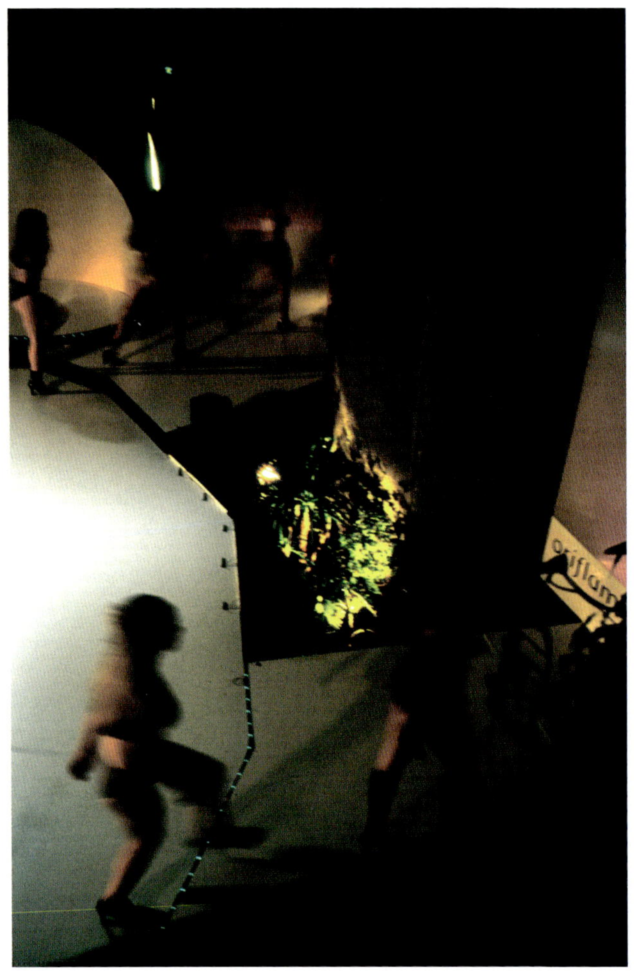

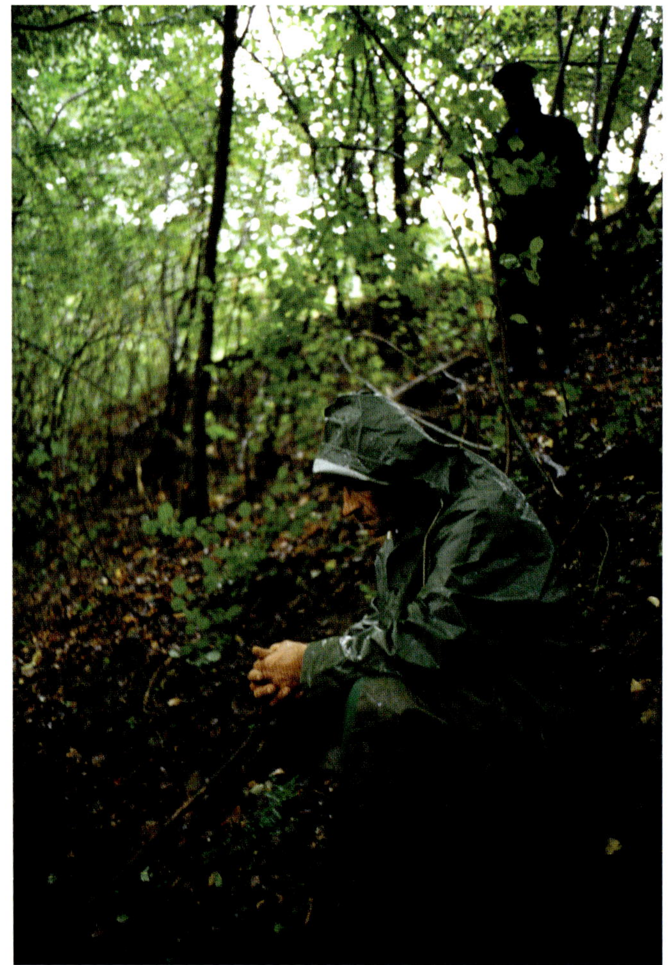

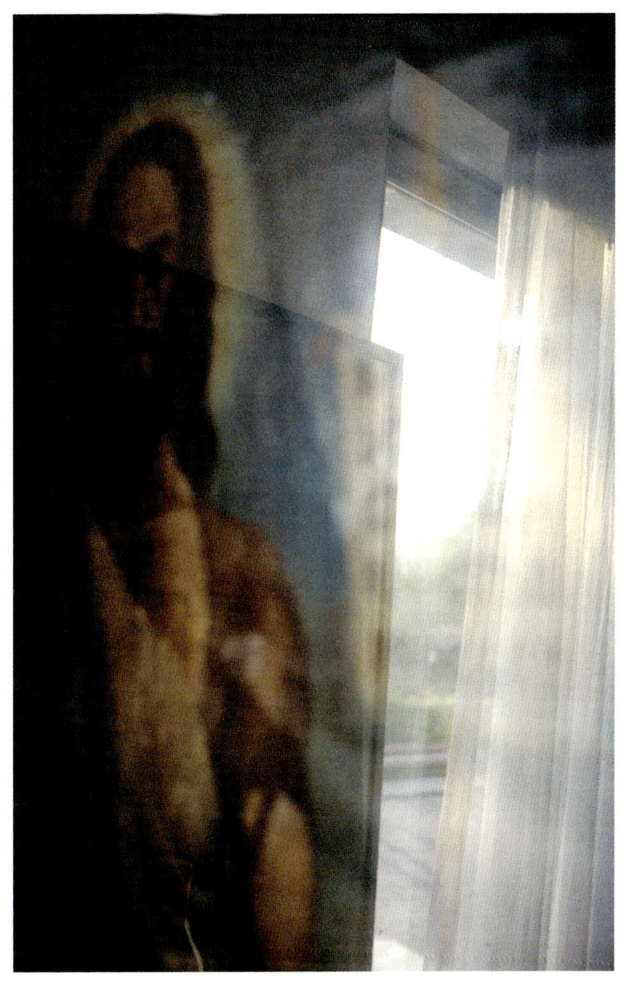

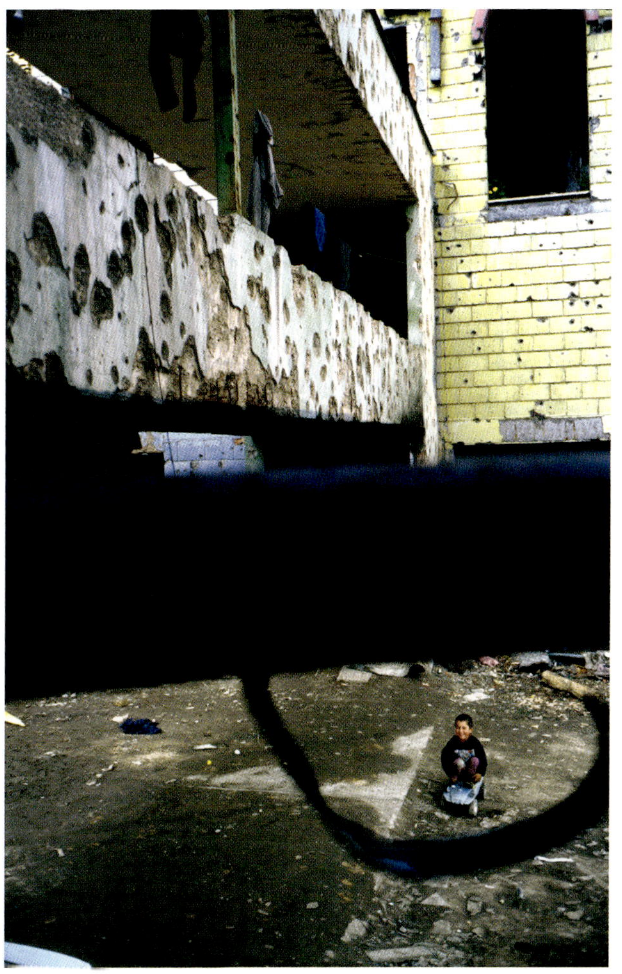

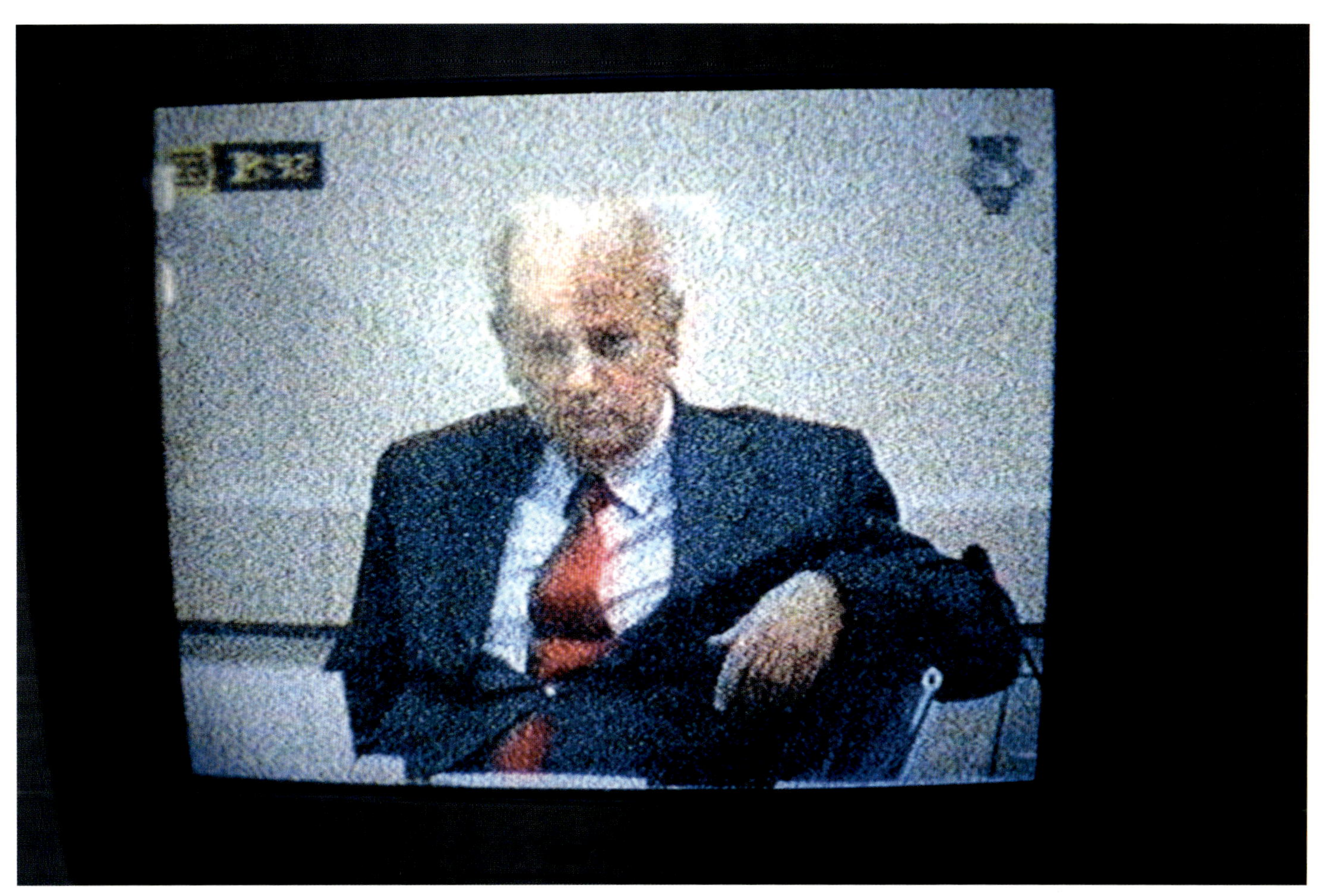

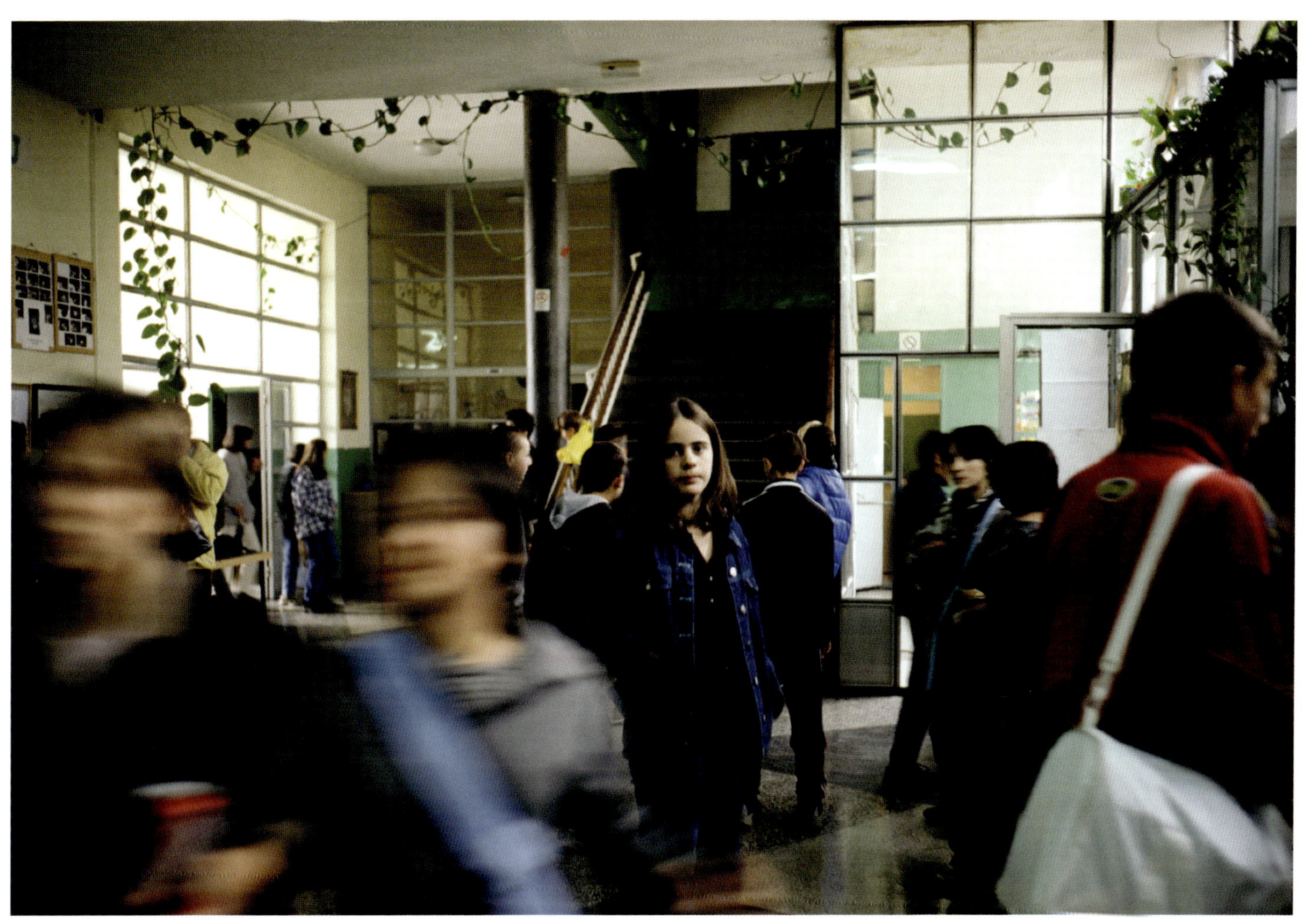

17 Muslim widow examines body bags containing the remains of recently exhumed victims of the 1992 "ethnic cleansing" campaign waged by Serbs against their Muslim neighbors. Exhumations of mass graves began in 1996 and are expected to last for many years to come. Nearly 30,000 Muslims—most of them civilians—were listed as missing at the end of the war; most are believed to have been victims of "ethnic cleansing." Sanski Most, July 2001.

19 Window reflection, beauty store. Sarajevo, April 2002.

21 Srebrenica widows on board a bus after groundbreaking ceremonies at the site of the memorial planned to commemorate the 7,000 to 8,000 Muslim men and boys who were massacred in July 1995, by Serb forces, who overran the U.N. "safe haven" of Srebrenica. Potocari, July 11, 2001.

23 This man has just helped to exhume his father, eight years after he was killed by Serb neighbors in May 1992. Muslim friends witnessed the killing–the first of several similar murders that were soon to follow–and later buried the man's father in a shallow grave in the forest of his village. Fearing for their lives, Muslims fled the village in the days that followed. The son was unable to return for his father's body until he came back to the remains of his village in 2000, determined to rebuild, along with a few former neighbors, and to recover his father's remains and bury them in the village cemetery. October 2000.

25 Muslim widows in prayer during dedication ceremonies for a planned memorial (which was completed in 2003) to the men and boys who were killed by Serb forces in July 1995. The site is across the road from a now abandoned factory where many of the victims were killed in the village of Potocari, just a few miles down the road from Srebrenica. July 11, 2001.

26 Two boys play a makeshift game of ping pong, with no net and no paddles. Travnik. July 28, 2004.

27 Squatters on the grounds of a building heavily shelled by Serb forces during the 1992-95 siege of Sarajevo. Serbs bombarded the city with mortars almost daily during the war. April 19, 2002.

28 A girl applies make-up for her scene in a student-made film. Sarajevo, July 2004.

29 Hundreds of red roses and carnations thrown in to the Drina river during ceremonies to mark the memory of the approximately 2,000 Muslim men and boys who were killed by Serbs in the town of Visegrad, which had a Muslim majority before the war. The ceremony, held on the bridge made famous by Ivo Andric in his Nobel Prize-winning novel, "Bridge on the River Drina," was attended by hundreds of Muslims, former residents of Visegrad who were bused in for the ceremony. Few Muslims have returned to their homes in what is now a hardline Serb community. May 25, 2003.

30 Putting green at the four-hole golf course in Sarajevo. An active minefield was cleared to make way for the course; on the far side of the putting green another minefield remains uncleared. Sarajevo, March 27, 2004.

31 Children play in the river that runs through the village of Vesela, which has had a refugee return rate of some ninety percent of its pre-war population of Muslims, Serbs and Croats. Vesela has been hailed as a success story by Bosnian officials; in the aftermath of a war marked by "ethnic cleansing" and genocide many towns and villages remain heavily populated by one group or another, with many refugees reluctant to return to the homes they fled during the war. Vesela, July 2001.

33 Members of the 3K Sarajevo wheelchair basketball team during a break from practice. Most of the players were wounded as civilians or as soldiers on the frontline during the 1992-95 war. The young man in the foreground was shot by a sniper when his parents let him go outside to celebrate his thirteenth birthday. Bosnia now has eight wheelchair basketball teams, made up almost entirely of young men wounded during the war. Sarajevo, April 16, 2002.

35 A policeman guards the entrance to the newly rebuilt Mostar Bridge the night before dedication ceremonies and the re-opening of the bridge, which was destroyed by Croat forces during the war. July 22, 2004.

37 A young boy plays on the recently-laid foundation of his grandparents' home in a mountain-side village in eastern Bosnia. Muslim villagers were forced to leave by Serbs who were "cleansing" the country of Muslims in an attempt to create a greater Serbia, which would join Bosnian Serbs with Serbia, which borders Bosnia to the east. Of the returning refugees, all are elderly; young people–including this boy's mother–are starting new lives in the towns where they lived as refugees during the 1992-95 war. Otricevo, April 10, 2002.

39 Tourists on top of one of the steep, rocky hills that ring the town of Medjugorje. The town has become a site for thousands of Catholic pilgrims from around the world, ever since six teenagers claimed to have received a message from the Virgin Mary in 1981. March 30, 2004.

40 Street scene. Sarajevo, April 2002.

41 Cat climbs along the rooftops of Bascarsija, the old Ottoman center of Sarajevo. April 2002.

42 Seven years after the end of the war, a Muslim man frames the roof of the home he is rebuilding, which was destroyed by Serbs who drove their Muslim neighbors from the town in the early days of the war. Bosanska Dubica, October 4, 2002.

43 Forensic anthropologists lay out the bones of a skeleton exhumed from a mass grave in eastern Bosnia, where Serbs killed thousands of Muslims as part of their "ethnic cleansing" campaign in the early months of the 1992-95 war. Visoko, July, 2001.

44a Contestants in the 2002 Miss Bosnia and Hercegovina contest, held at the Holiday Inn, the hotel which was known for housing foreign journalists during the war. Sarajevo, September 21, 2002.

44b A gravedigger takes a break during an exhumation. October 2000.

45a A Serb Orthodox icon hangs on the wall of a room being used as a temporary location for services. The local Orthodox church was deliberately destroyed by Croats (Catholics) during the war. Bugojno, May 24, 2003.

45b A Roma boy plays in the rubble of a building that was heavily mortared during the 1992-95 siege of Sarajevo by Serb forces. In 2002 squatters moved in to the complex, a senior citizen home which was completed just before the war began and never used. April 2002.

47 Televised proceedings of the trial of Slobodan Milosevic, the former president of Serbia, who was handed over to the International Criminal Tribunal for the Former Yugoslavia and sent to The Hague in 2000. Milosevic was indicted in November 2001 for genocide in Bosnia during the war; by early 2005, his trial was still ongoing. Brcko, May 22, 2003.

49 Serb and Muslim students in the hallway of a Sarajevo school. The children had been brought together for the first time since the end of the war as part of a fledgling parent-teacher organization program fostered by an international non-governmental organization. The students, who attend separate schools, put on a program of skits and songs for each other. October 2000.

prošlost i sadašnjost
PAST AND PRESENT

> notes and observations

october 2000

I'm finally collecting some thoughts on this place – realizing, for example, that when the Iron Curtain fell, most other countries got on with democracy and capitalism, places like the Czech Republic, Poland, Hungary. But Bosnia imploded almost immediately in war, meaning that in addition to having to get over the trauma and destruction of this war, with its "ethnic cleansing" and genocide, Bosnia still has a communist system mind-set. In other words, there was no strong democratic infrastructure in place to help Bosnians recover because they didn't have much of a chance to start creating a democratic way of life before the war started. It's like a double blow. I don't think Americans understand this at all. Can you imagine what the U.S. would have been like after the Civil War, if there had been no functioning economy? And on top of that, no real functioning democratic institutions? Would we have become the nation that we are today? I'm not so sure.

And yet we somehow expect that in five short years, Bosnia should be fully recovered and ready to stand on its own.

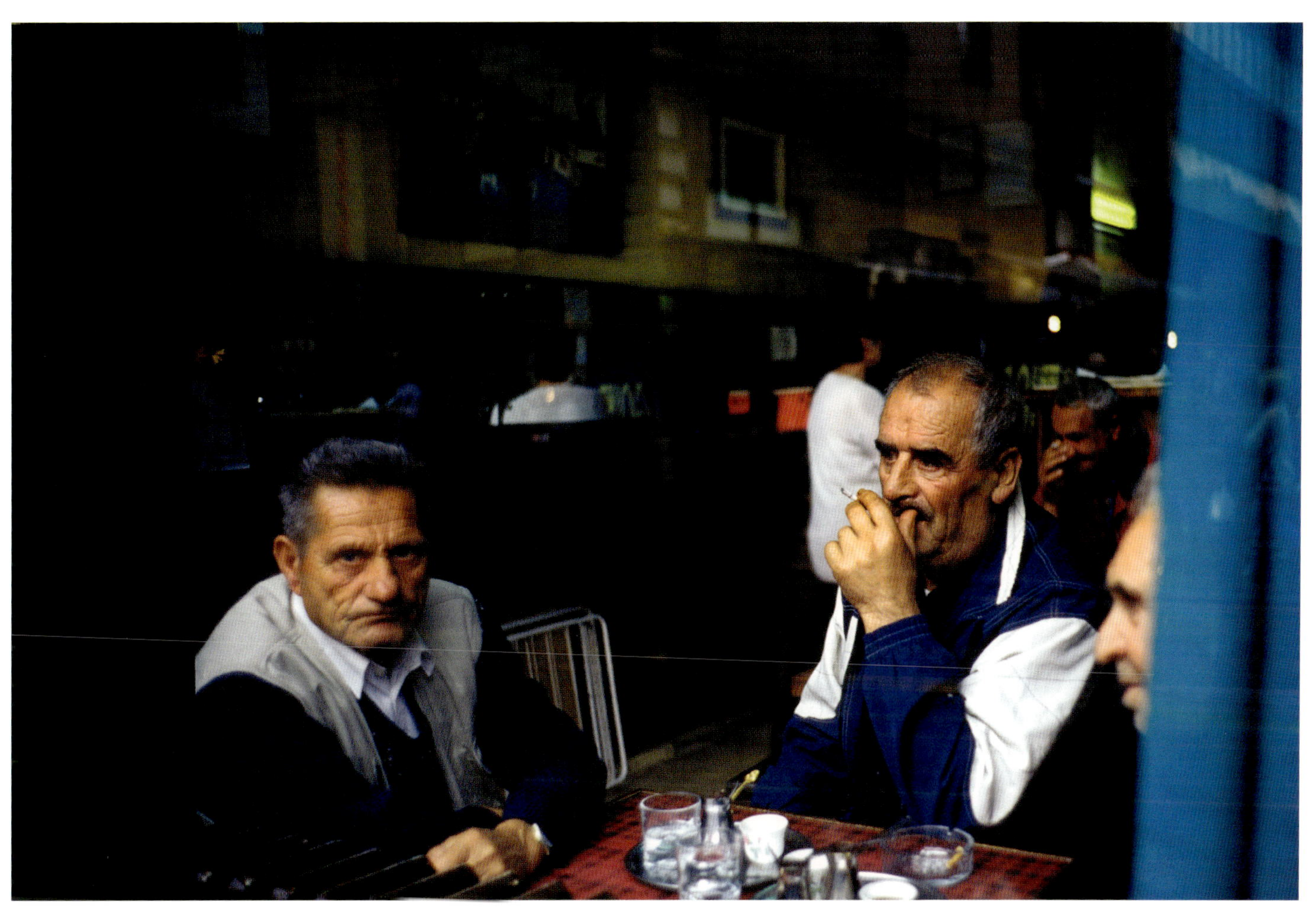

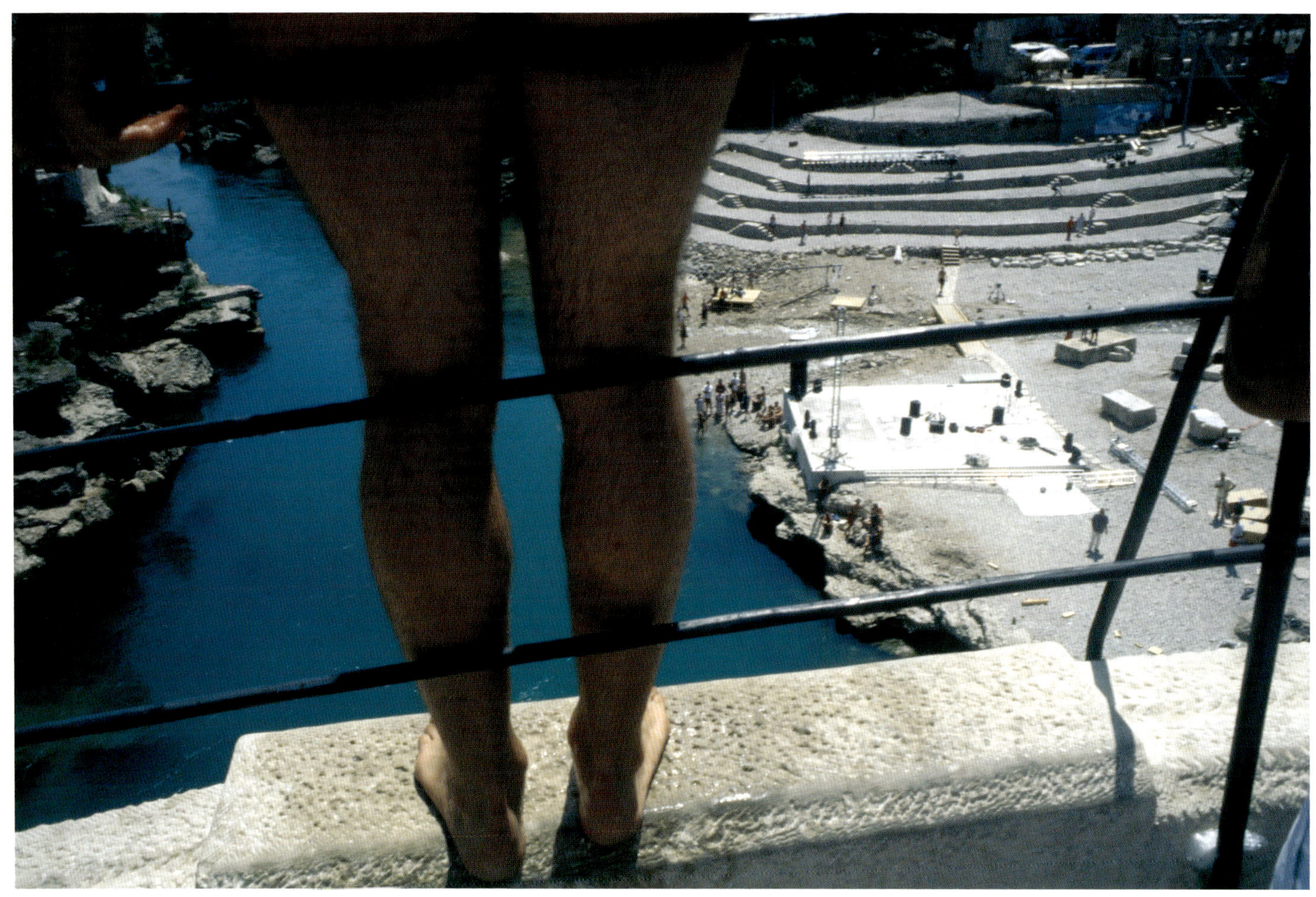

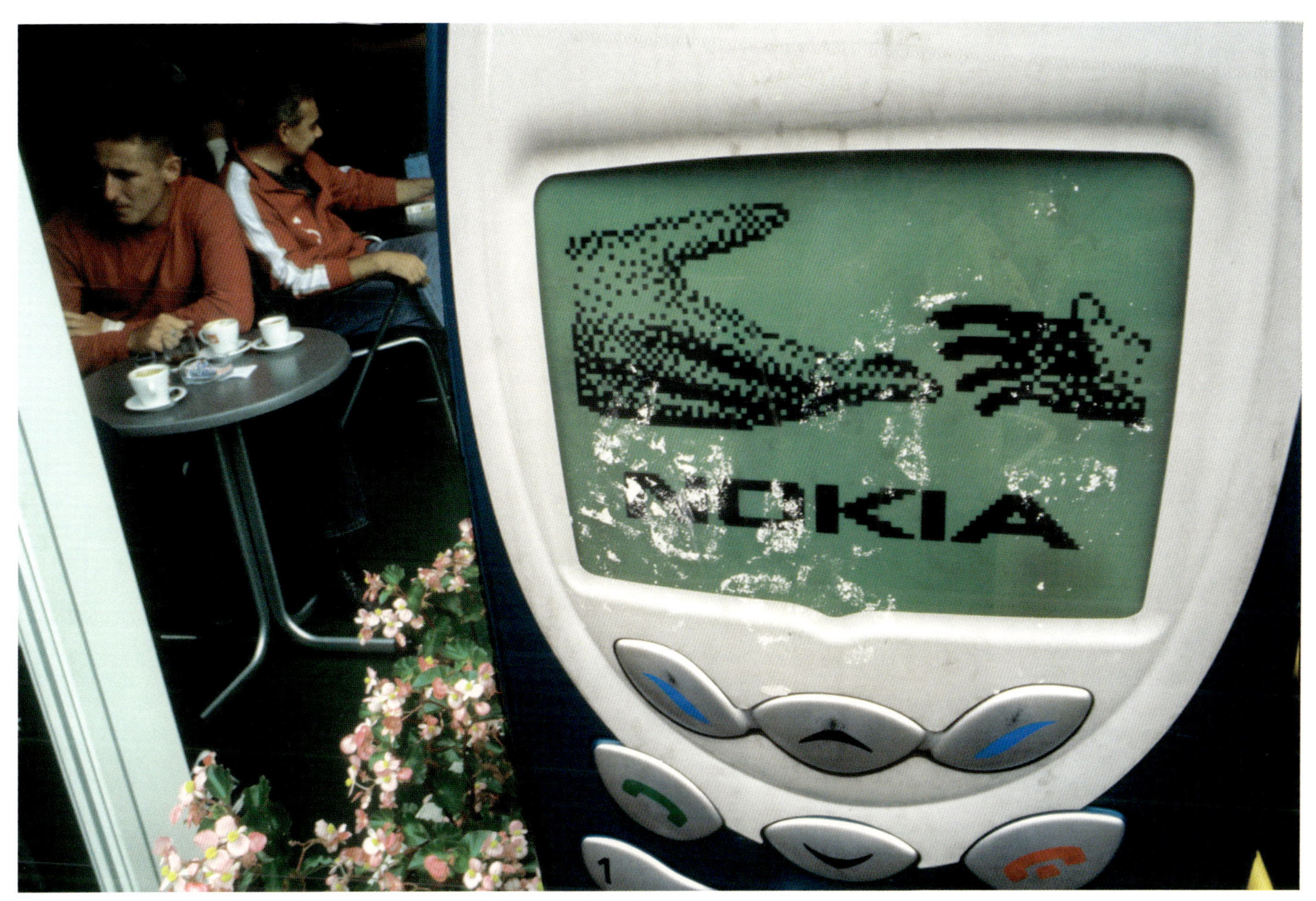
NOKIA

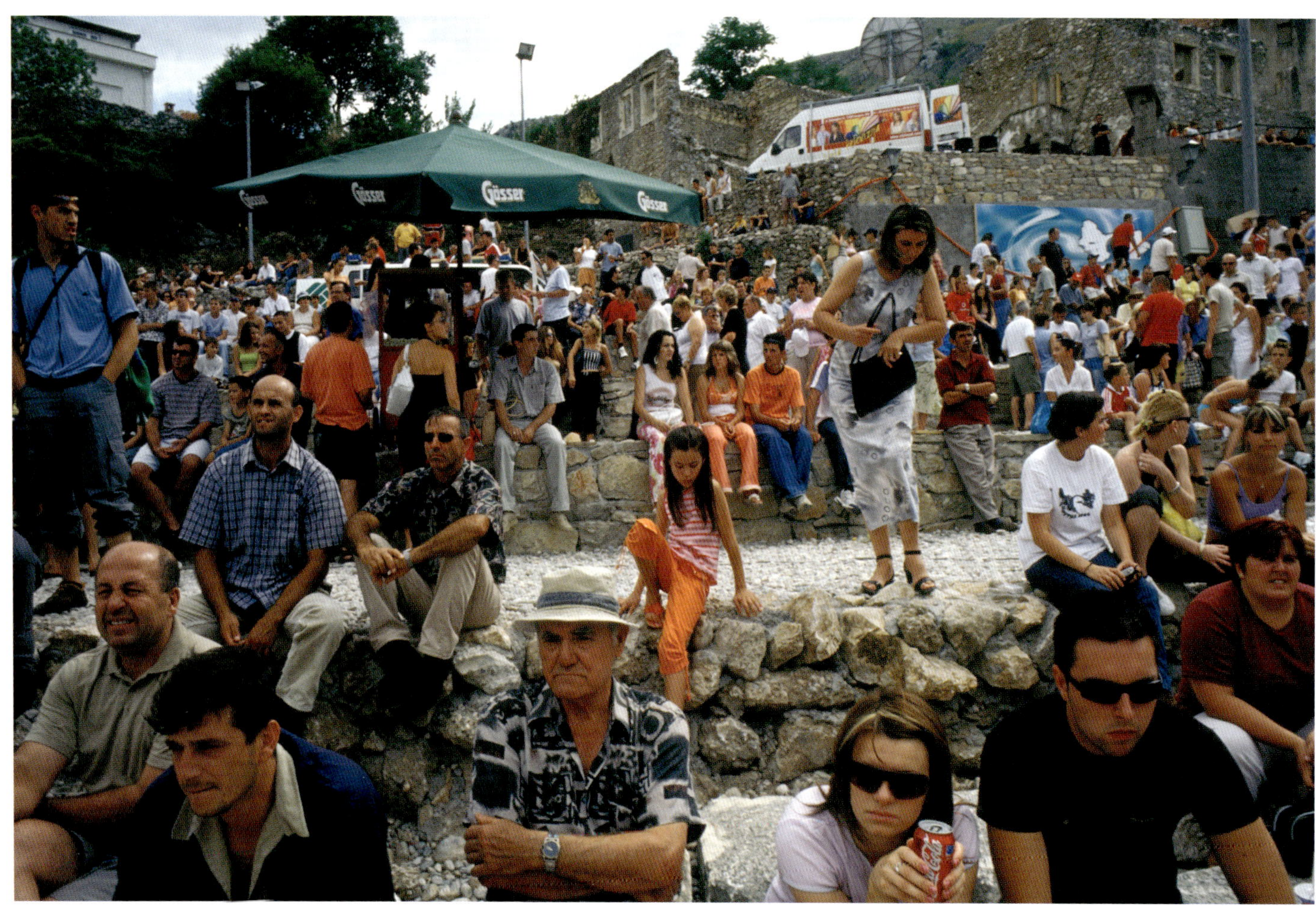
Gösser

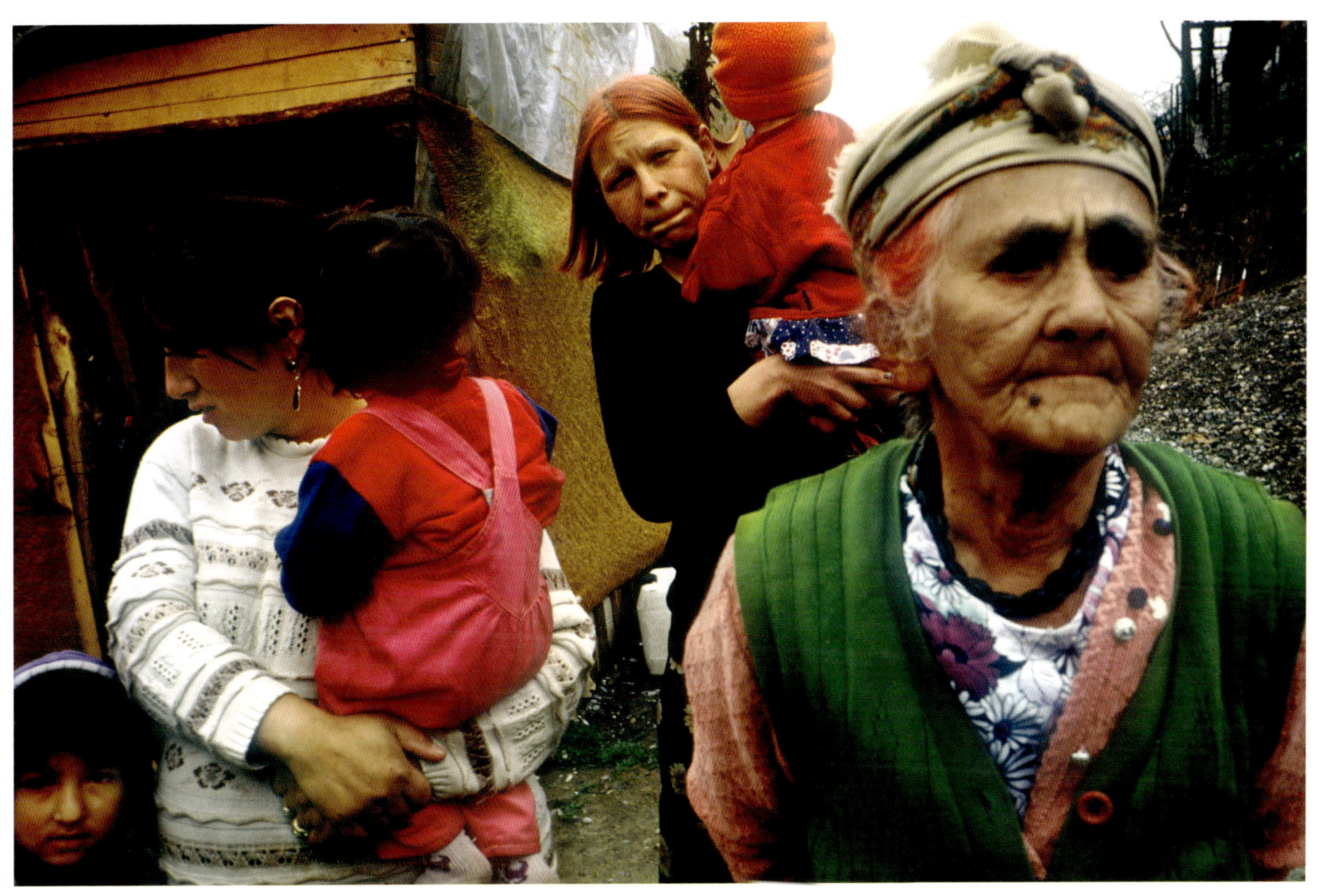

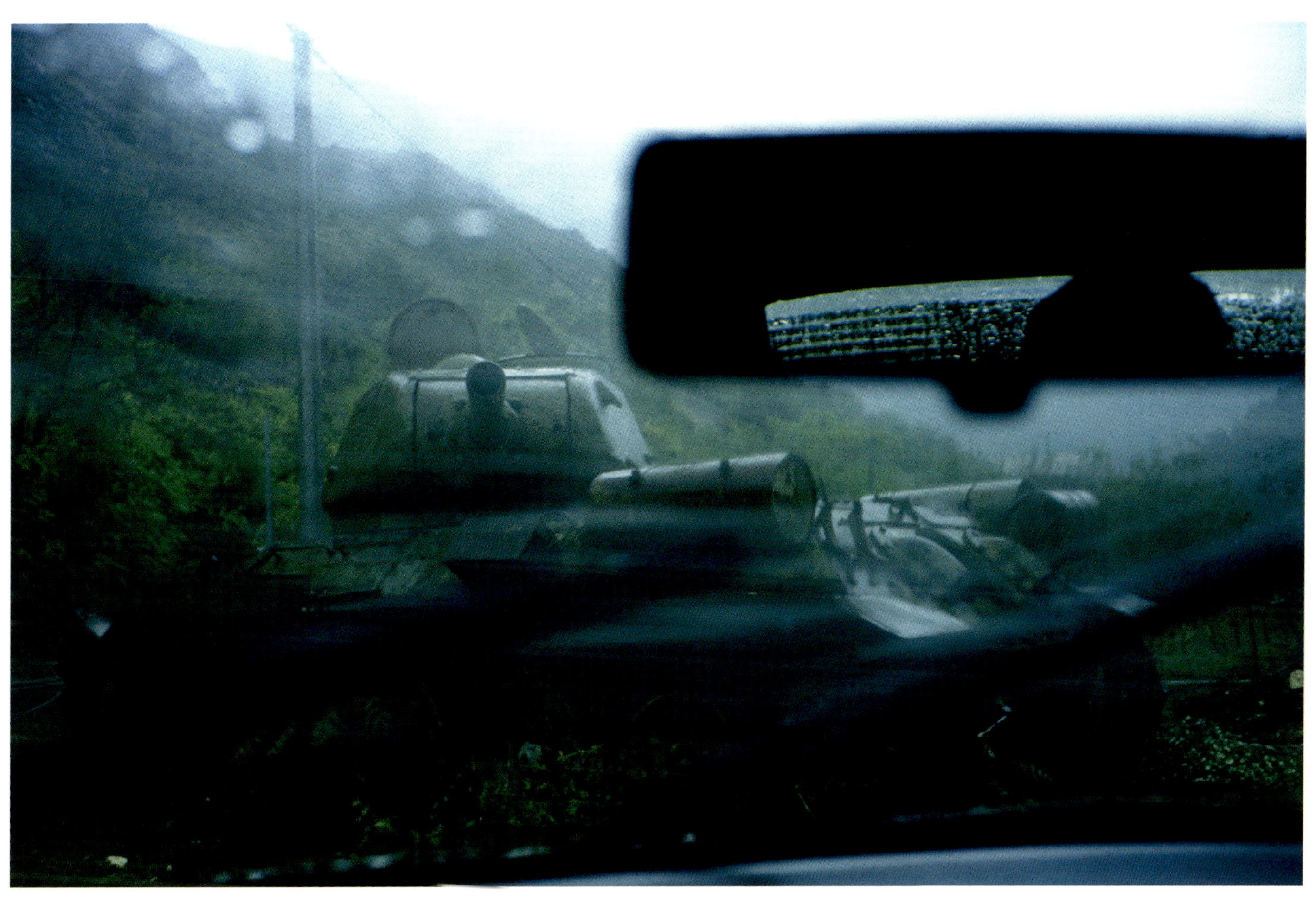

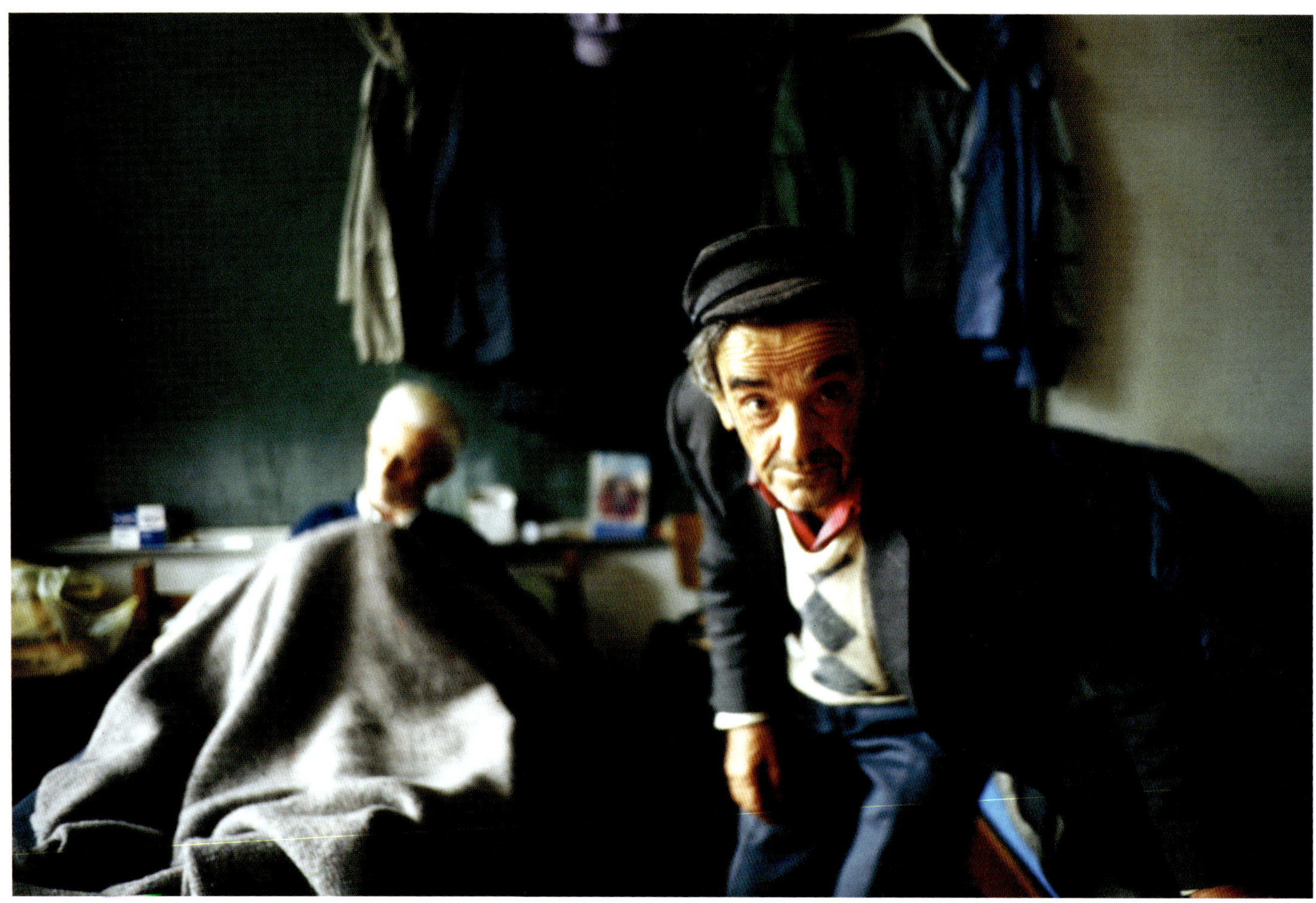

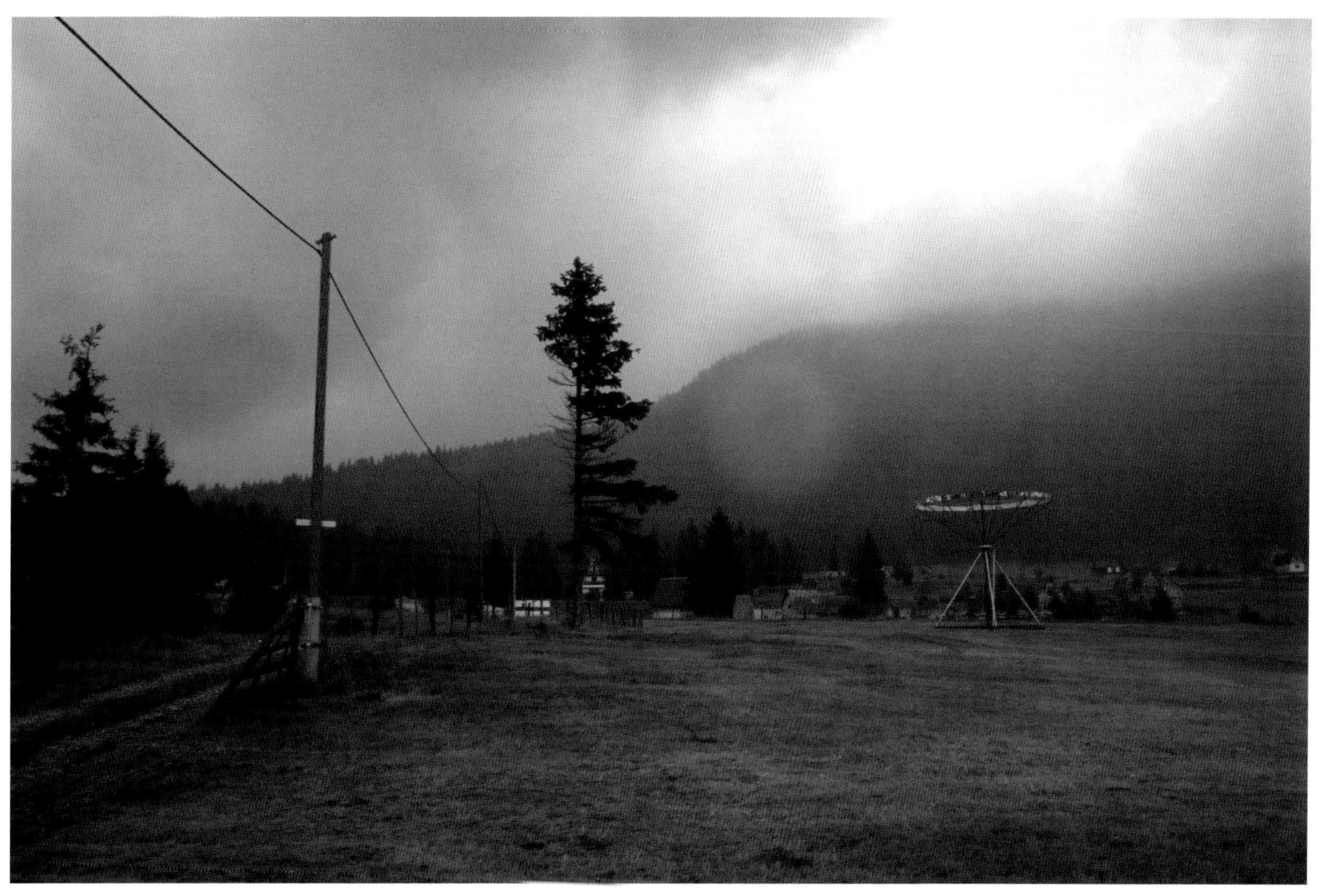

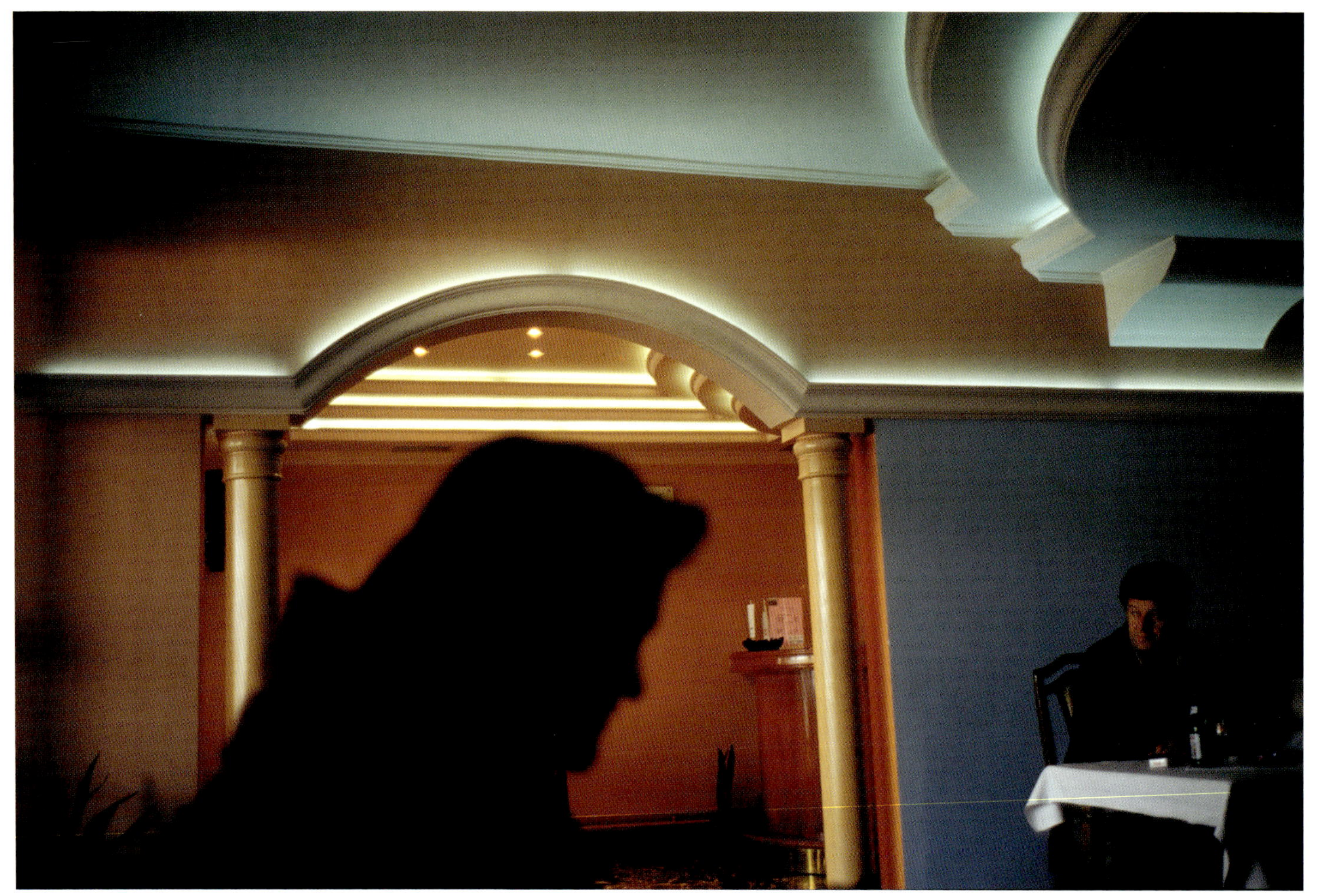

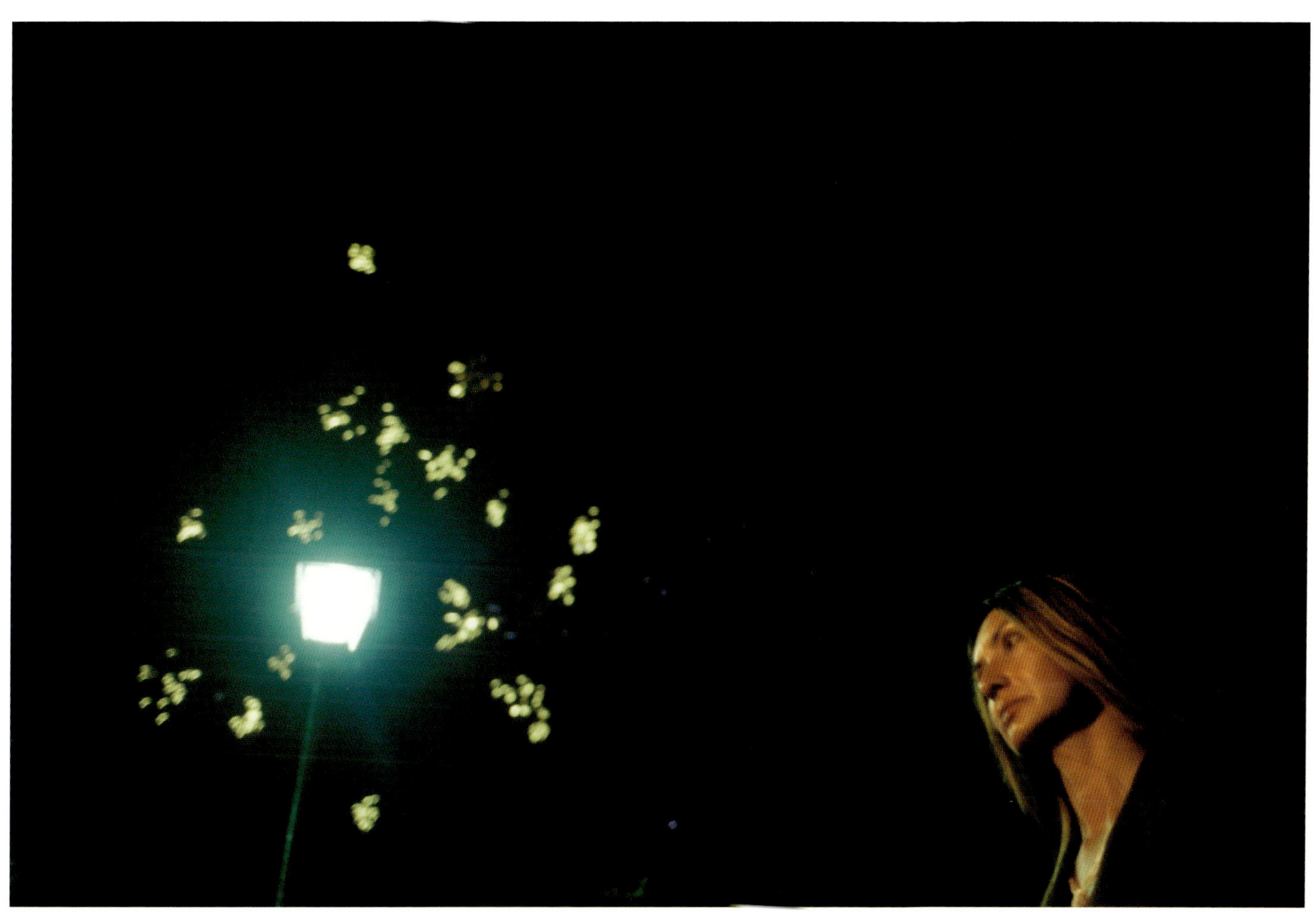

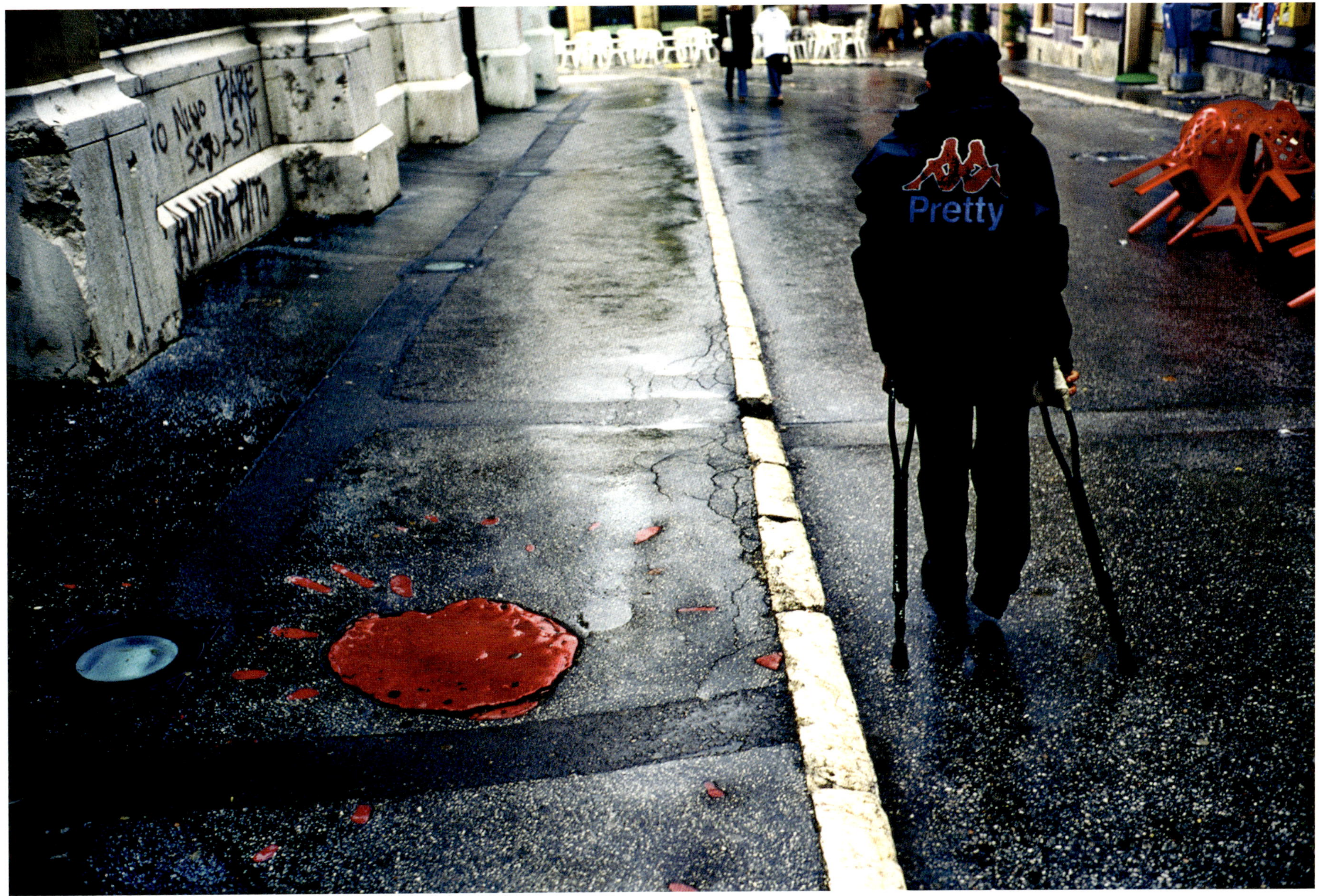
Pretty

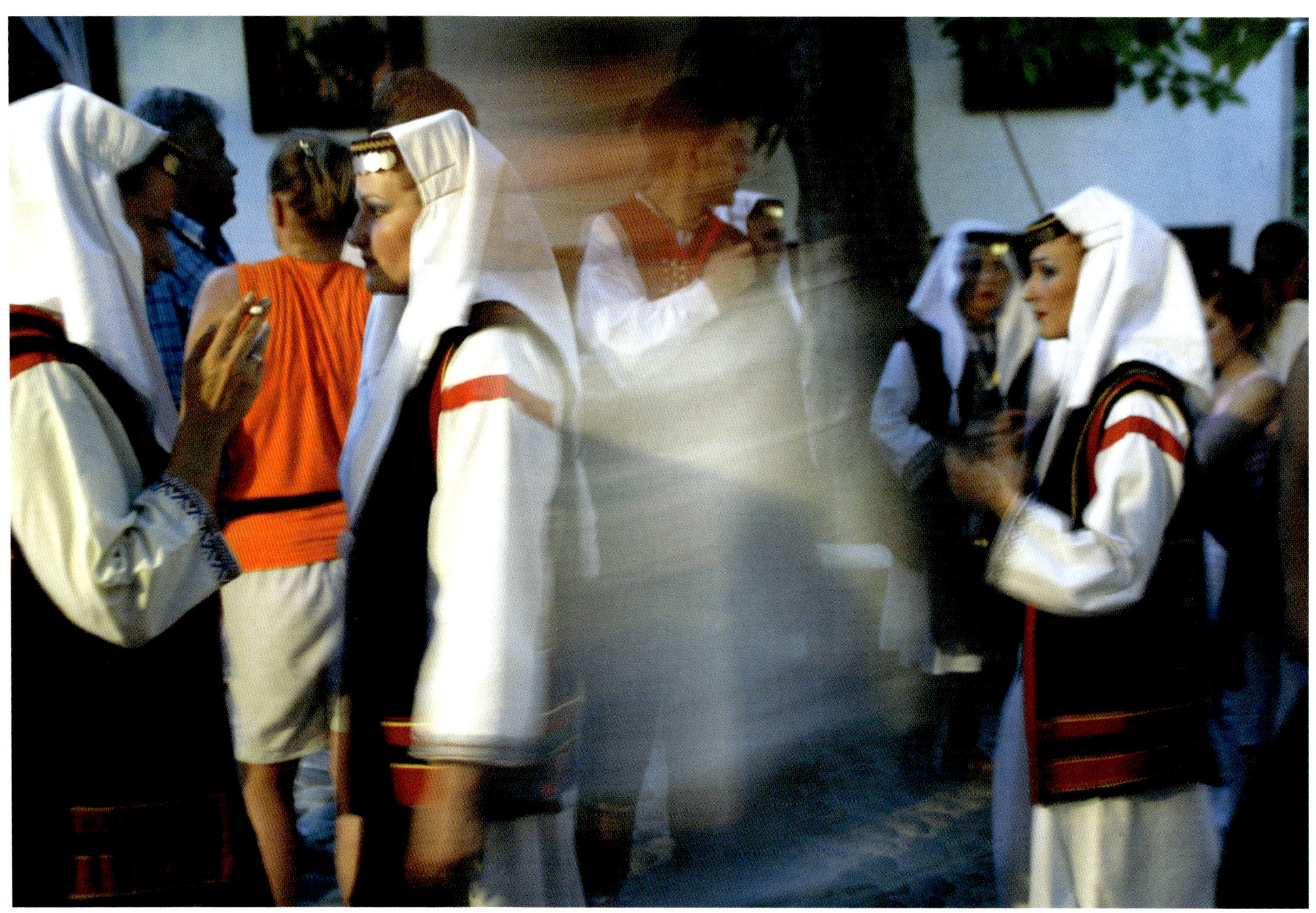

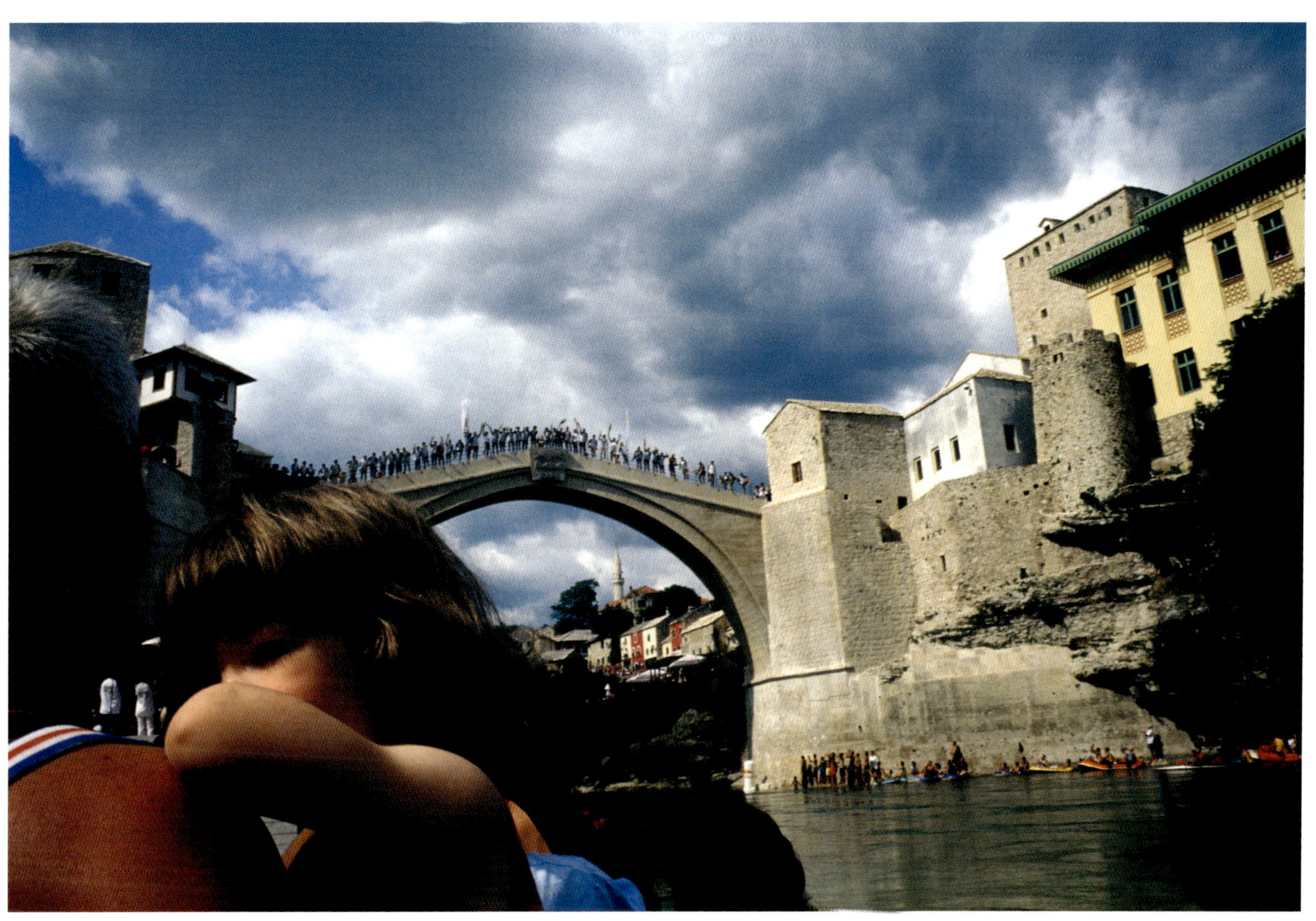

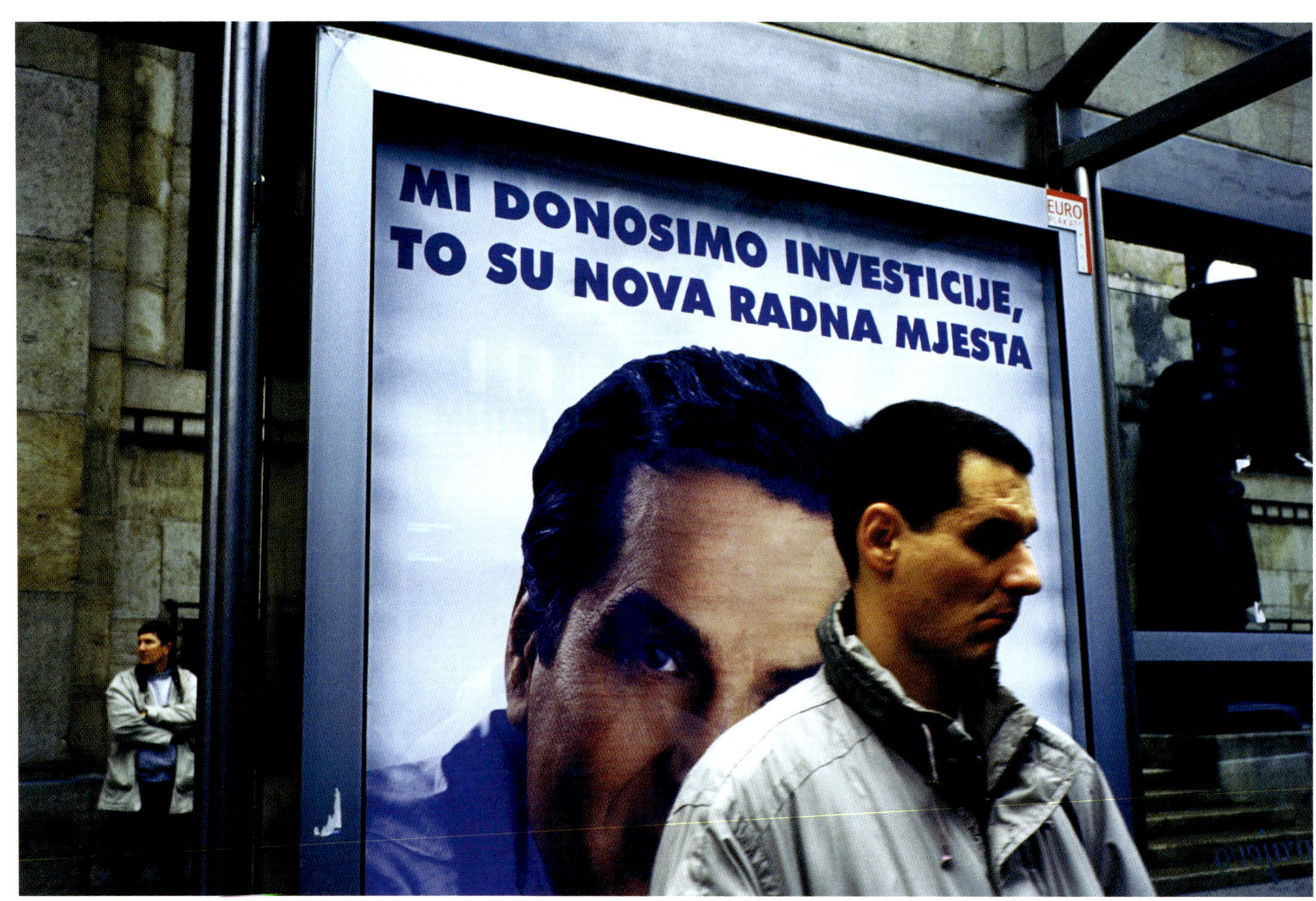
MI DONOSIMO INVESTICIJE,
TO SU NOVA RADNA MJESTA
EURO

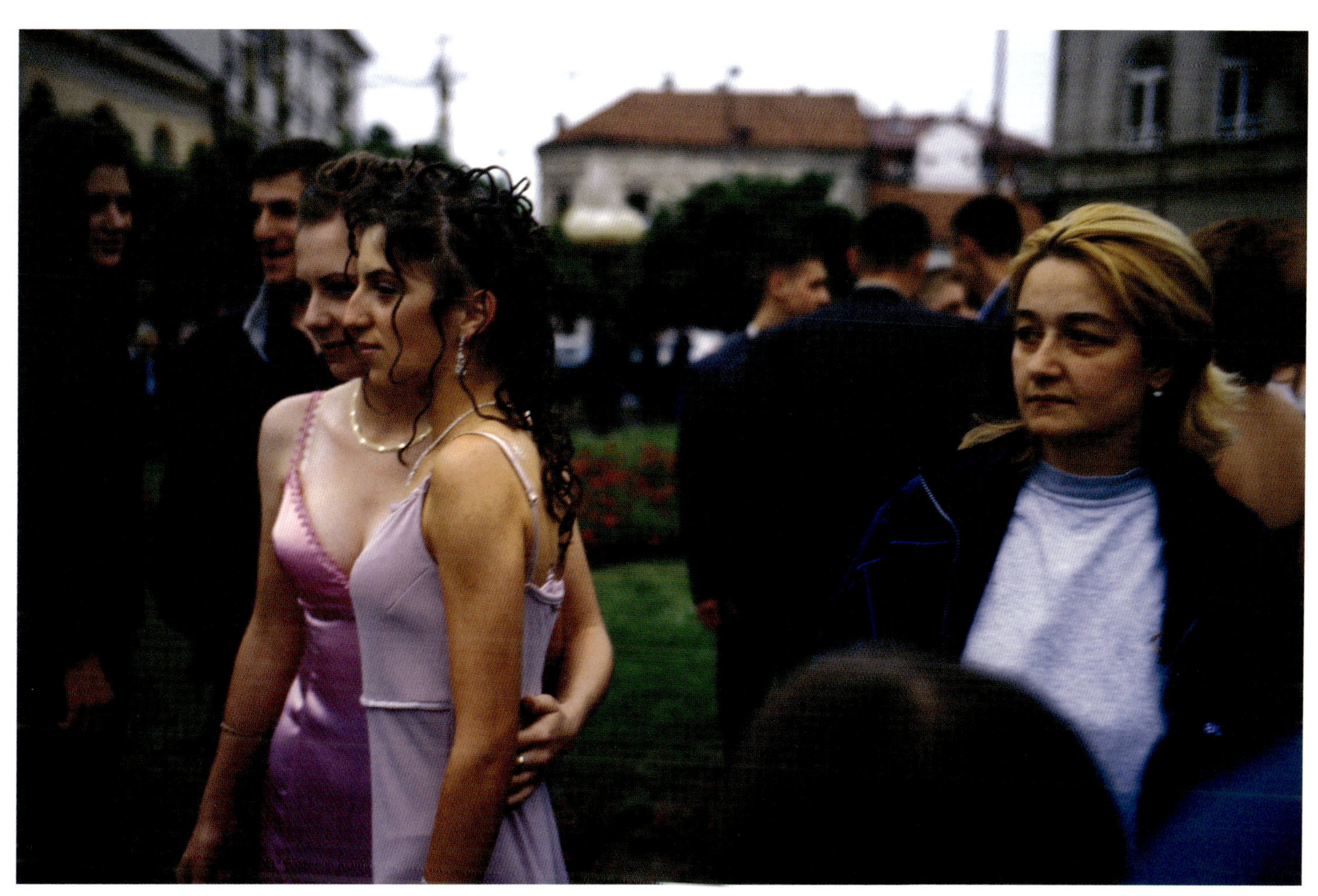

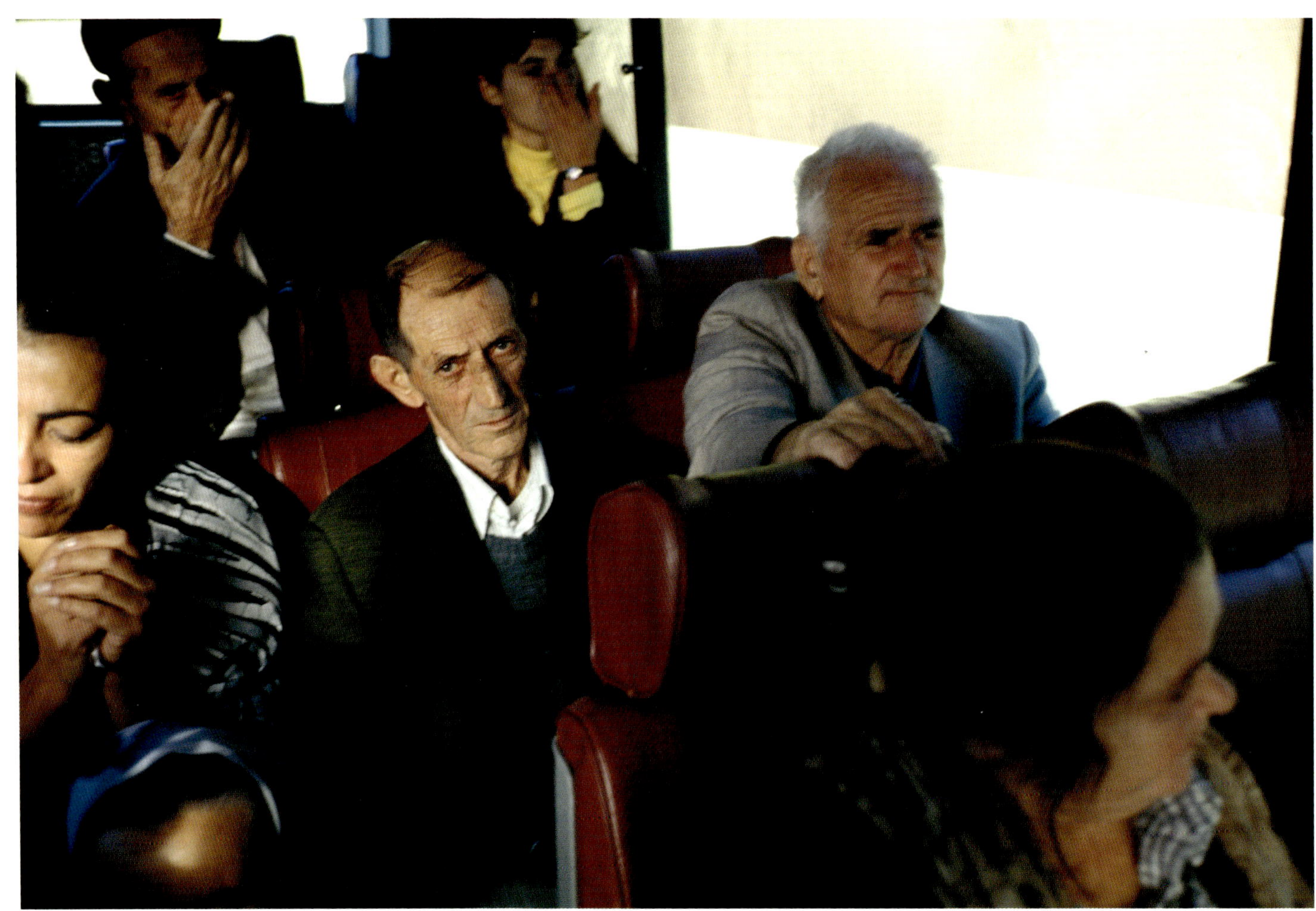

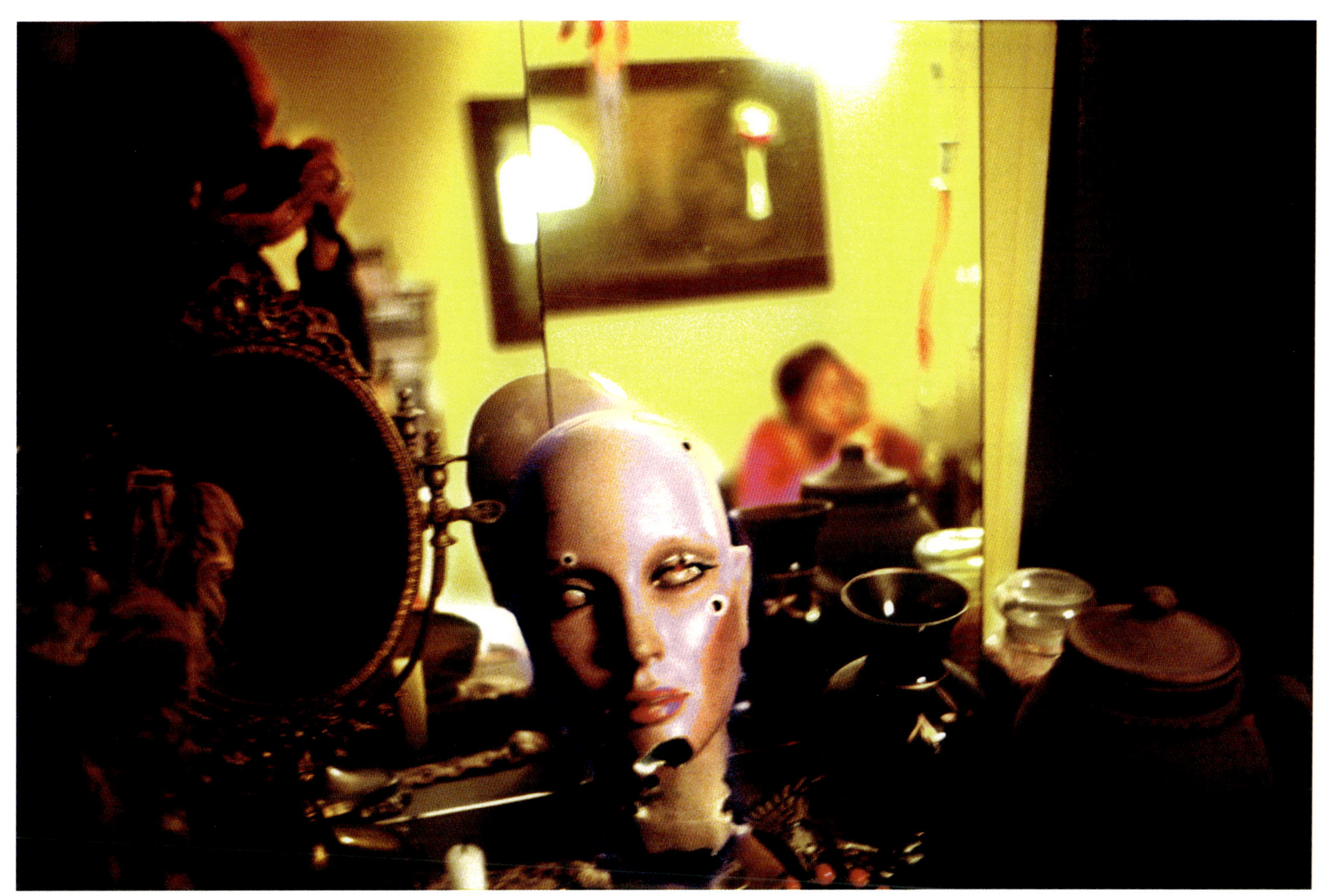

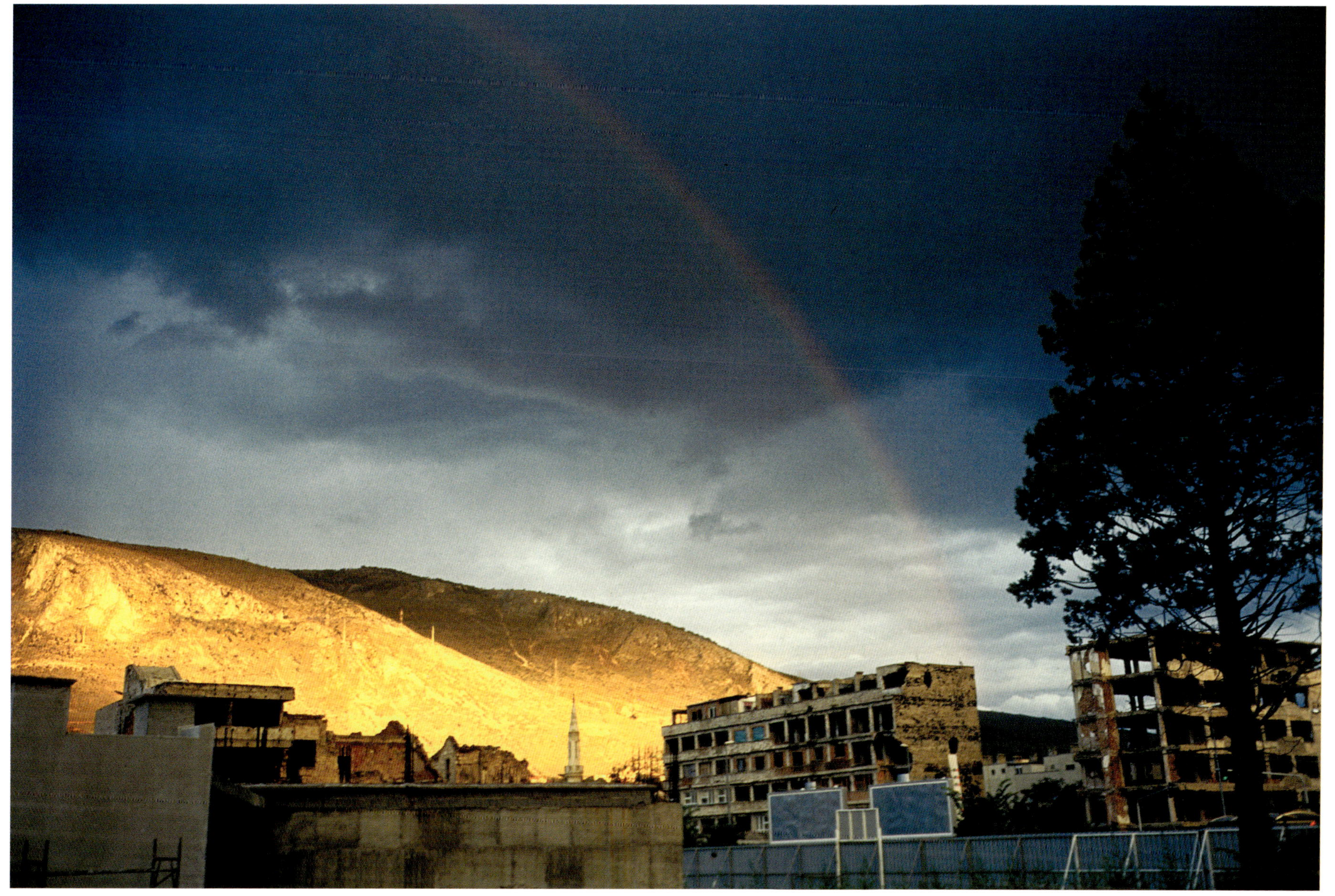

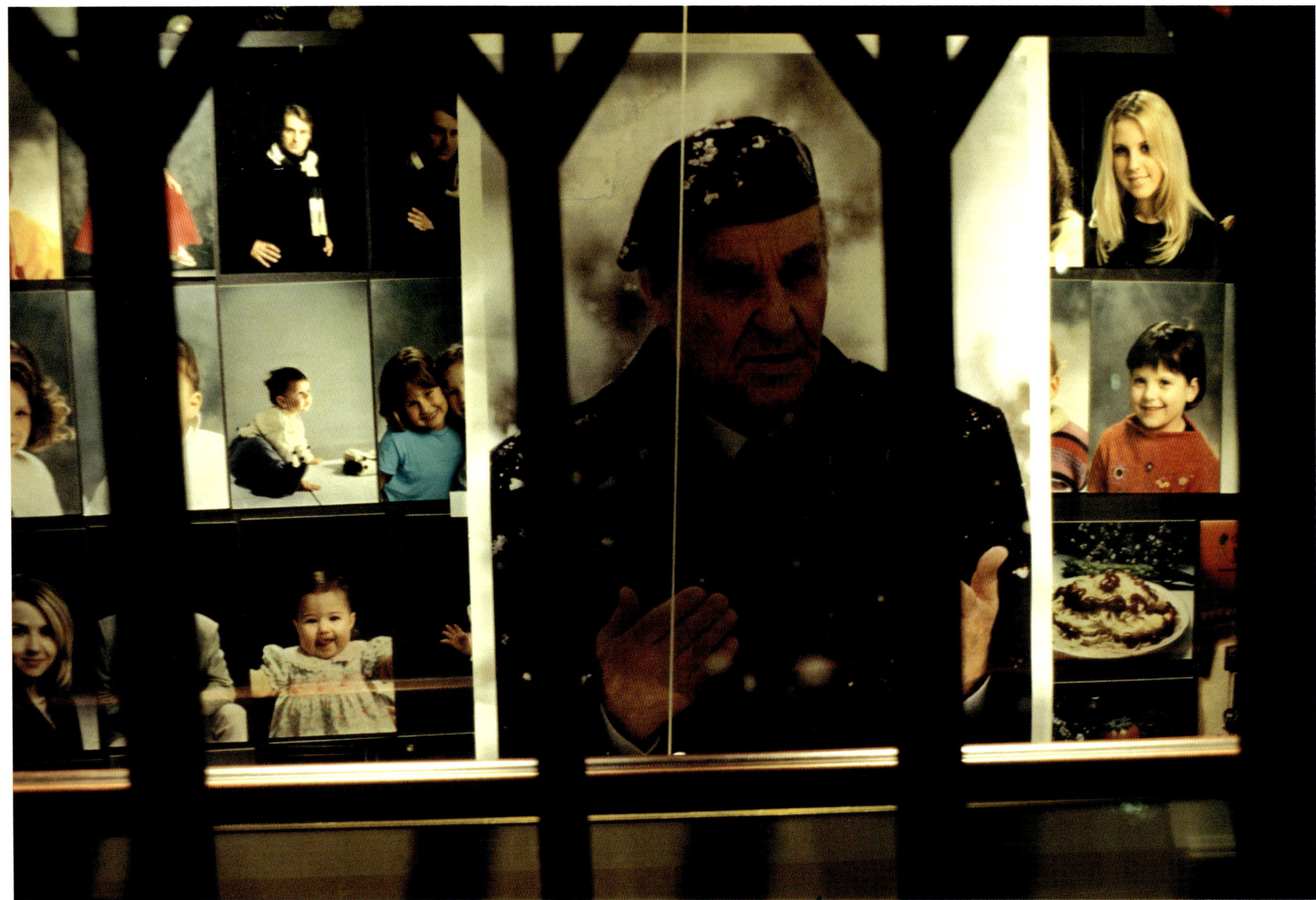

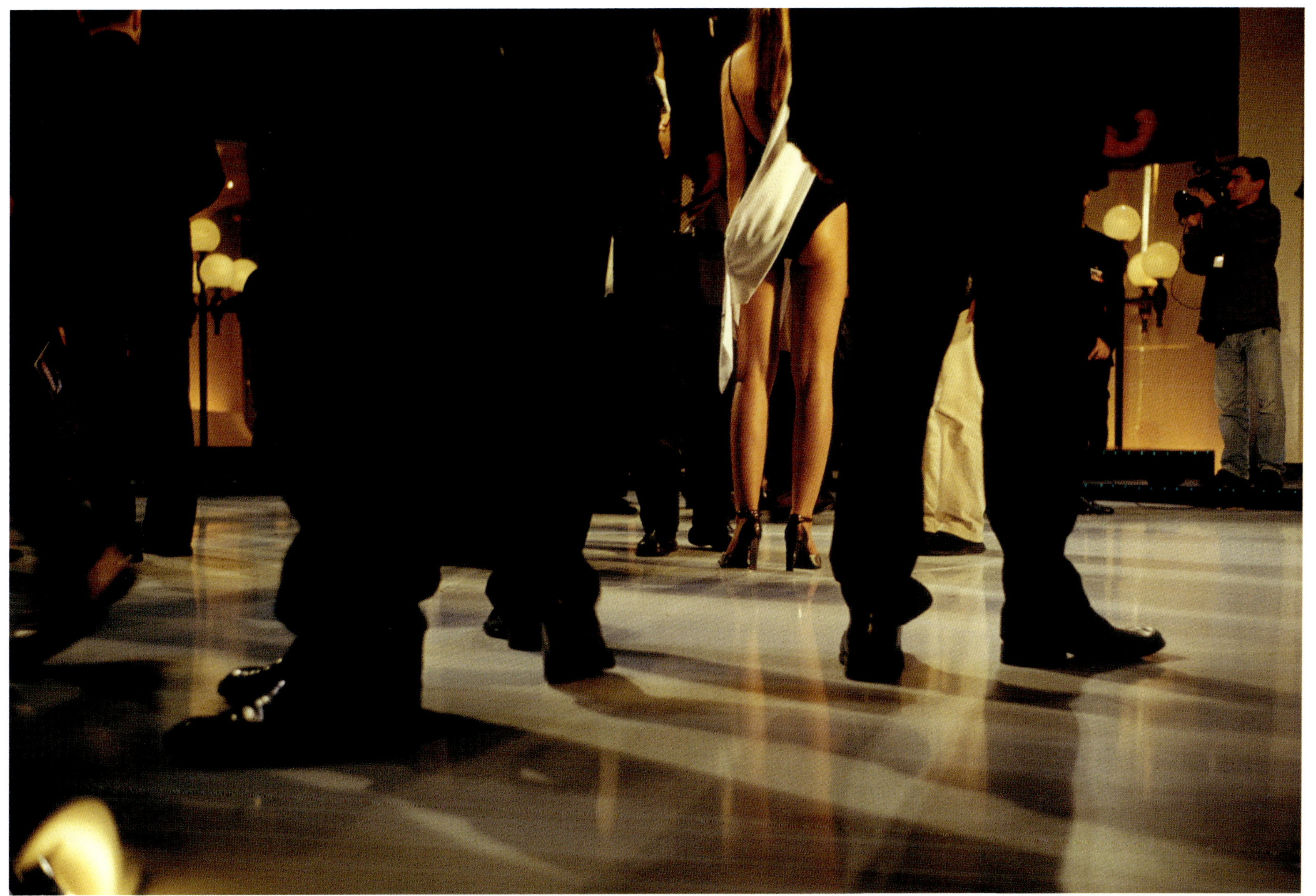

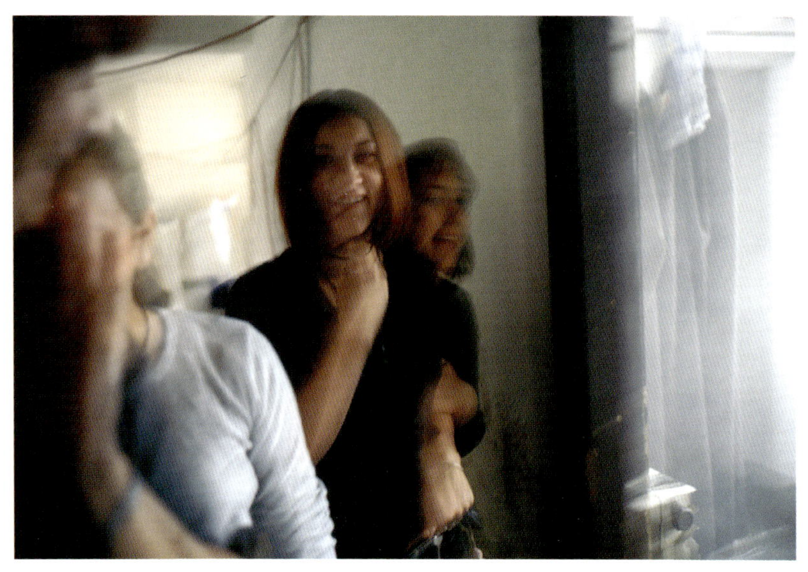

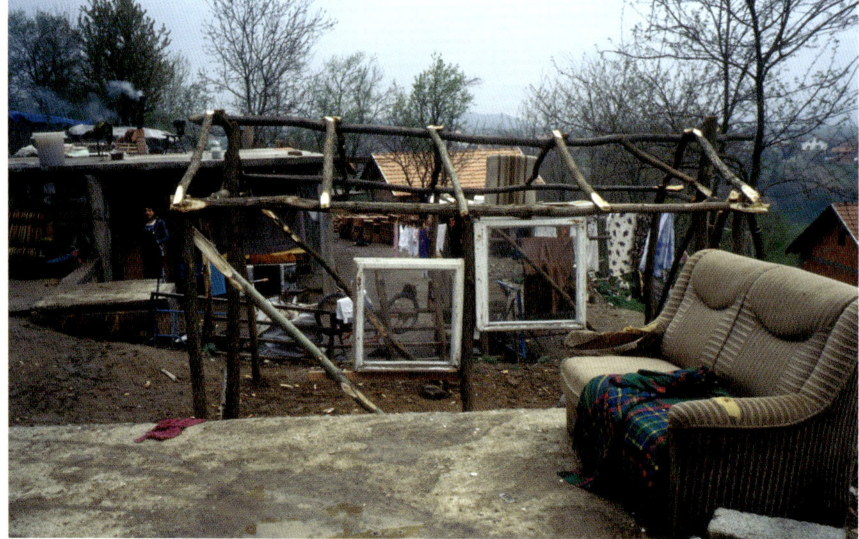

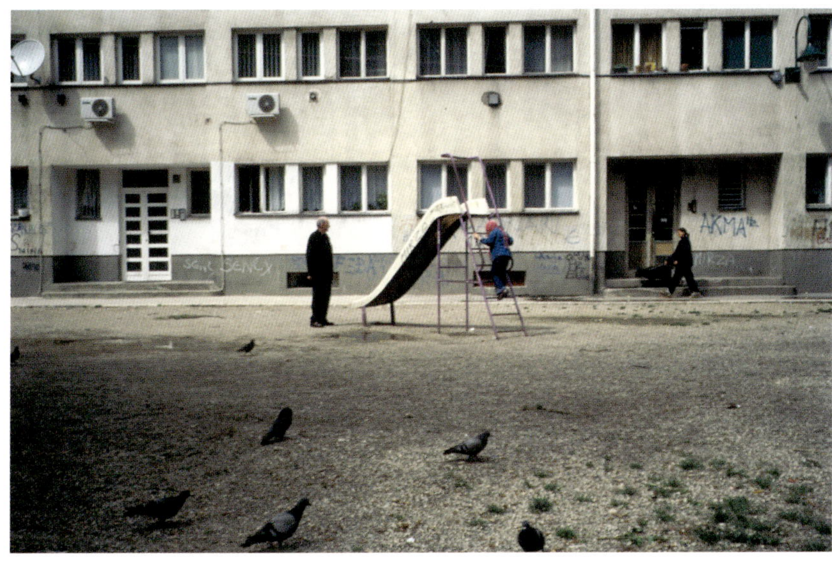
AKMA

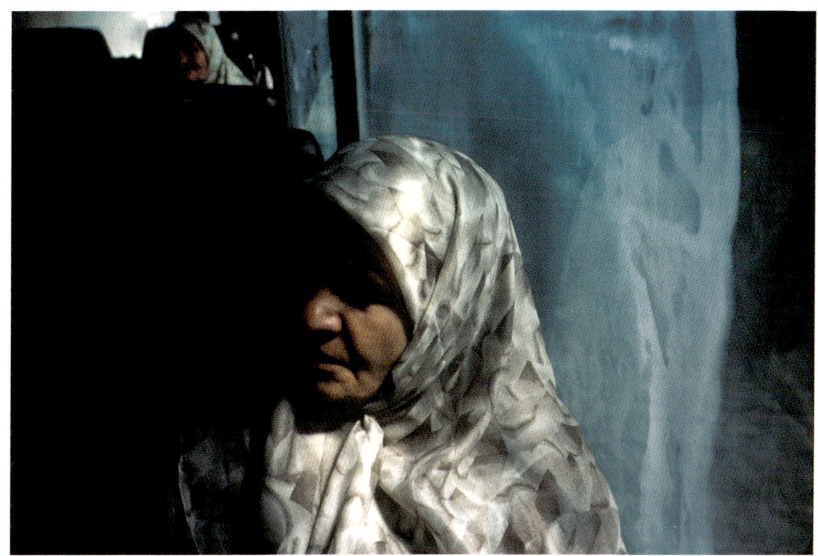

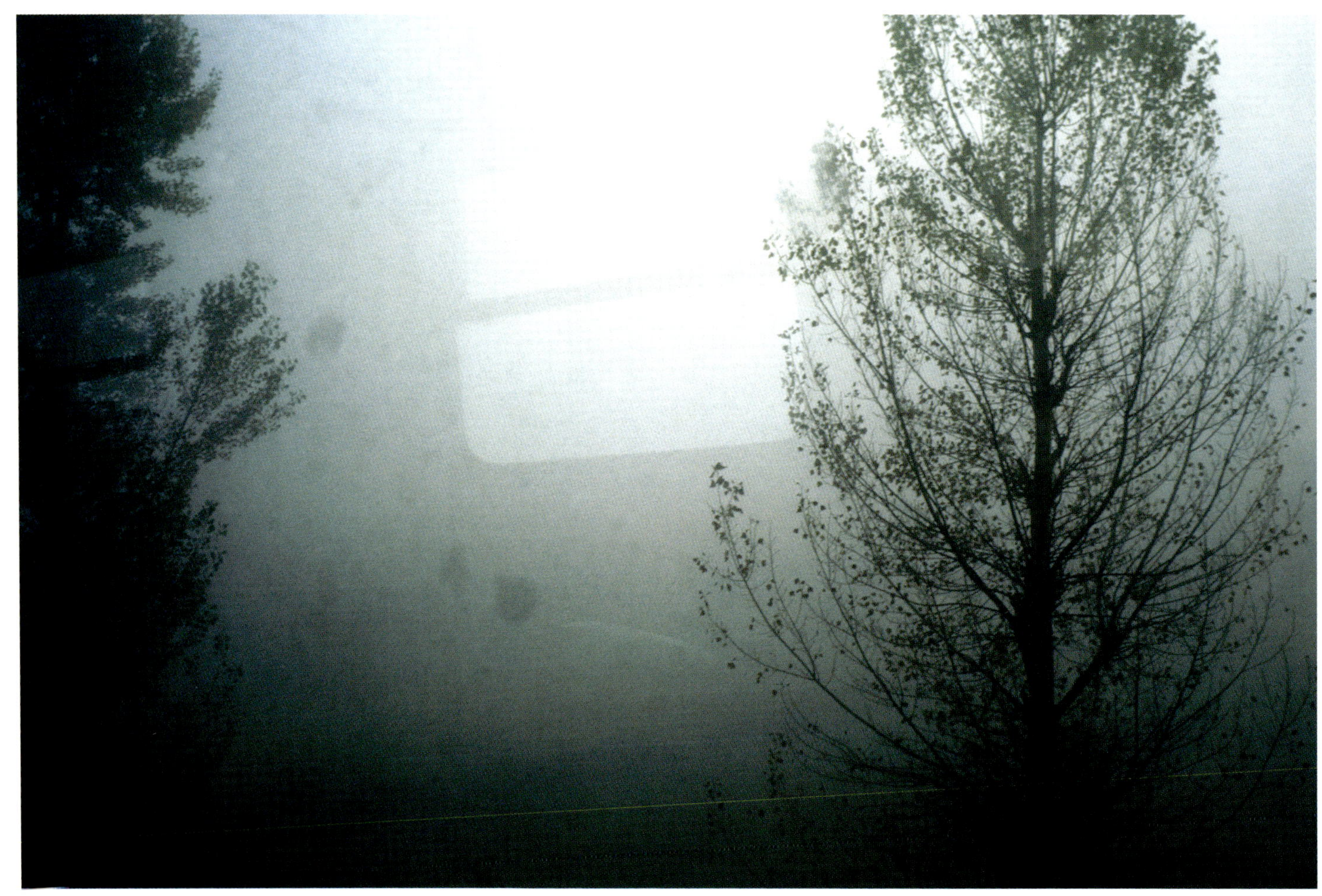

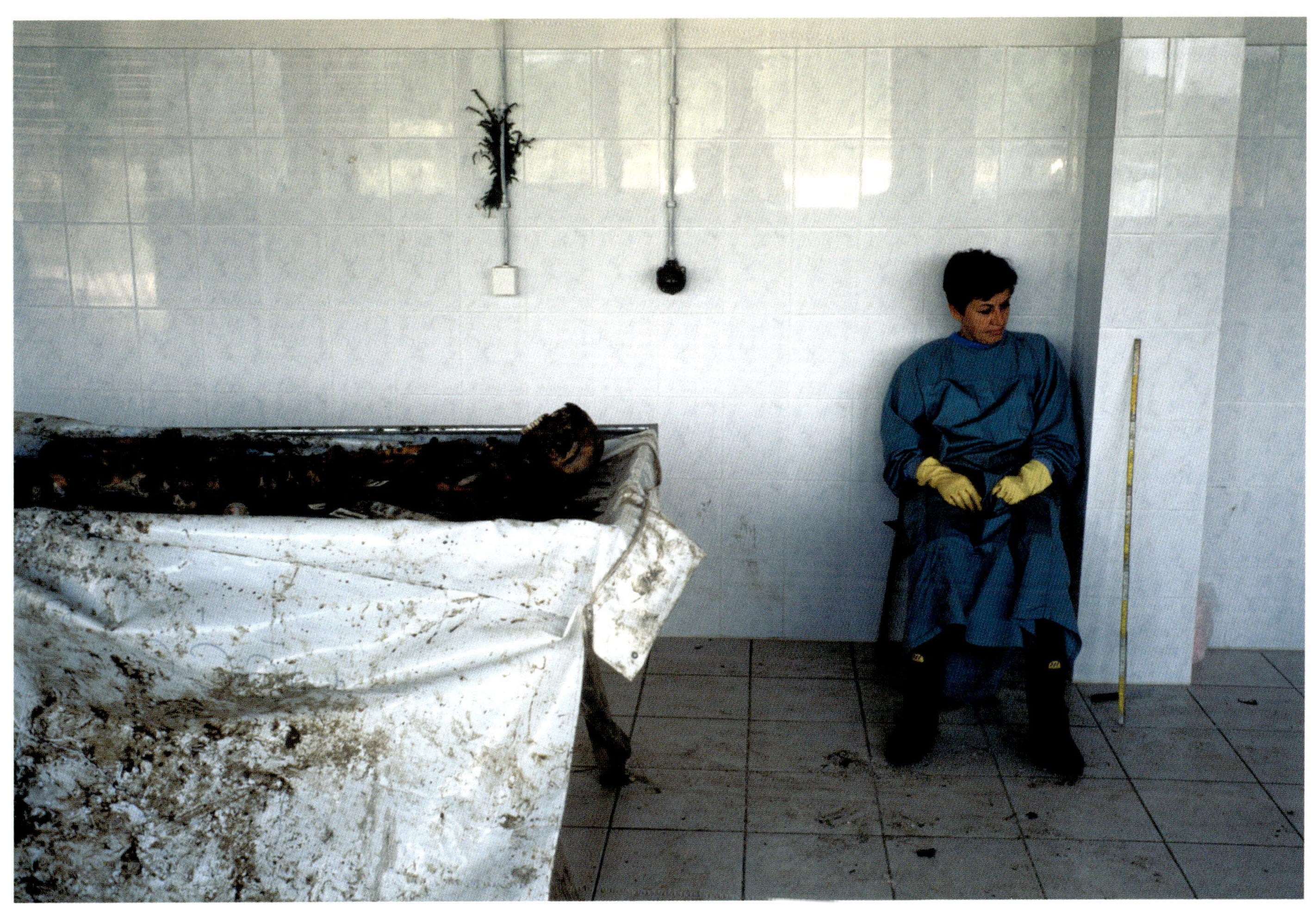

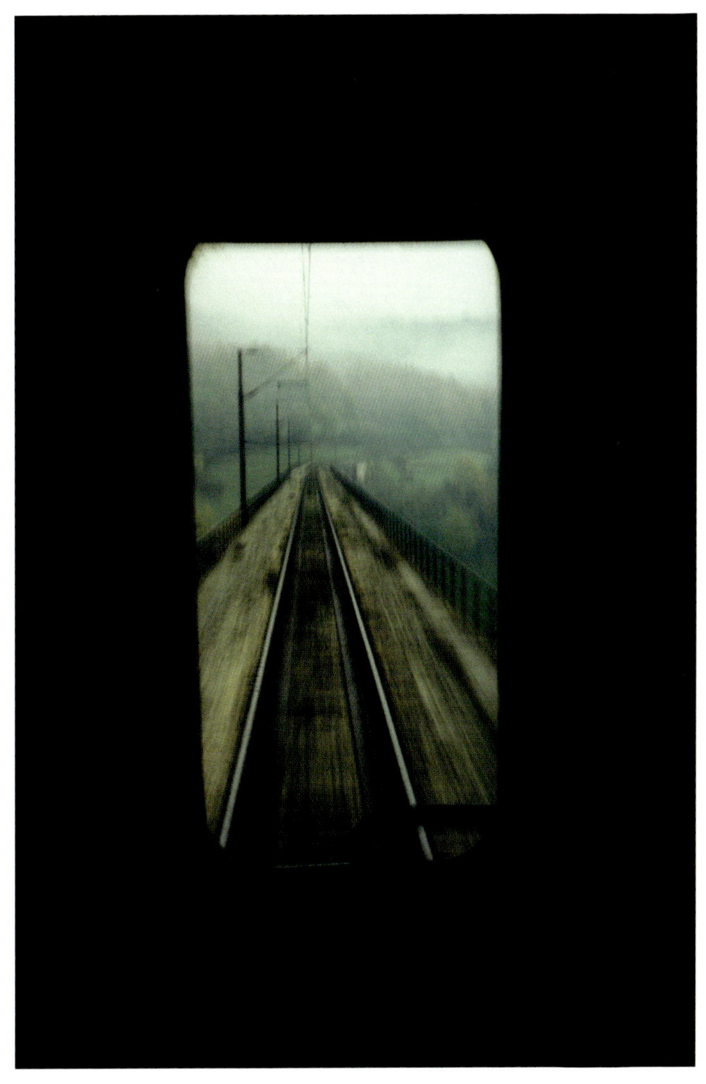

55 Coffehouse. Sarajevo, April, 2002.

56 The day after ceremonies marked the opening of the rebuilt Mostar Bridge, one of the town's legendary jumpers prepares to throw himself off the more than eighty-foot-high bridge. The old bridge, built during the Ottoman Empire, was long a symbol of Bosnia's cultural heritage before it was destroyed in the 1992-95 war. July 24, 2004.

57 Street scene. Banja Luka, July 28, 2004.

58 Crowds line the banks of the Neretva River, waiting for what locals say is the 448th annual jumping and diving competition in Mostar. Local youth have proved their athletic prowess on the more than eighty-foot-high bridge for years. Even during the 1992-95 war, when the bridge was destroyed, they continued to jump from the side of where the old bridge once stood. July 31, 2004.

59 A Roma, or gypsy, woman, with her daughters-in-law and grandchildren, stands in front of a makeshift home in the village of Strazenica. During the war, gypsies were also "cleansed" by Serbs; these gypsies were forced to leave their homes and have returned to rebuild. Strazenica, April 11, 2002.

61 An abandoned Serb tank still stands on the side of the road near the town of Stolac, which saw heavy fighting during the war. September 26, 2002.

62 Serb refugees, living in a schoolroom being used for "temporary" housing. After the end of the war "collective centers" were set up all over the country, in schools, gymnasiums, old warehouses and other spaces to house thousands of refugees. The centers were meant to provide housing for three months only, but five years after the end of the war, more than 10,000 people were still living in extremely difficult conditions in these centers. Kosorac, October 2000.

63 A carnival-type ride stands unused along the side of a road. Near Travnik, July 28, 2004.

64 Dining room of one of the many "motels" that have been built along the roads outside towns across the country. Banja Luka, October 4, 2002.

65 A television reporter waits to do a live report as fireworks light up the sky during the dedication ceremonies of the rebuilt Mostar Bridge. July 23, 2004.

67 A "rose" of Sarajevo marks one of the thousands of deadly mortar blasts fired at the city by Serb forces during the 1992-95 siege. Mortar blasts leave a pattern that looks like a flower; after the war, some blasts were filled in with red as a commemoration to those who died. Sarajevo, September 2002.

68 Dancers in traditional Bosnian dress take a cigarette break while waiting to perform in the ceremony that marked the opening of the rebuilt Mostar Bridge. Despite the symbolic significance of the reconstructed bridge, which joins the eastern Muslim half of the city with the Croat, or Catholic, western half, Mostar remains a bitterly-divided community, with little mixing between the two groups. Local Croats chose overwhelmingly to have little to do with the dedication ceremonies. July 23, 2004.

69 While crowds line the banks of the Neretva river, competitors line the top of the famed Mostar Bridge ready to begin the city's 448th annual jumping and diving contest. The competition was held just eight days after the newly rebuilt bridge was opened. July 31, 2004.

70 At a bus stop in Sarajevo, an election poster for the moderate "Stranka za BiH" party ("Party for Bosnia Hercegovina") reads, in rough translation, "Through Investment, to New Jobs," a reference to the country's troubled economy, and its unemployment rate of nearly fifty percent. The man in the poster is Haris Silajdzic, who served as prime minister during the war. September 2002.

71 High school prom night in the town of Bjeljina, where "ethnic cleansing" began in April 1992, when Serbian paramilitary forces and local Serbs attacked the city's Muslim community, killing many people and forcing the rest of the Muslim population to flee. Some 8,000 Muslims have returned to the city, which is in the northeastern part of the country, along the border with Serbia. May 22, 2003.

72 Srebrenica refugees on a bus taking them from Sarajevo to their home town, to inspect the homes they fled in 1995 and to begin legal proceedings to reclaim their property. September 2000.

73 A mannequin head used for target practice during the war sits on a bureau in an apartment in Grbavica, a Sarajevo neighborhood that was a frontline during the war. July 2001.

75 A rainbow crosses the late-afternoon sky in Mostar; the destroyed buildings in the foreground mark the war's frontline, which divided the Catholic and Muslim sections of the city. September 25, 2002.

76 A photo of Alija Izetbegovic, who served as president of Bosnia during the war and who resisted Western efforts to force him to agree to demands from Serbia and Croatia to carve up the country. After Izetbegovic died in November, 2003, photos of him in his trademark beret sprang up all over Sarajevo, and remained in place months later. March 2004.

77 The winner of the 2002 Miss Bosnia and Hercegovina contest. Sarajevo, September 21, 2002.

78a Muslim teenagers in the hall of a university dormitory wing still being used for "emergency" housing, five years after the end of the war. Each room housed one family. Tuzla, October 2000.

78b Rebuilding a Roma village destroyed by Serbs during the war. Strazenica, April 11, 2002.

79a Playground in front of an apartment building. Sarajevo, April 2002.

79b Srebrenica widow. July 11, 2001.

80 Window reflection from a one-car passenger train that runs between Sarajevo and the town of Konjic, about forty-five minutes to the south. Before the war, the former Yugoslavia had one of the best rail transit systems in Europe. Bosnia's rail system was virtually destroyed during the conflict, and is only slowly being rebuilt. October 7, 2002.

81 A forensic anthropologist takes a break from cleaning the remains of a recently-exhumed victim of the Serbs' 1992 "ethnic cleansing" campaign against Muslims. Sanski Most, July 2001.

83 View from the back of the one-car passenger train that runs between Sarajevo and Konjic. October 7, 2002.

ljubav i smrt
LOVE AND DEATH

> journal notes and observations

If I have become comfortable in the presence of bones, it is because of Ewa and Piotr. I have spent many long days with them as they examined the skeletons they have helped exhume from mass graves, victims of the 1992 "ethnic cleansing" campaign waged by Serbs against their Muslim neighbors. Neither Ewa nor Piotr is Bosnian – they are Polish-born forensic anthropologists – but they are committed to the people of Bosnia, to finding their hidden dead, so that they may finally be laid to rest.

On my first trip to Bosnia, in the fall of 2000, I walked into a warehouse in the town of Sanski Most, which was full of skeletons, laid out with the clothing which had been found still clinging to the bones in the mass graves where they had been hastily buried. People came and paced the aisles that day, looking for something they could recognize of a loved one – a shirt, a shoe, a lucky charm – the first step in the identification process, which could then be confirmed with a DNA test. Ewa and Piotr were there, although I did not know them then. It wasn't until later, after I'd met them during another trip, that I recognized them in the background of a picture I took that day. That first time, I only stayed an hour or so – overwhelmed, I suppose, by all those remains, by the stench, by the awfulness of what had been done to them, by the heavy sorrow of those who came looking for those they had lost, by the muffled sob of recognition of the woman who knelt at the feet of one skeleton, picking up the sweater she knew had been worn by her husband the last day of his life. I cannot believe now that I stayed so short a time, but then I was still new to the story of Bosnia, still uncertain of the pictures that were waiting to be seen.

It was on my next trip, in July of 2001, that I met Piotr and Ewa. I spent days at exhumations of mass graves and in warehouses where remains were cleaned and autopsied, then laid out, each one numbered and marked by the location of the grave where it was found, so that families could come to try to make identifications.

It's the shoes that make me cry, a pile of them on a stainless steel table, some torn, some missing a lace. I ask Ewa why they are so poignant, and she says it's because they are so personal, like a handprint or a signature. For Ewa, this work is a mission, I think. She says, "These people were killed and stripped of their identity. They have a right to their identity. We are trying to return their identities to them. These bones are somehow living." It's from Ewa and Piotr – who say to the skeletons, Excuse me, or, I'm sorry, if they accidentally step on a bone – that I begin to see this part of Bosnia's story as something more than a tale of death. Piotr says, "It's about families. It's about Bosnia. It's a story about life. These were people who were living. They cannot tell the story that brought them here. But their skeletons tell stories – where they were shot, what happened when they were killed. And the story of these remains is part of the story of the living – of the families who have been searching, waiting, needing to know."

It wasn't until more than a year later – on another trip, in the fall of 2002 – that I finally began to see this story as a story of love. I was with Ewa and Piotr again, this time at one of the mass graves of victims of the 1995 Srebrenica massacre of some 7,000 to 8,000 Muslim men and boys. This grave was huge – with several hundred partial remains and bodies – and the exhumation had been going on for weeks by the time I arrived. I had come on this trip knowing that I had yet to take a picture of an exhumation that I felt was a definitive image. And I knew why I had failed. I hate exhumations. I hate the smell, the muck of the pit, the horror of decomposing bodies, the thoughts that stream through your mind about what it must have been like for these people in the final frightening moments of their life. Most of all, I hate the hatred that put them there. Up until this time, I had kept my distance from the exhumation pit, taking pictures from the rim, or of the people who gathered to watch. And the pictures showed that detachment, that reluctance. I was prepared to be closer this time – but not as close as Ewa wanted me to be. She called me into the grave one cloudy afternoon, on to a dirt patch surrounded by partially exposed skeletons. She and Piotr had spent hours working to free the partially preserved arms and hands of what had once been a teenaged boy, and she wanted me to take a picture for her with her small cheap camera. Reluctantly, I balanced myself in the grave and looked through the lens. I nearly threw up. But I looked again and saw Ewa's white-gloved hand and arm as it reached to lift the decaying hand of a long-dead boy. What I saw, I realized, was the image I had been waiting for. I lifted my own camera and snapped a few frames. I knew what I had, and it felt right. Today, when I show this photo to people, they often flinch and turn away. But I always say, Please, look again. For me, this is a photo about life, about love. Yes, the dead hands are horrific, unbearable. But there is also a living hand in that grave, gently drawing the dead from an anonymous pit back to the possibility of life – of identity restored. This hand tells a different story of aftermath. It speaks of an unyielding faith in the human spirit. It speaks of a living goodness that does not cower before the evidence of evil, one that refuses to give the final word to death or to the hatred that caused it.

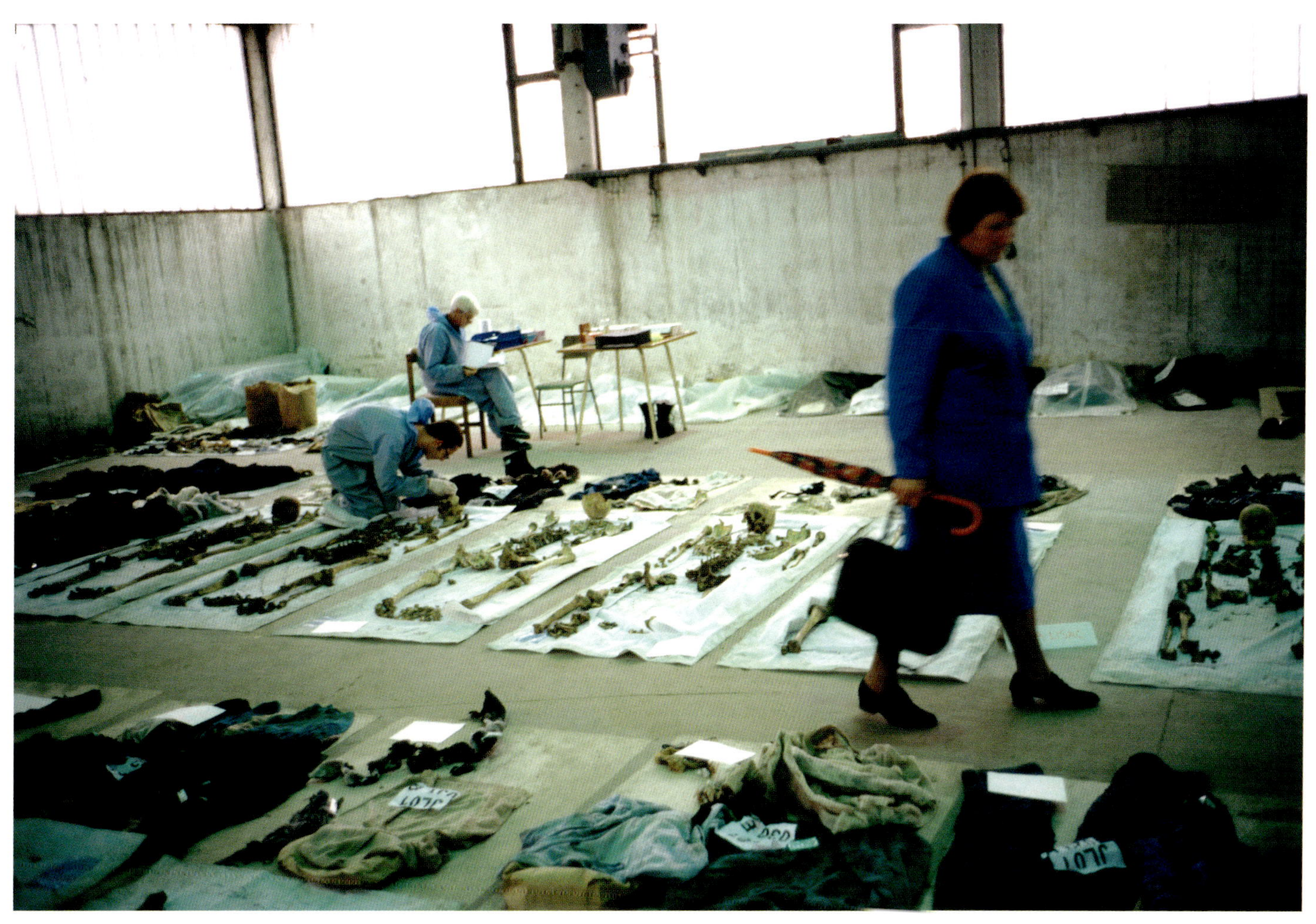

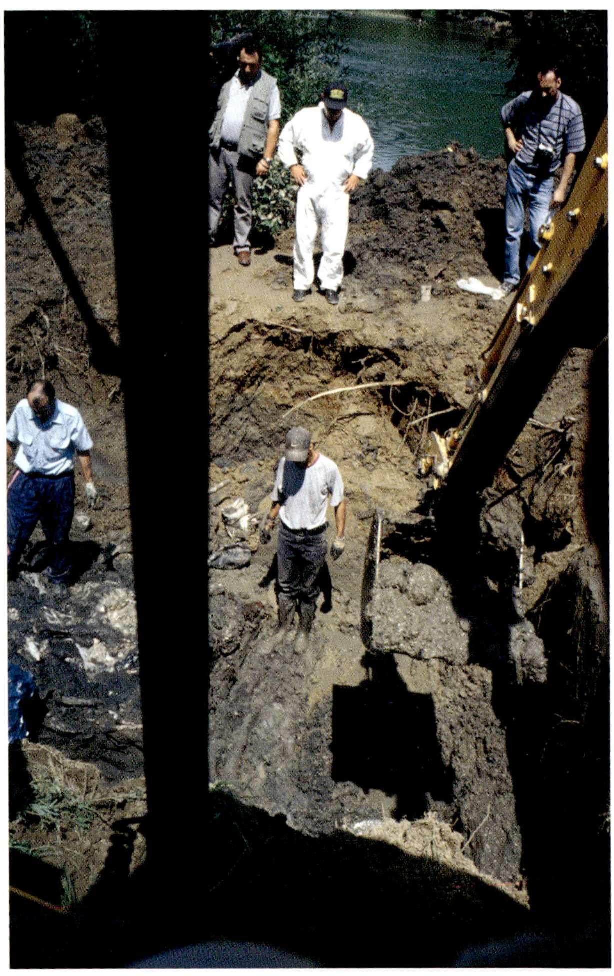

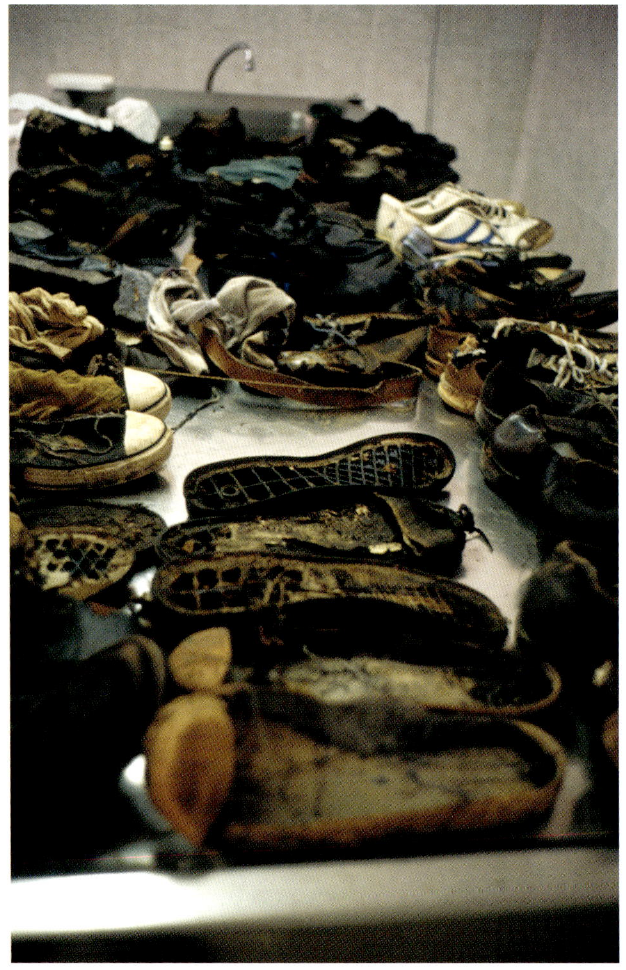

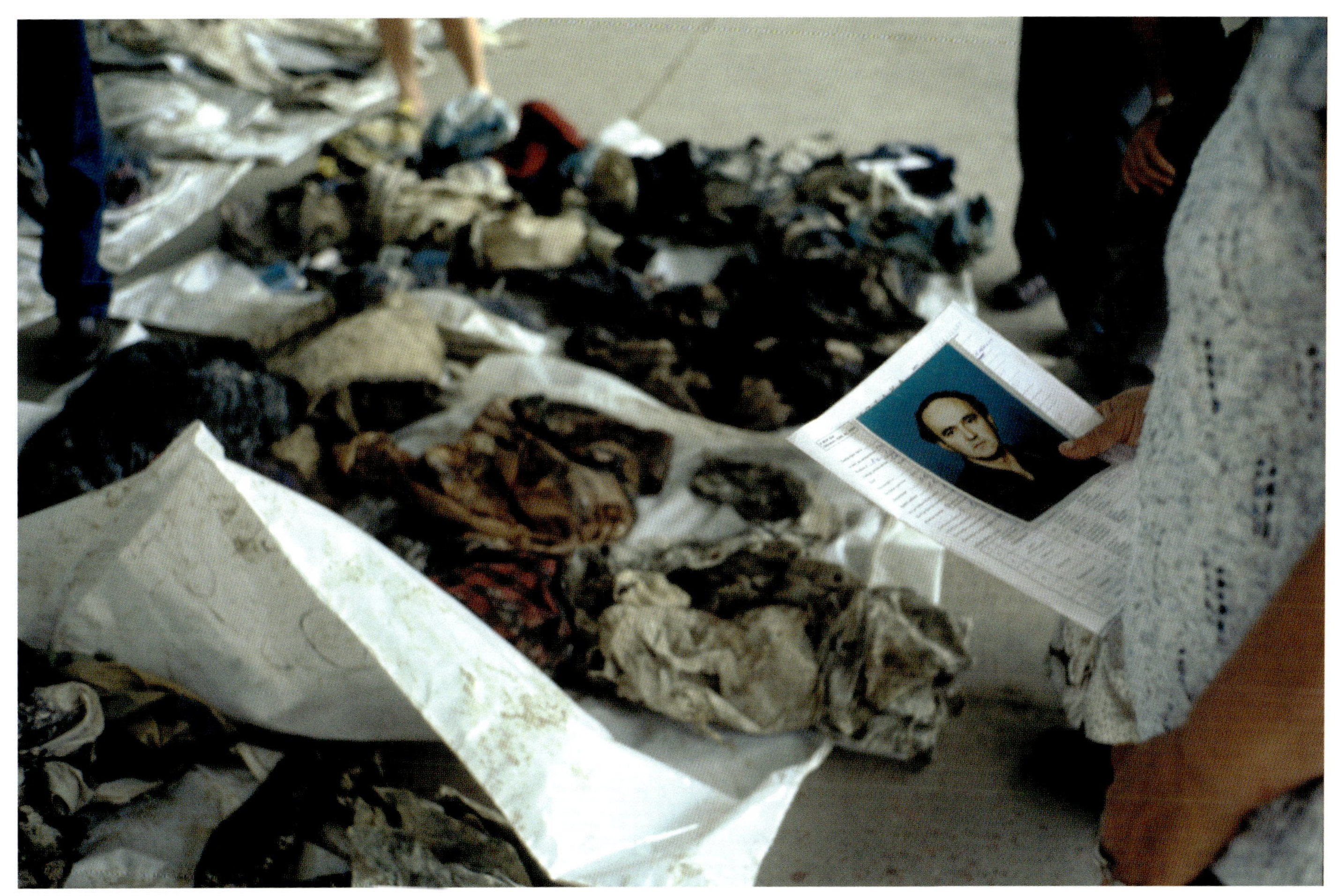

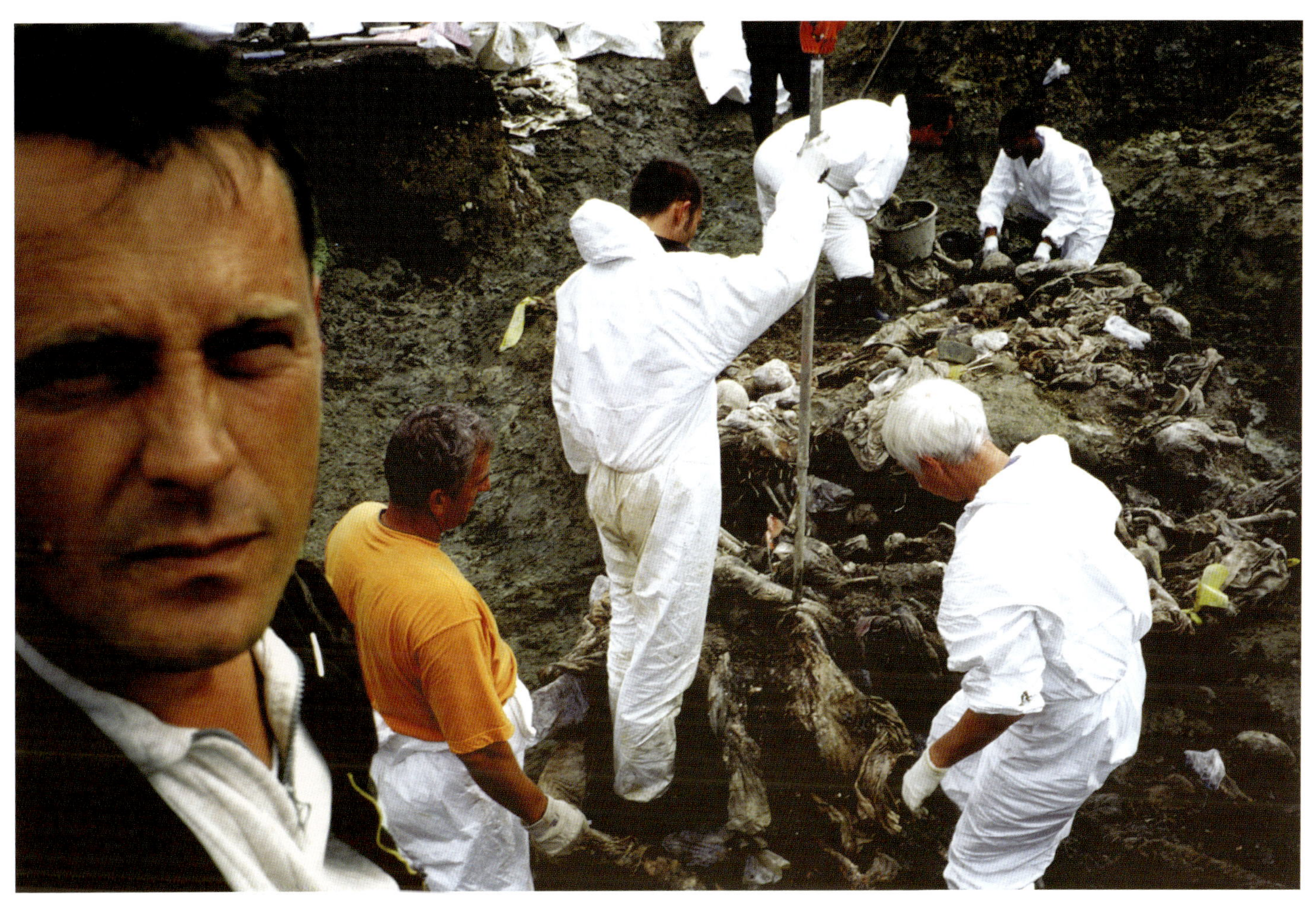

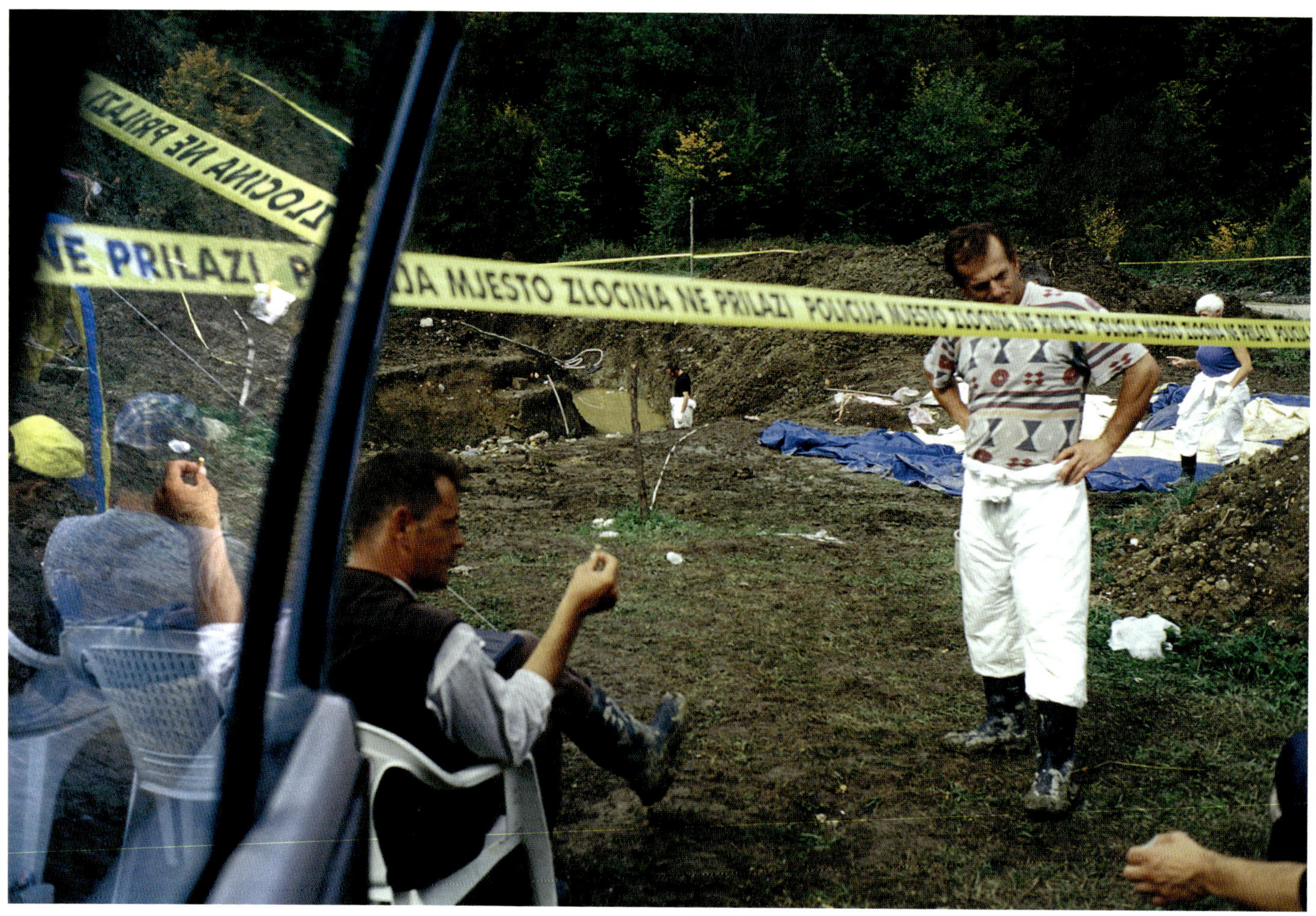
ZLOCINA NE PRILAZI
NE PRILAZI
JA MJESTO ZLOCINA NE PRILAZI POLICIJA MJESTO ZLOCINA NE PRILAZI

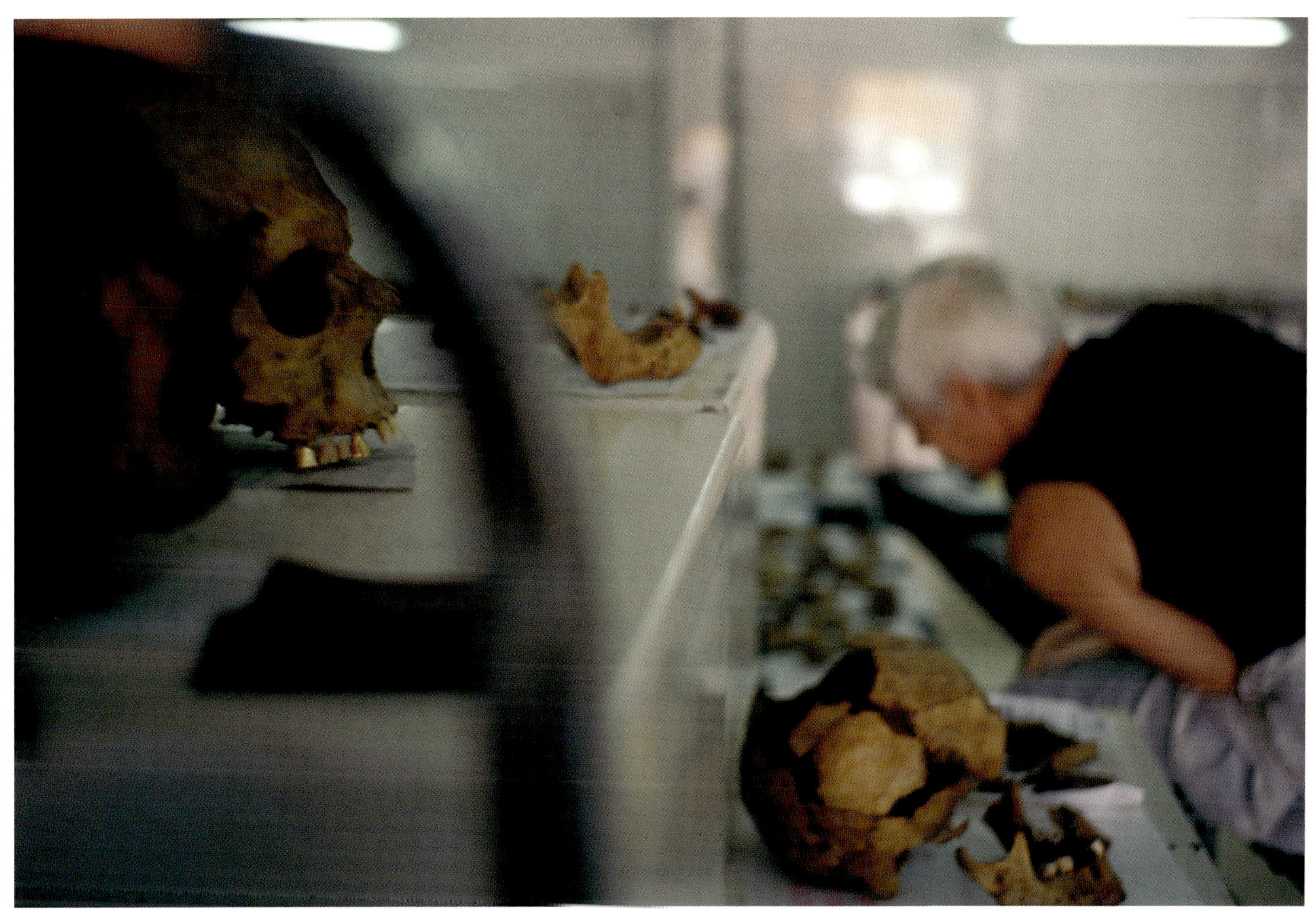

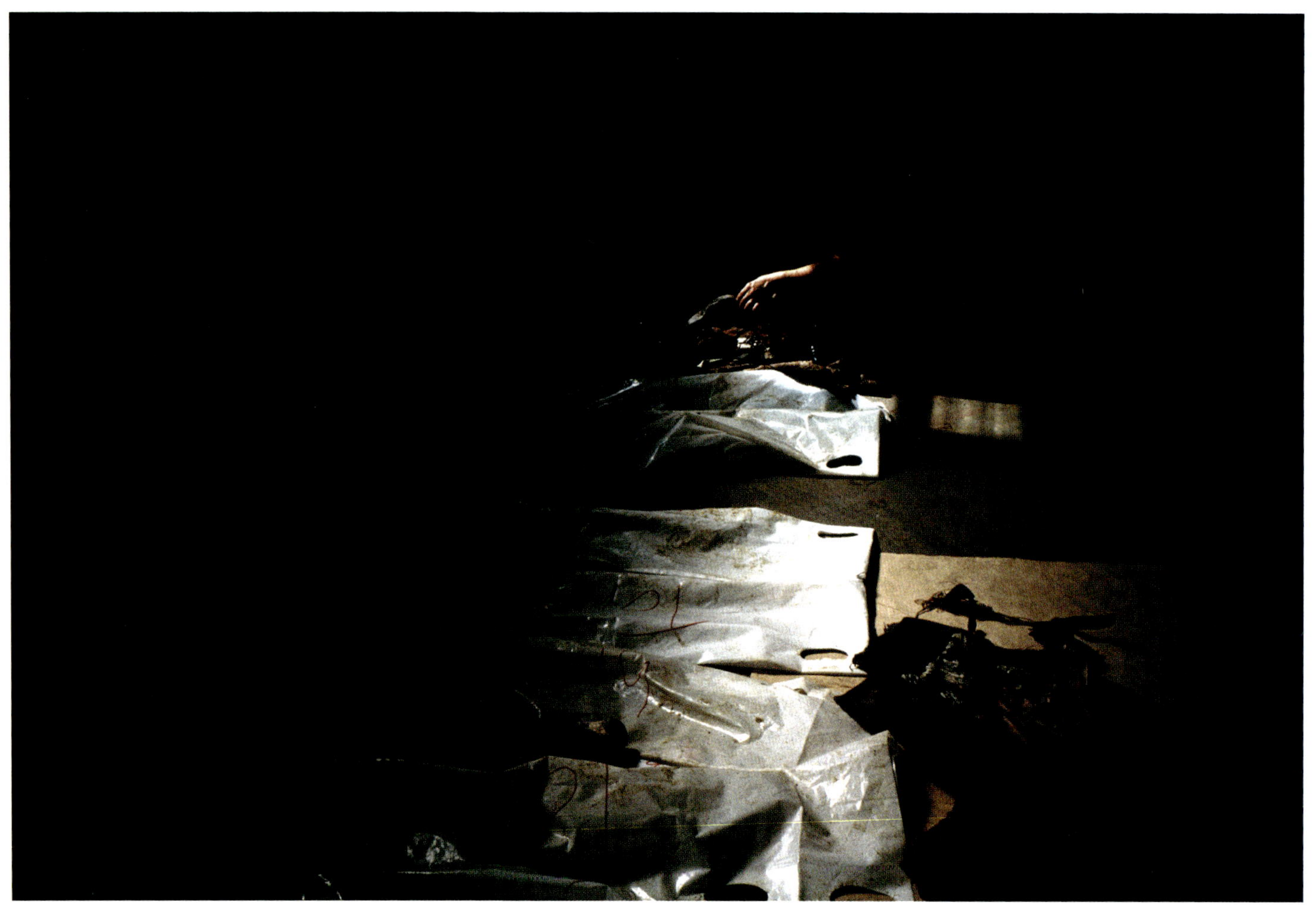

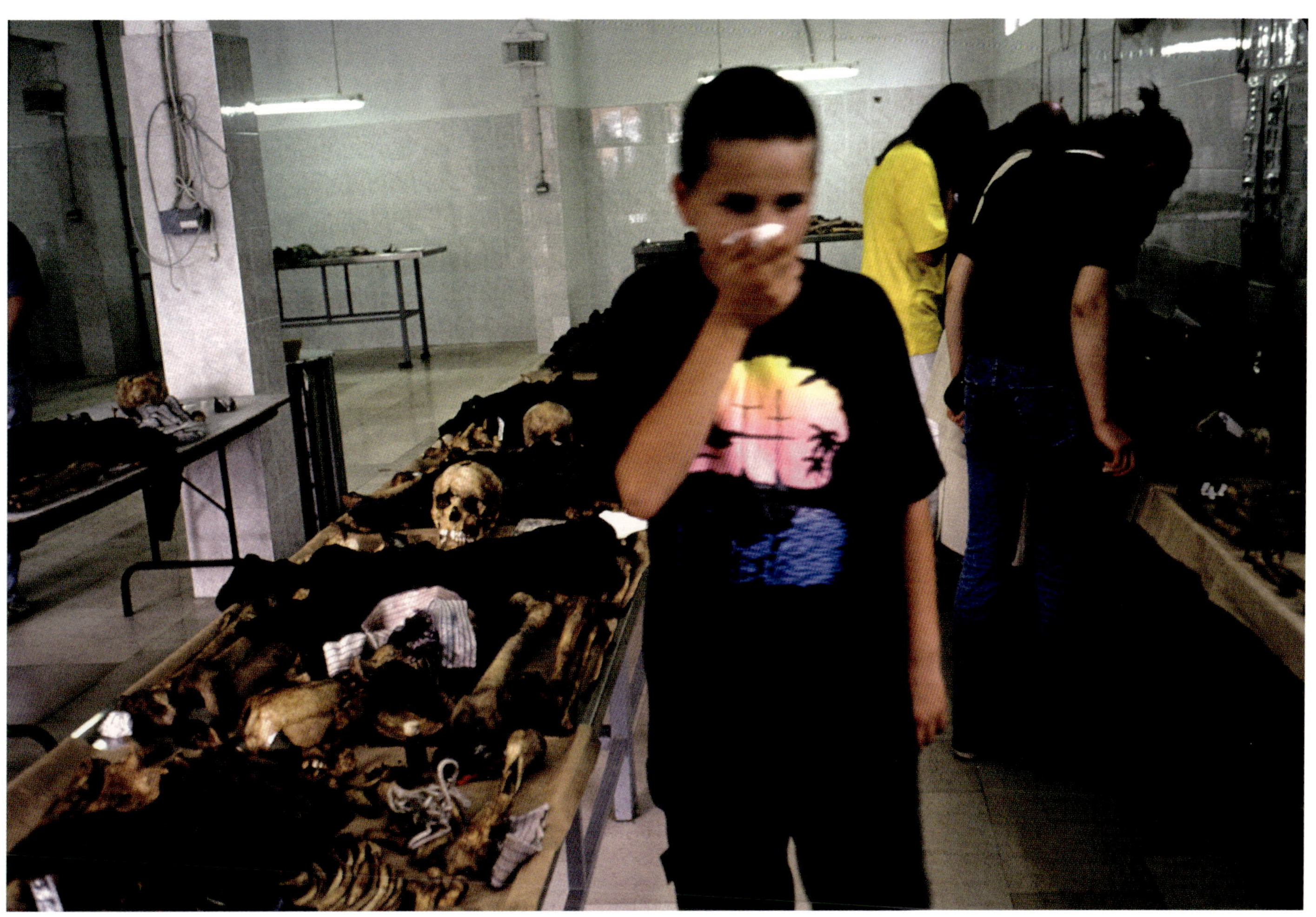

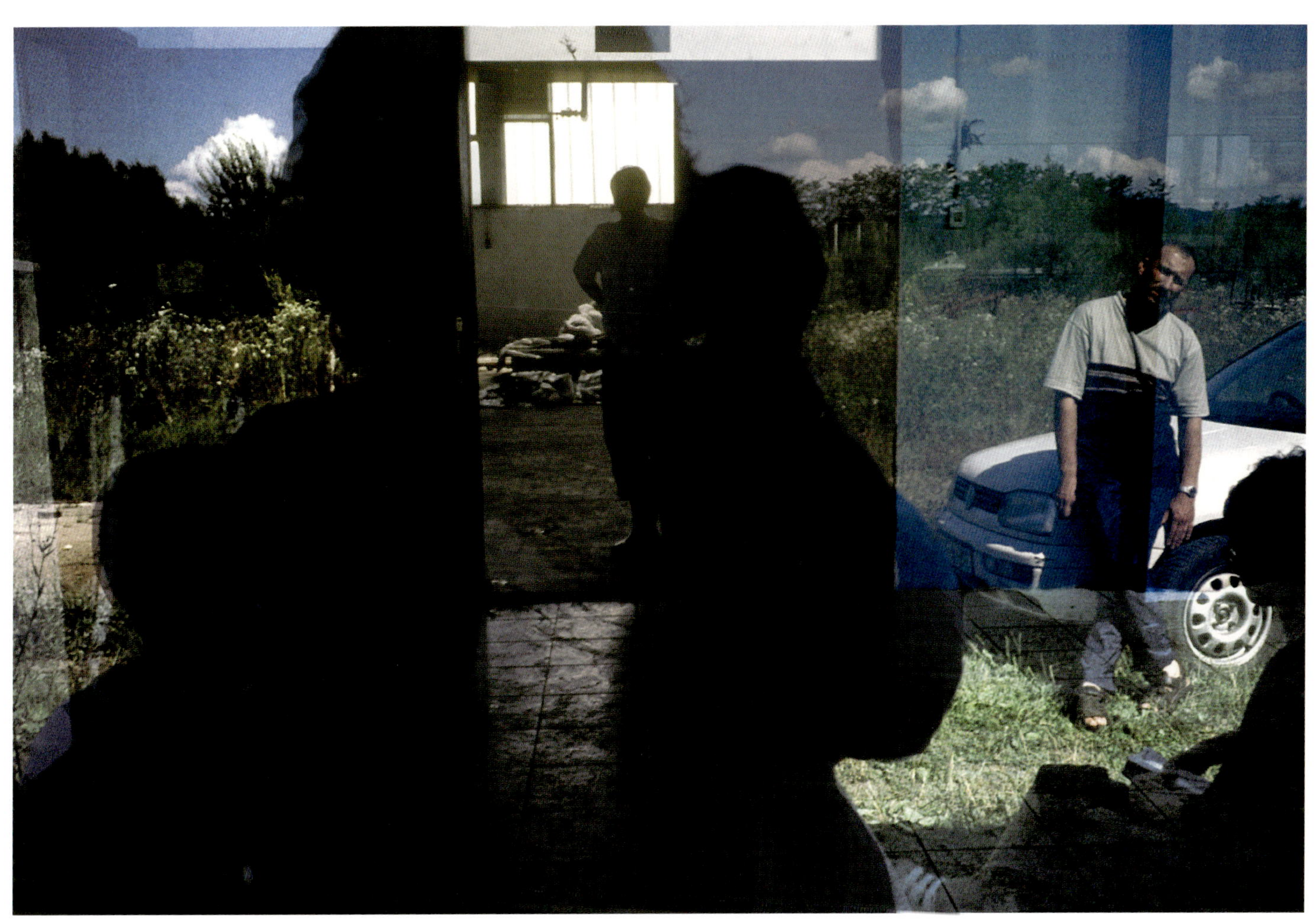

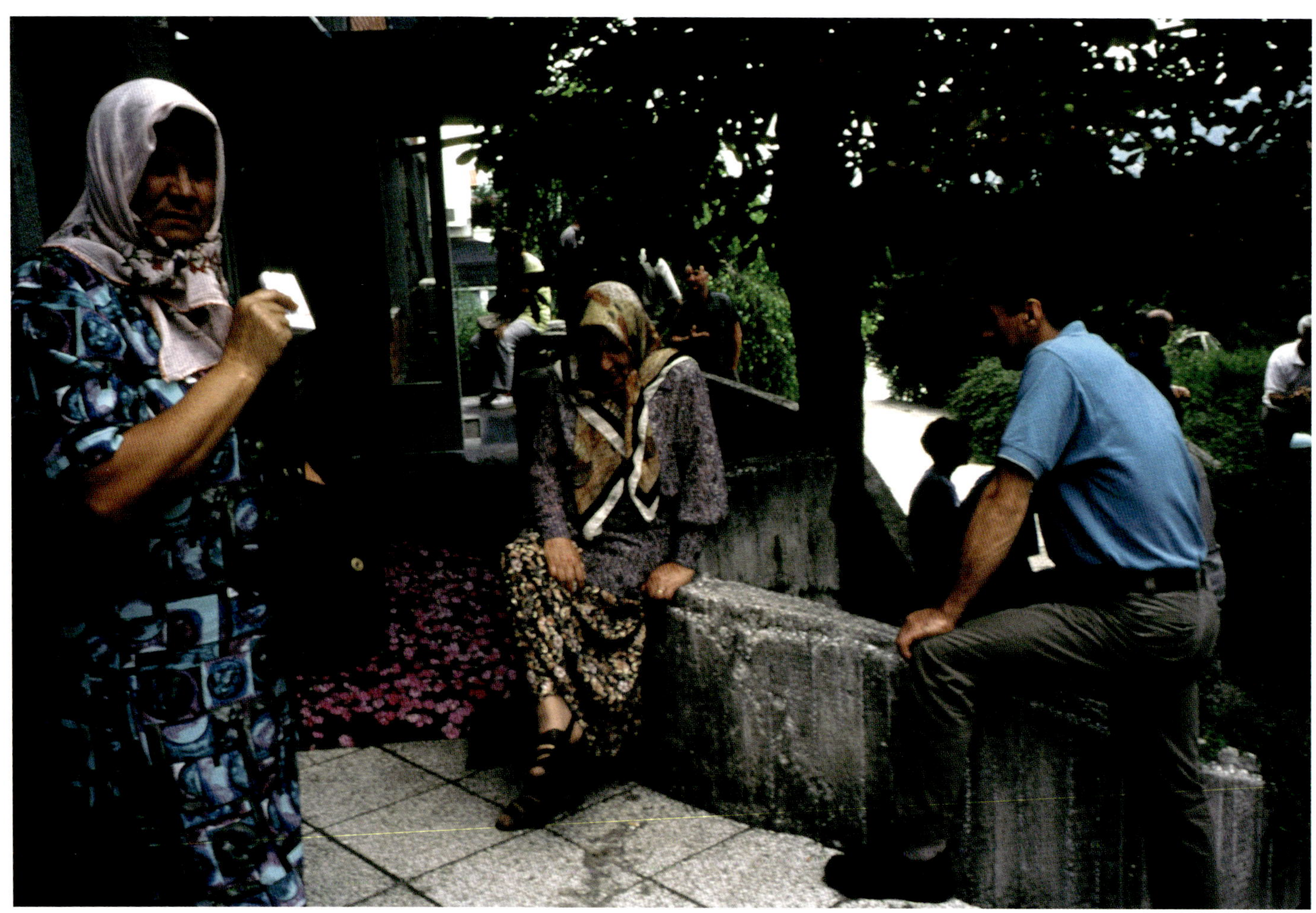

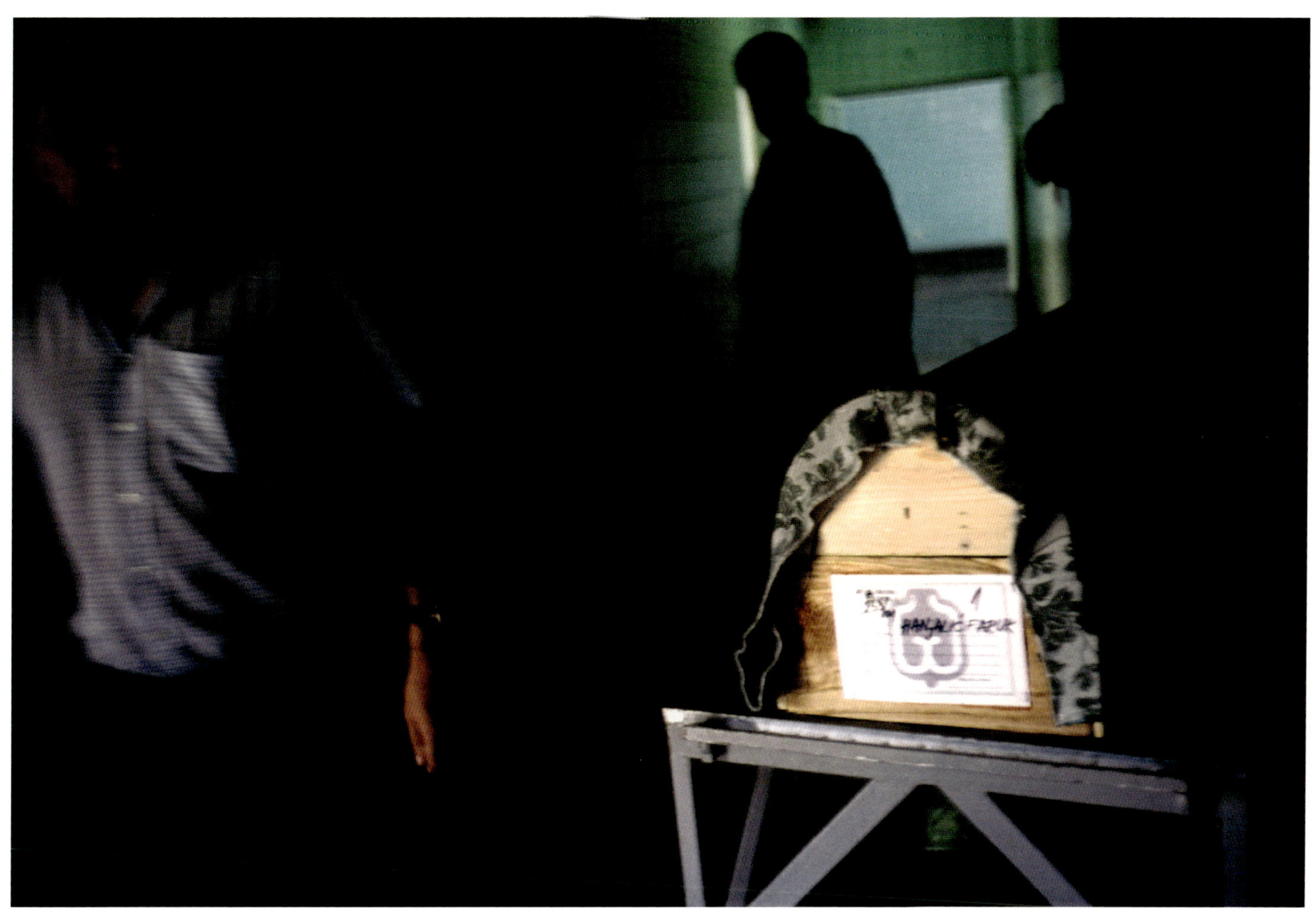

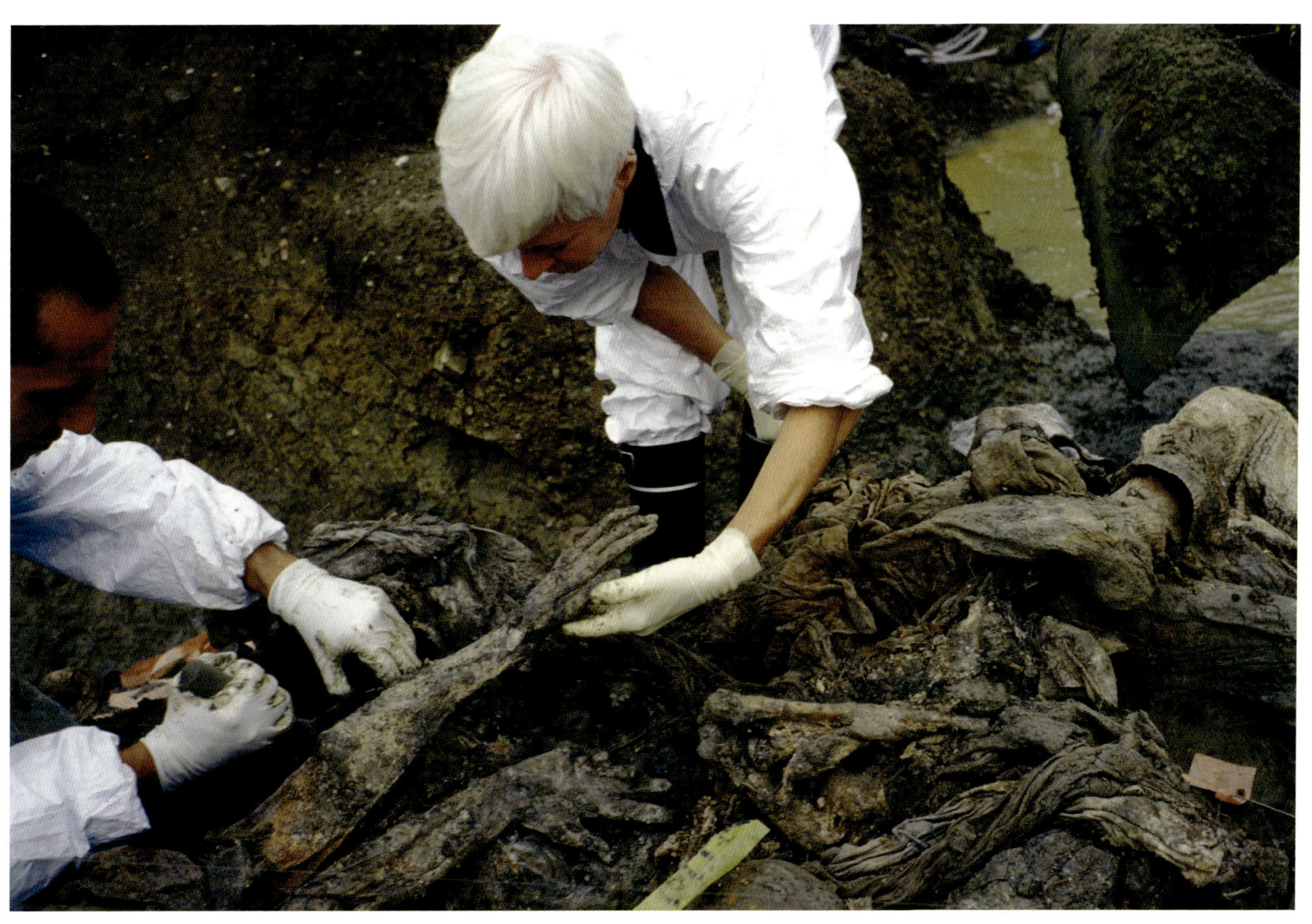

91 As forensic anthropologists Ewa Klonowski and Piotr Drukier work in the background, a woman walks among the rows of remains laid out with the clothing found with each skeleton during the exhumation of mass graves. Relatives looking for loved ones often recognize a piece of clothing first; a formal identification is made through forensic data and DNA samples. Thousands of Bosnians—the majority of them Muslims—remain missing years after the end of the war. Sanski Most, October 2000.

92a A steam shovel removes mud and dirt away from a site identified as a mass grave, thanks to a tip from a Serb informant. Exhumation officials say that as more time passes since the end of the war, Serbs are increasingly offering information—often anonymously—about where to find mass graves. Many of the informants say they want to clear their consciences, according to authorities. The exhumation of this grave yielded about two dozen remains. Sanski Most, July 2001.

92b Shoes retrieved from a mass grave. Visoko, July 2001.

93 During a public viewing of exhumed remains, a woman holds a photograph of her brother, who disappeared during the 1992 "ethnic cleansing" campaign waged by Serbs against their Muslim neighbors. At her feet is a pile of clothes found with bodies exhumed from a mass grave. Sanski Most, July 2001.

95 Asim Hadzic, a police crime technician, stands at the rim of a mass grave of Srebrenica victims, as forensic anthropologists work to free remains of bodies from the compacted soil. This grave, one of twelve found along a rural road, is a "secondary" grave—meaning that the bodies were originally buried elsewhere, and then dug up, moved and hastily buried again by Serbs who were trying to cover up evidence of the 1995 massacre of some 7,000 to 8,000 Muslim men and boys who were killed when the U.N. "safe haven" of Srebrenica was overrun by Serb forces. Kamenica, September 24, 2002.

96 Workers take a break from the exhumation. Kamenica, September 23, 2002.

97 Forensic anthropologist Ewa Klonowski examines skeletons exhumed from a mass grave near Foca, in eastern Bosnia. Visoko, July 2001.

98 A family member looking for remains of a loved one reaches towards bones in a body bag, during a public viewing of exhumed remains. Visoko, August 2001.

99 Public viewing of skeletons exhumed from a mass grave near Foca in the eastern part of Bosnia, where many Muslims were killed in a 1992 "ethnic cleansing" campaign by Serbs who wanted to create an ethnically "pure" state. At public viewings, the stench from the remains can be so strong that those viewing the bodies sometimes clasp handkerchiefs to their mouths and noses. Visoko, July 2001.

101 Window reflection of a warehouse where exhumed remains of victims of "ethnic cleansing" are cleaned and examined. In the reflection, in the background, a police officer takes a break from his work. Sanski Most, July 2001.

102 Families gather outside a mortuary where autopsied remains of victims of ethnic cleansing have been laid out in several rooms for public viewing. Visoko, August 2001.

103 The identified remains of a victim of "ethnic cleansing" have been placed in this makeshift pine coffin, to be released to family members for burial. Visoko, August 2001.

105 Forensic anthropologists Ewa Klonowski and Piotr Drukier examine the partially preserved hands of a teenage boy, found in a mass grave of victims of the 1995 Srebrenica massacre of some 7,000 to 8,000 Muslim men and boys by Serb forces. The grave, which contained more than 150 intact bodies and some 350 partial remains, was one of the largest mass graves uncovered in Bosnia since the end of the war. September 24, 2002.

ogromna radost
HUGE JOY

"It's all about merak. It's a very common Bosnian word. It's joy, but it's more than that. It's a huge joy. Can I say huge joy? We're like, Oh, hey, don't be yelling, let me buy you a beer. We're either like that or we're killing each other over little things. Why? I don't know. Because we are upside down...Merak, it's joy. We have lots of songs about it. When you're in a cafe, with friends, that's the best time of day. Merak is connected with friends, being surrounded by them. You love everybody, and they love you. You would do anything for them. You can also say merak when you mean life. Merak is when people are happy... [Having lived through the war] means I know more how to appreciate life and to express it. Joy and happiness are what matter, not fighting."

> **adela hrlovic,** high school senior

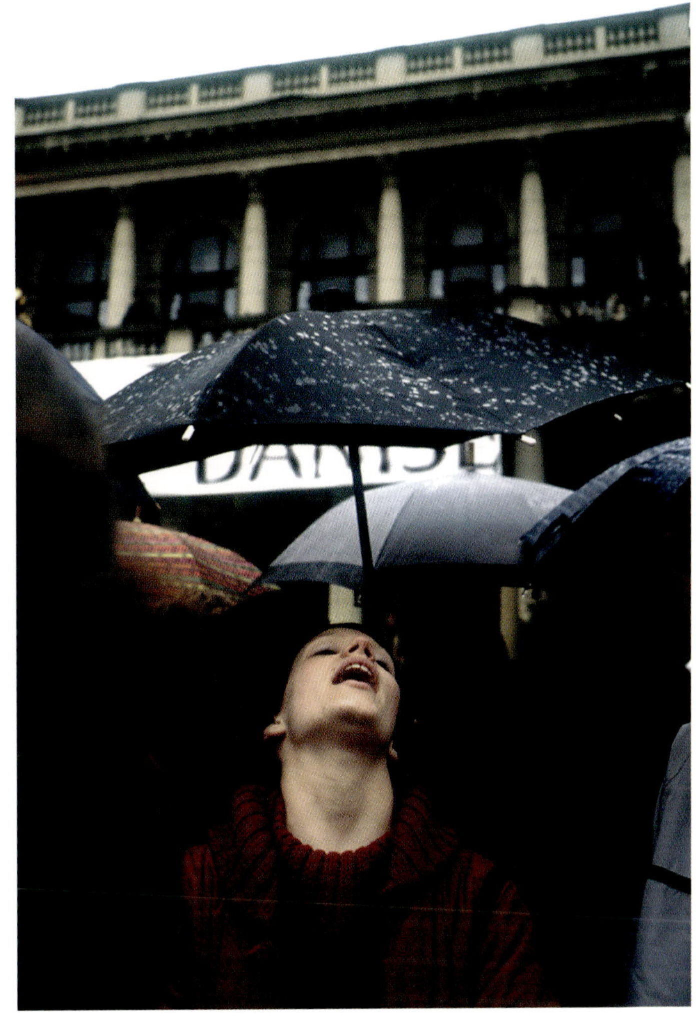

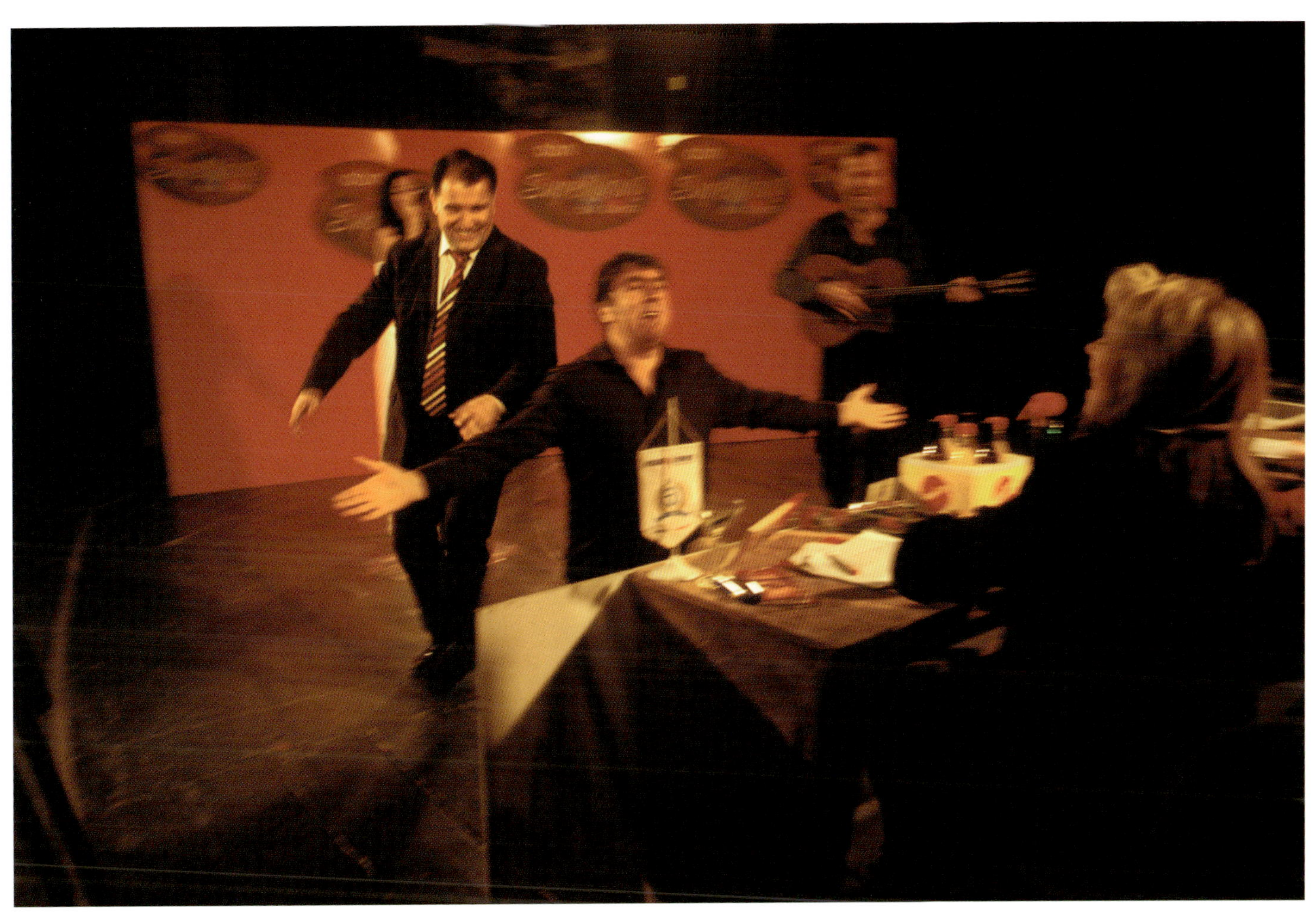

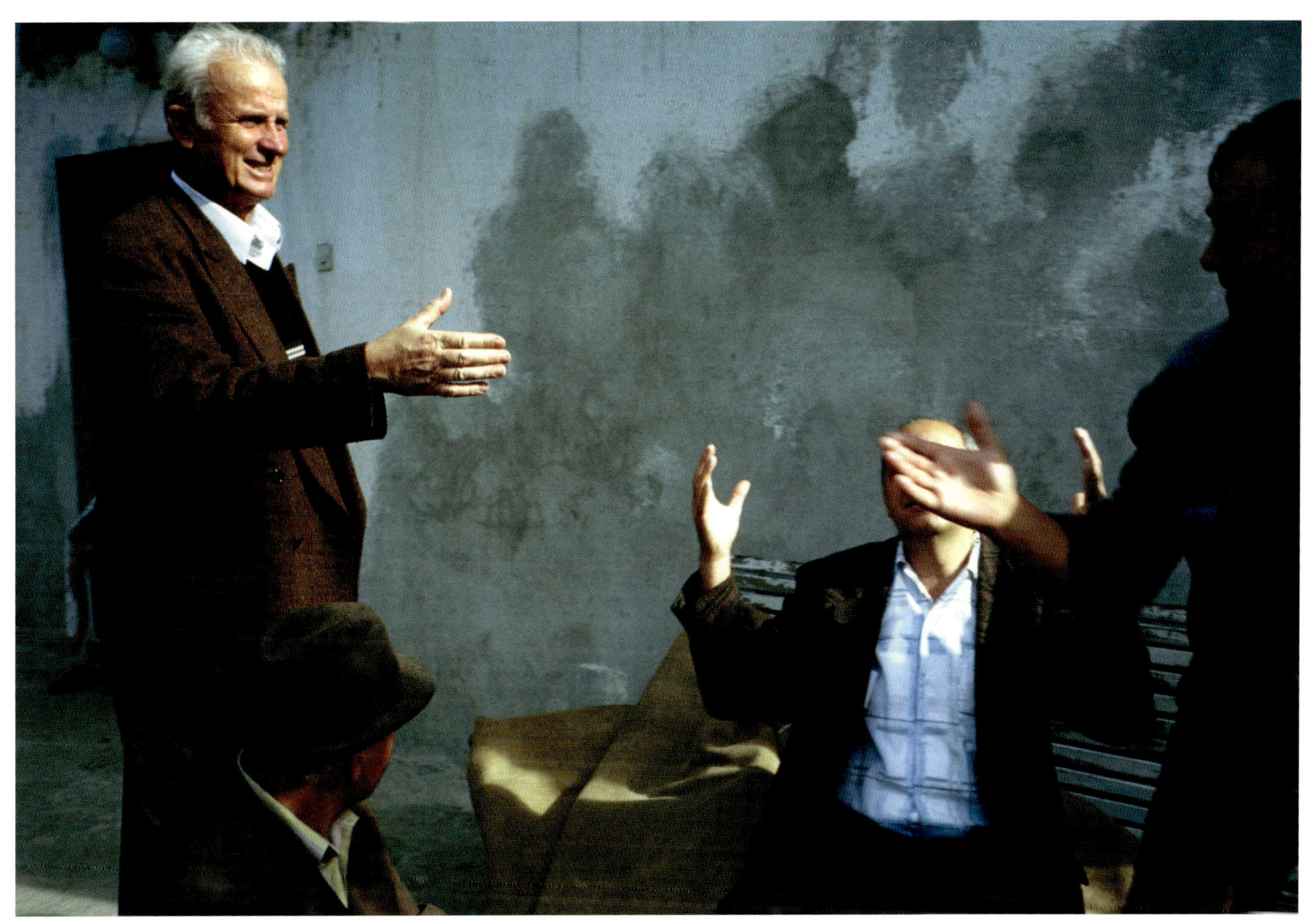

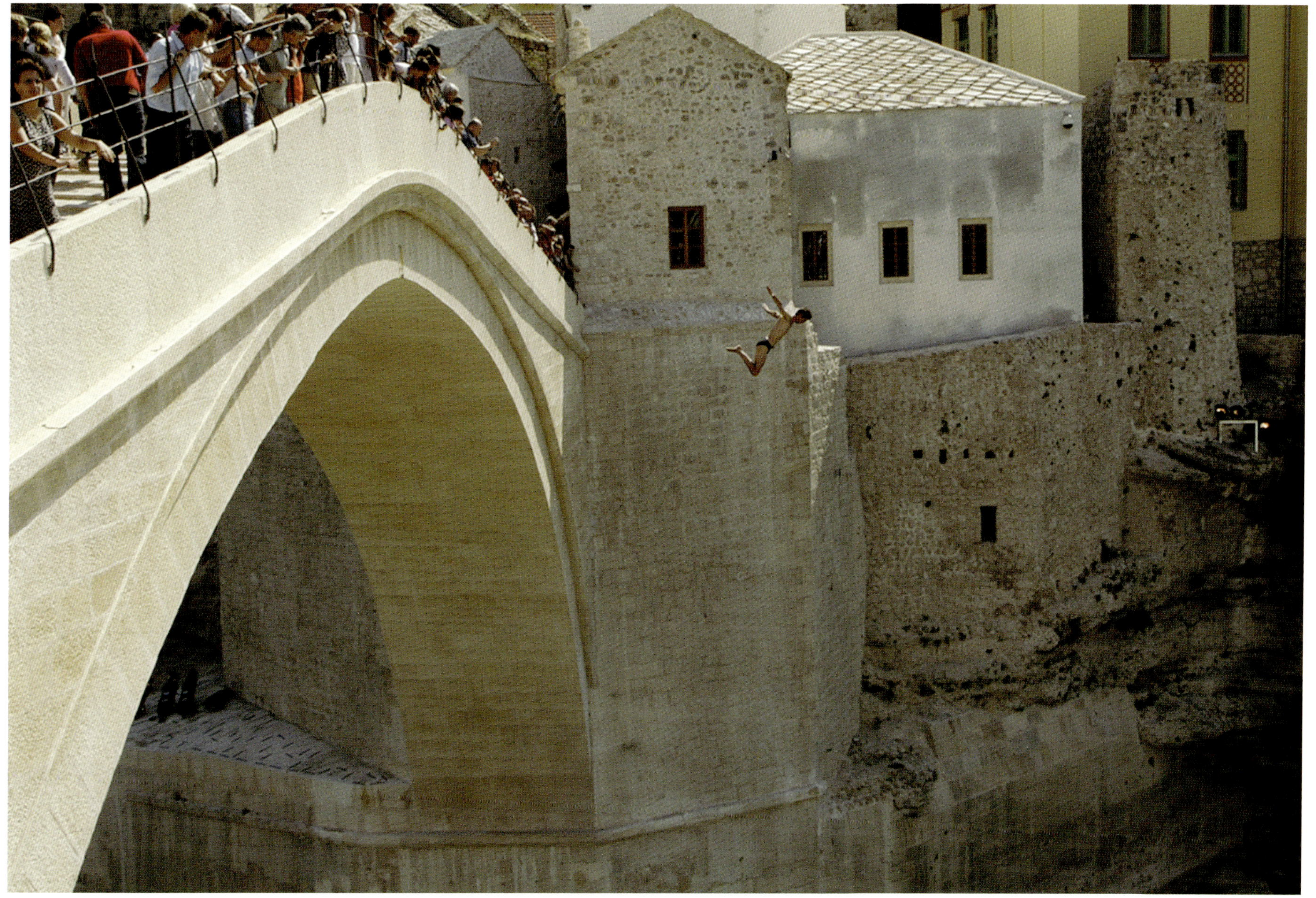

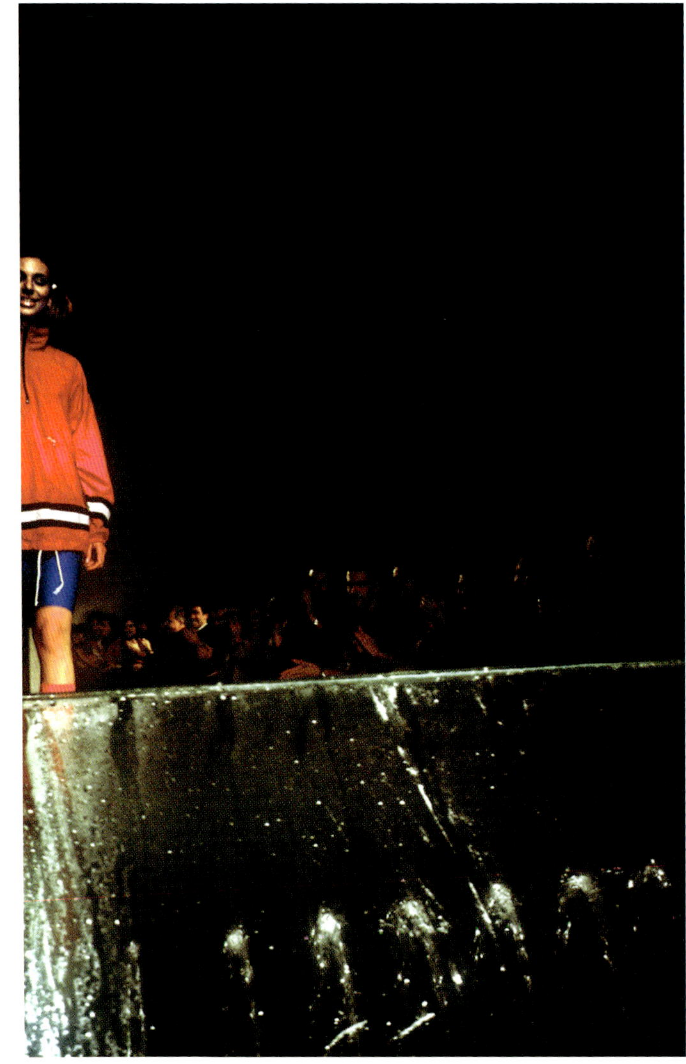

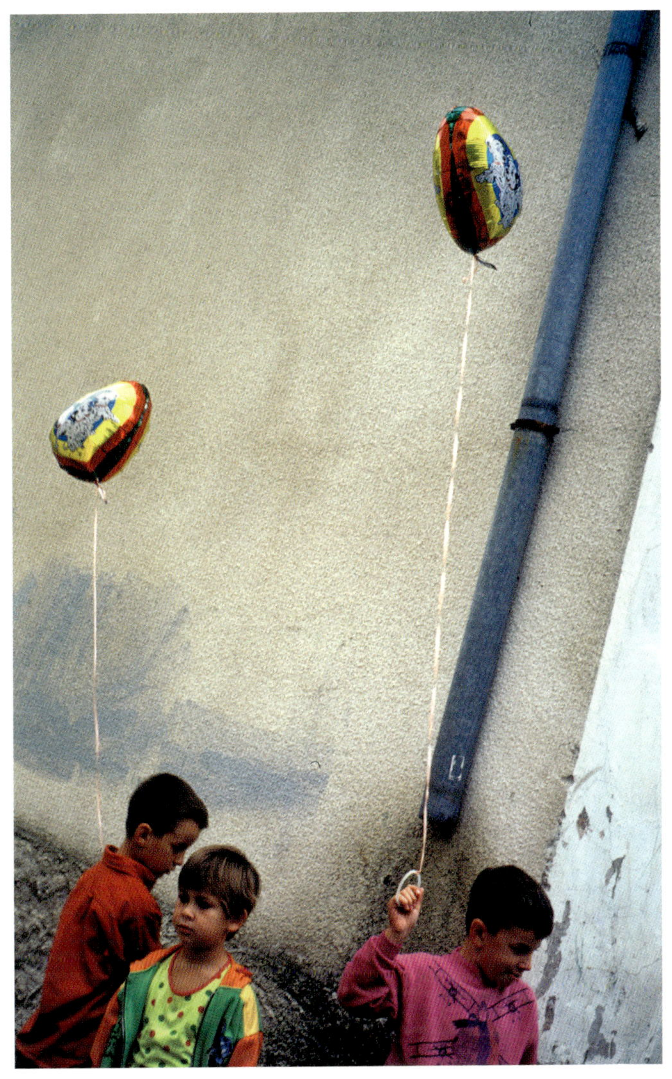

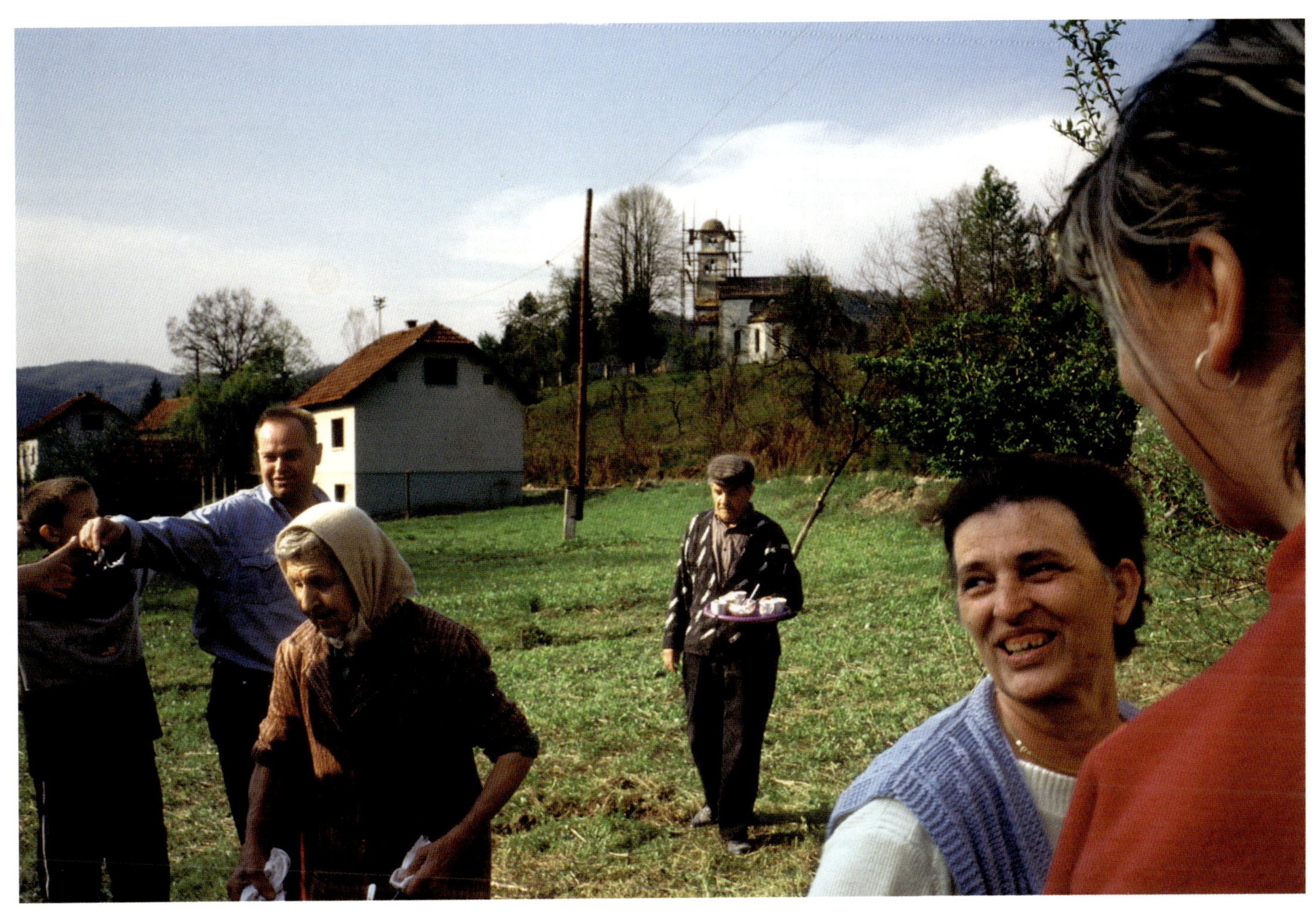

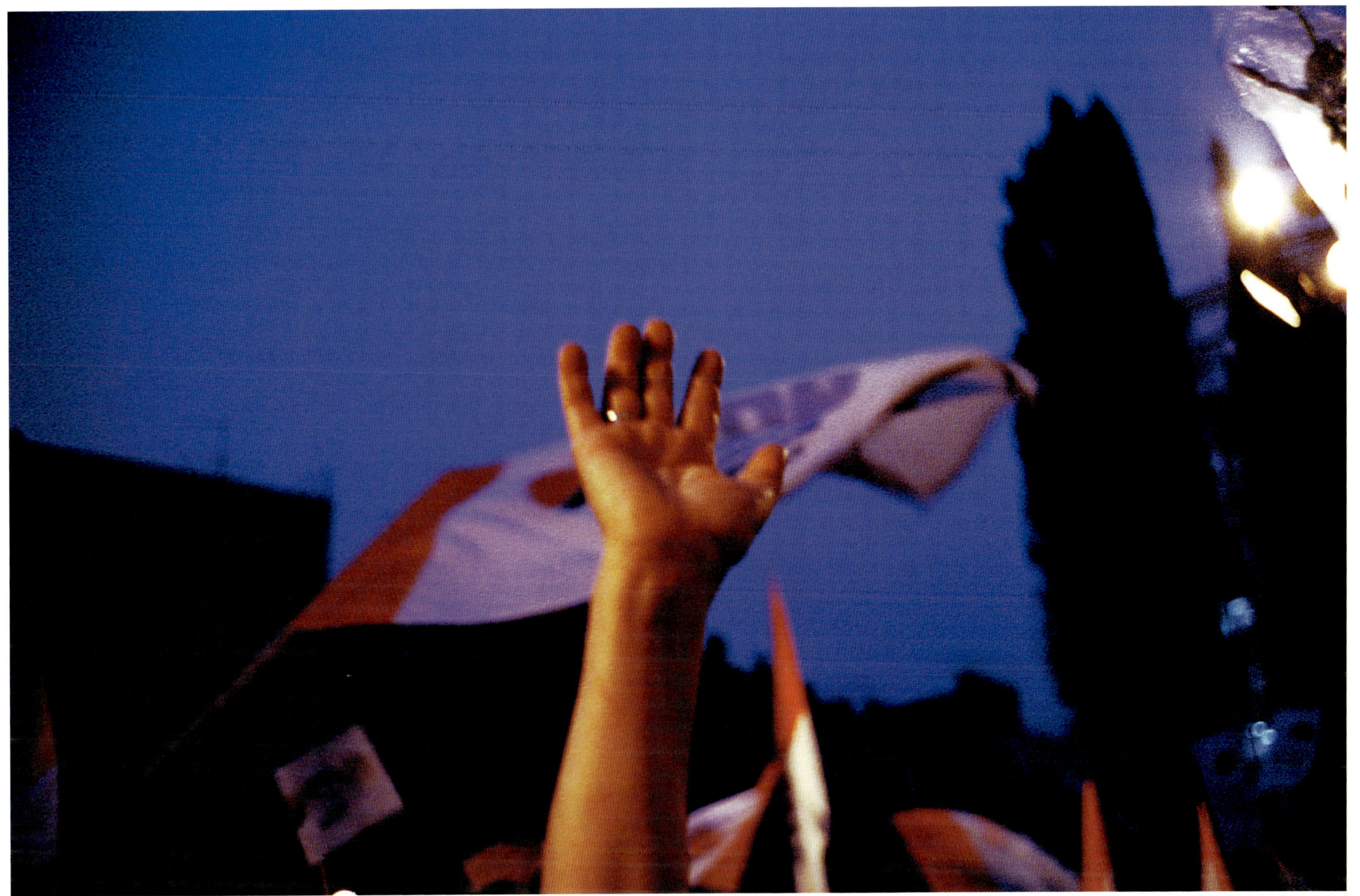

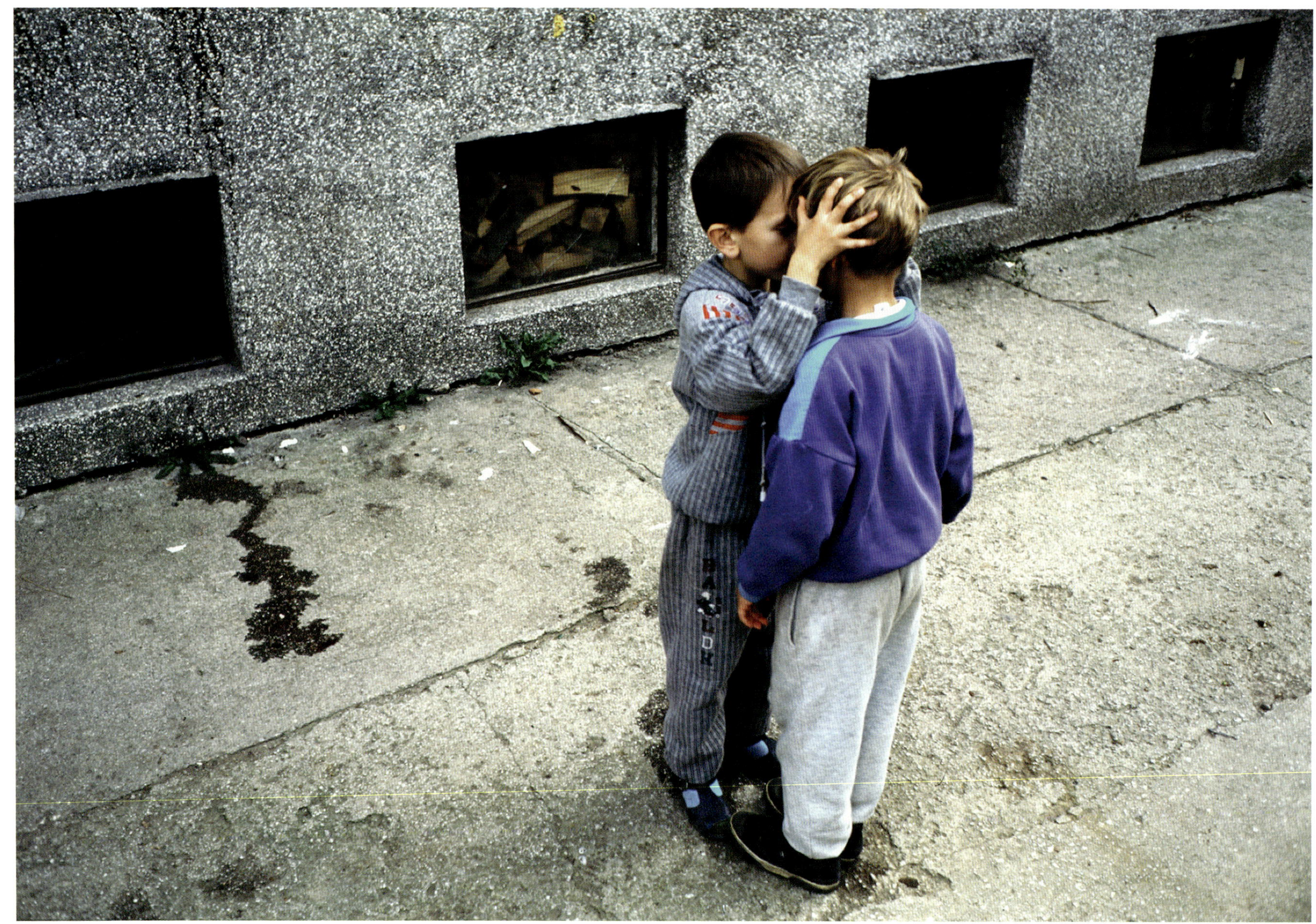

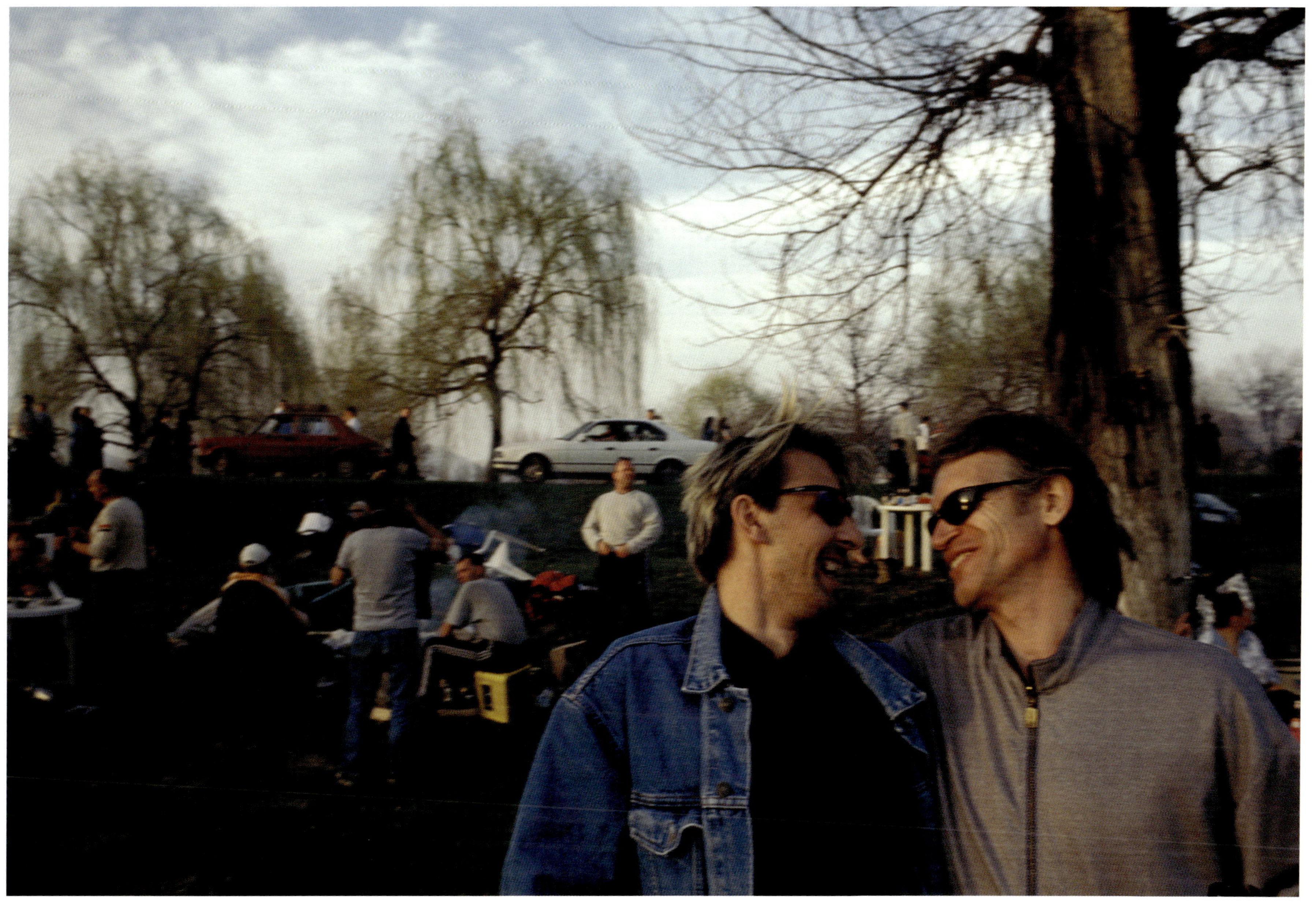

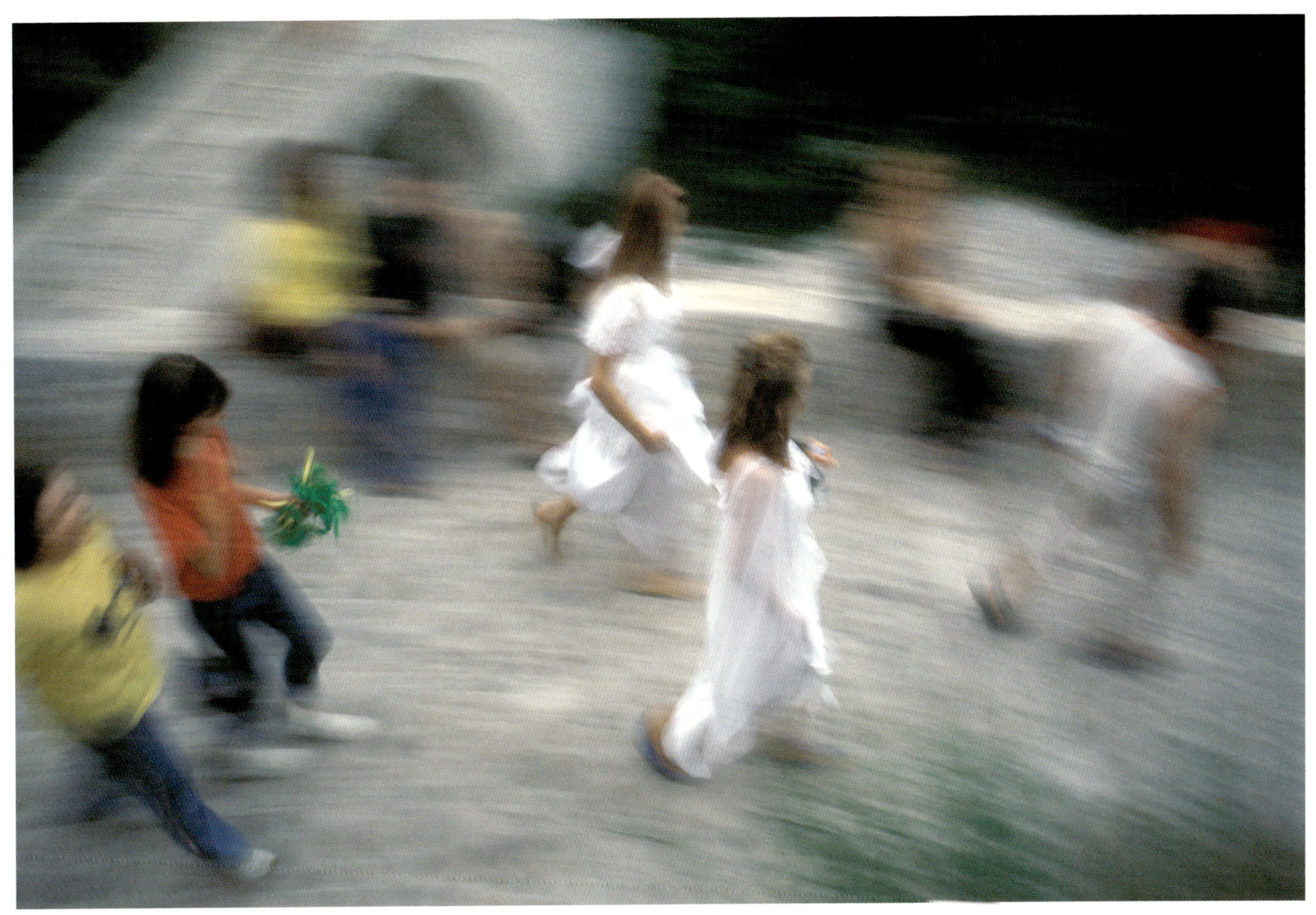

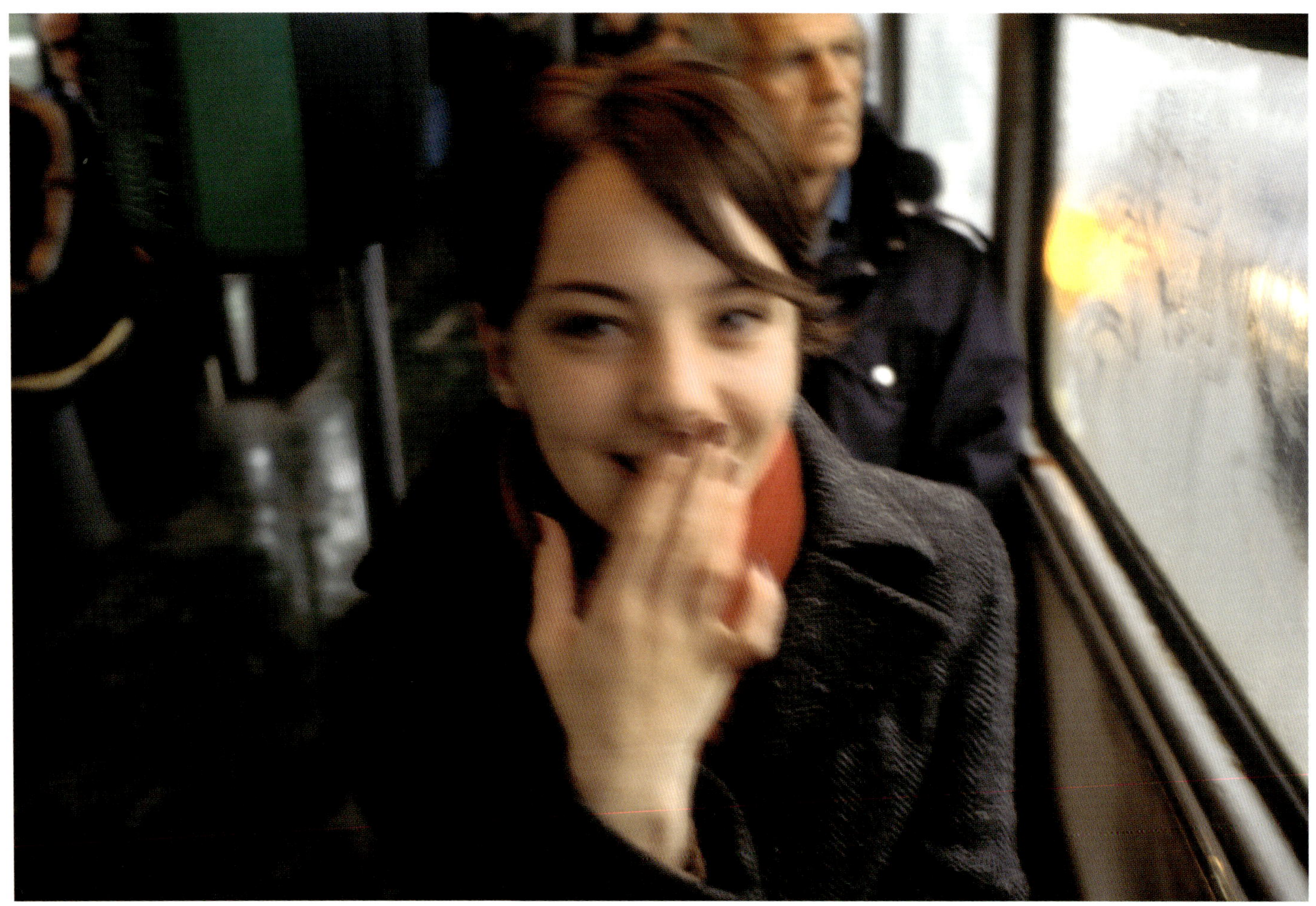

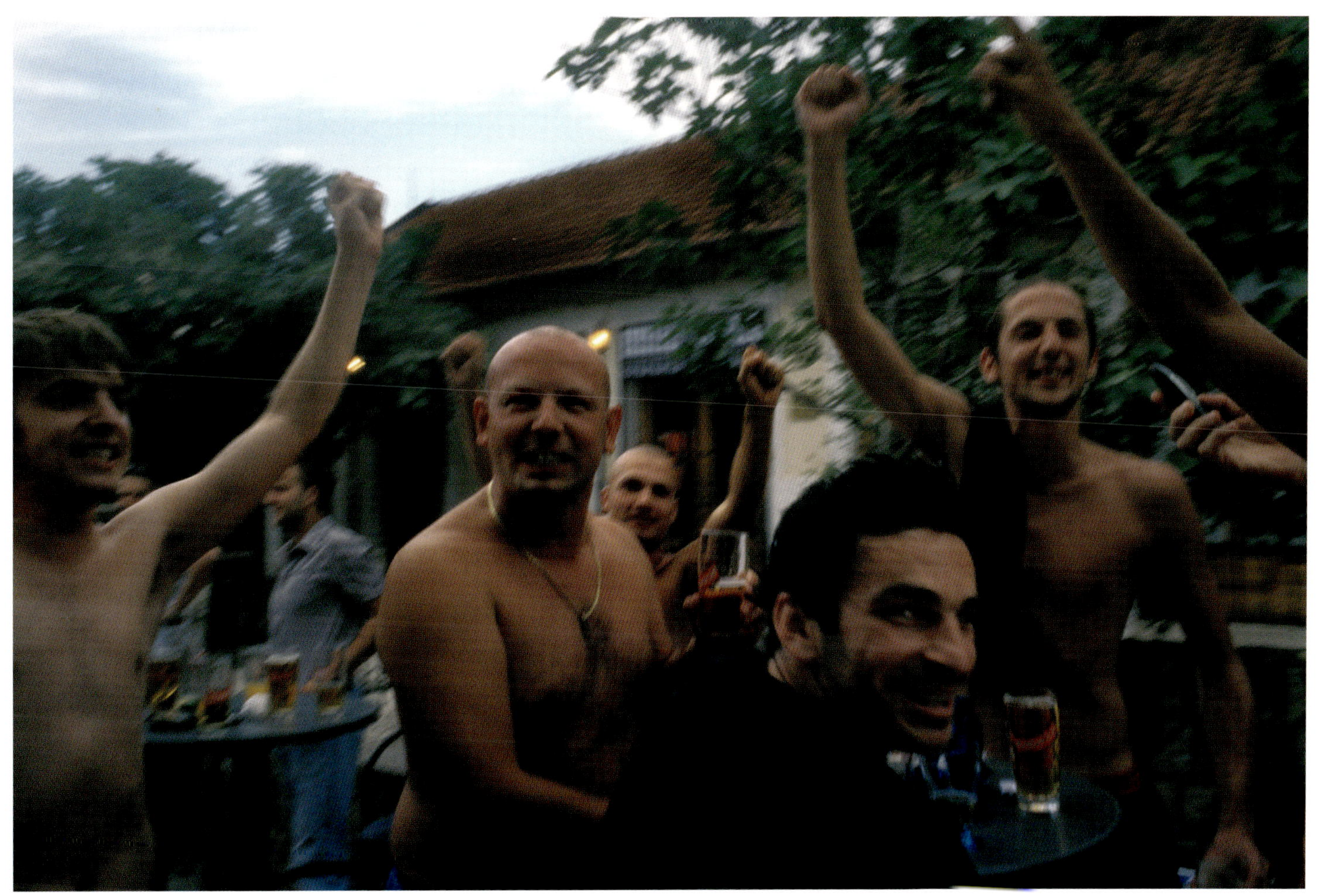

111 A girl throws back her head in the rain while waiting for film director Danis Tanovic to appear at a rally in his honor. Tanovic, who won an Oscar a few days earlier for his film about the war in Bosnia, 'No Man's Land,' came home to celebrate, arriving the day before the tenth anniversary of the beginning of the siege of Sarajevo. Sarajevo, April 5, 2002.

113 The set of the Bosnian version of American Idol. Mostar, March 20, 2004.

115 Muslims and Serbs, who have remained friends, greet each other in the town of Srebrenica. Although the Muslim man who introduced me to his friends had not yet returned to live in the town where his brother and father were among the 7,000 to 8,000 Muslim men and boys killed by Serbs, he praised his Serb friend, a former colleague of his father's. He said he had no anger towards the man, who had helped look out for the Muslim's home after the 1995 massacre. "This man did not kill my father or my brother," he said. "If I met the man who did kill them, that would be a different story." October 2000.

117 One of Mostar's legendary jumpers throws himself from the town's famed bridge, which stands more than eighty feet high. Eleven years after it was destroyed during the 1992-95 war, the rebuilt bridge was opened to the public after a dedication ceremony that drew many foreign officials, including Prince Charles. Local jumpers and divers wasted no time returning to one of their favorite pastimes before the war—collecting change from tourists who watch them jump. Local athletes also used the week to prepare for the 448th annual jumping and diving competition, held the following week. July 24. 2004.

118 A fashion show staged at midnight on the eve of the tenth anniversary of the beginning of the siege of Sarajevo. Although there were few events sponsored by the city to mark the occasion, artists and young people—many of whom lived through the siege as children— put on the fashion show, which featured clothes worn by famous people during the war—including the beret of former president Alija Izetbegovic, filmmaker Danis Tanovic's sleeping bag, and the track suits worn by two Olympic athletes who snuck out of Sarajevo during the siege and marched in the opening ceremony of the Barcelona Olympics, to remind the world of the tragedy that was unfolding in Bosnia. Sarajevo, April 6, 2002.

119 Children at play in the Muslim section of the town of Stolac. For several years after the end of the war, the town was known for its hardline, nationalist Croat sentiments; Muslims who attempted to return to their homes were frequently attacked. By 2002, however, nearly a thousand Muslims had returned, although the two groups continue to lead essentially separate lives in separate parts of the town. September 26, 2002.

121 Serb neighbors gather for coffee in the village of Bocinja. Although Serbs lived in the village throughout the war, they fled once the cease fire was signed in the fall of 1995. Several Islamic mujahideen, who had come from Arab countries to fight during the war, moved in to the village and refused to leave when Serb owners wanted to return. International and Bosnian officials finally intervened and removed the mujahideen. As they left, the mujahideen damaged several houses, as well as the Orthodox church in the background, which was being repaired at the time this photo was taken. April 21, 2002.

123 The last election rally to be held before election day by the SDP, the popular, moderate Social Democratic Party of Bosnia and Hercegovina, which was part of the ruling coalition in government at that time. The international community had pinned high hopes on these elections, which were the first to be run entirely by Bosnian officials since the end of the war. But voter apathy and frustration with the slow pace of change led to an outcome that many political observers felt was a setback for the country: moderate parties, including the SDP, lost heavily on election day, as voters returned to power the same three nationalist parties who controlled the country at the end of the war. Sarajevo, October 3, 2004.

124 Two boys on a sidewalk in a suburb of Sarajevo are among the thousands of refugees from Srebrenica who fled to the city at the end of the war, after the massacre of some 7,000 to 8,000 Muslim men and boys at the hands of Bosnian Serb forces. The fathers of both boys were killed in the massacre. Vogosca, October 2000.

125 Two friends are among the thousands of people who turned out to celebrate "cimburijada," which is held in the town of Zenica every year on the first day of spring. The celebration begins at dawn when the hardiest revelers turn out to cook scrambled eggs on the banks of the river. It lasts all day, turning into a giant picnic and party. Although locals proudly boast that the tradition is unique to Zenica, and has been observed since the end of World War II, no one seems to know exactly who started it or why. March 21, 2004.

127 Children dressed in white run to take part in the dedication ceremonies of the rebuilt Mostar Bridge. Croat and Muslim schoolchildren were supposed to participate in the opening, but Croat parents decided to take their children out of the ceremony because, they said, they were afraid the children would slip on the paving stones on the bridge. The weak excuse was widely seen as a reflection of the reluctance, especially among Croats, to re-integrate the two communities. July 23, 2004.

128 Adela Hrlovic, the girl whose words can be found at the beginning of this chapter, was a high school senior when I met her in Sarajevo in 2002. She loves "classic" movies—"Pretty Woman" is a favorite—and wishes she could be like Carrie on "Sex in the City," able to buy a $400 pair of shoes on days when she's feeling down. Adela lived through the siege of Sarajevo as a young girl and still remembers things like making salad from grass when there wasn't enough to eat. Her father wants her to run his successful printing business when she finishes college; Adela wants to see the world. Sarajevo, April 9, 2002.

129 With temperatures topping 100 degrees Fahrenheit, shirtless young men sing and drink beer on the day of what locals say was Mostar's 448th annual bridge jumping and diving competition. It marked the first time that Mostarians were able to jump from the full height of their beloved bridge since it was destroyed during the war by Bosnian Croat forces. Although locals continued to jump from the remains of the bridge during the war, and later from a temporary bridge built after the war, they had to wait more than a decade before the bridge was rebuilt according to its exact original style and dimensions. July 31, 2004.

viera i izdaja
FAITH AND BETRAYAL

"My best friend was from Zenica. She was a Serb. She called me once during the war and said, Look what your president is doing to you. She believed all the propaganda...She came to see me after the war, in my home, and she cried. I cried, too. And she heard the sounds of the mosque, calling people to prayer, and she said, It's so long since I heard this sound. But she still believed all the propaganda of the Serbs. And here she was in my living room, saying, Oh, I missed the sounds of the mosque. It was the last time I saw her."

> **adela,** temporary office worker, sarajevo

I would like to know when will you take/show pictures of Serb widows and their kids? I would like to know when will you tell stories of all those Serbs massacred? When there was muslim festivites, Serb forces would back up and freeze the front line, but in gratitude, scores of Serbs got their throats cut on Orthodox Christmas and Easter. When will we hear about that? When will we here about those Serbs castrated and tortured before being beheded? When will your rightous self present the real reasons for all this "mess"? And don't ask me how I know...

> **tomek,** guest book entry,
Bosnia Aftermath website

In response to Tomek's comment about "Serb widows, etc..." and other people's comments about "bias" and all that nonsense, I would just like to say that 250,000 Bosnian Muslims were killed, masacred...(need I mention Srebrenica or Markale in Sarajevo) during this aggression, ethinc cleansing OR as the rest of the world likes to say "CIVIL WAR" So, to those masacred serb widows and children, I am sorry but that is what happens when you send your serb sons, serb children and serb husbands to clean out Bosnia from Muslims.

> **hadzija,** guest book entry,
Bosnia Aftermath website

It's sad that after the worst has happened people are using this website for childish arguing. I'm Bosniak and if my army (to what my father belonged) commited war crimes against ANYONE – I want that out on the open. People of Bosnia need to know the truth – and you can't ignore Srebrenica, Zepa, Gorazde, Bihac, Sarajevo, and destruction of ALL non-Serb-Orthodox religous objects in Serb-controlled part of Bosnia when you are telling the story of Bosnia. And if I don't know parts of the story – I want to learn them. And then accept the past for what it is! We all want to be able to live off our work, to be able to support our families, to live in peace – we have lived together before (coexisted) and we still can. My parents' best friends are Serbs and Croats as well as Bosniaks. I REFUSE TO HATE! I WILL NOT GO THAT LOW TO HATE! NE CU SE PONIZITI I BITI COVJEK KOJI MRZI!

> **Sanjin,** guest book entry,
Bosnia Aftermath website

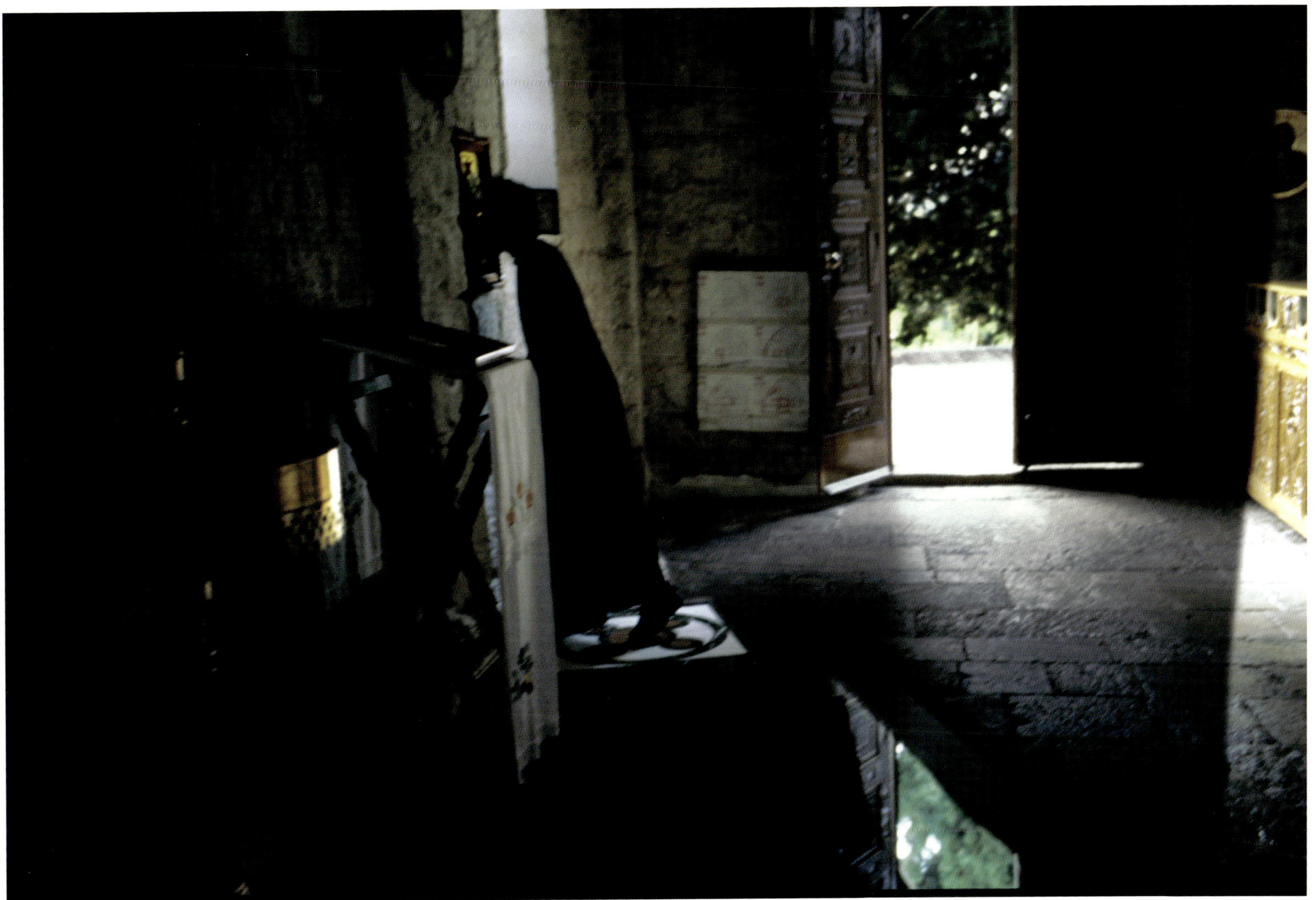

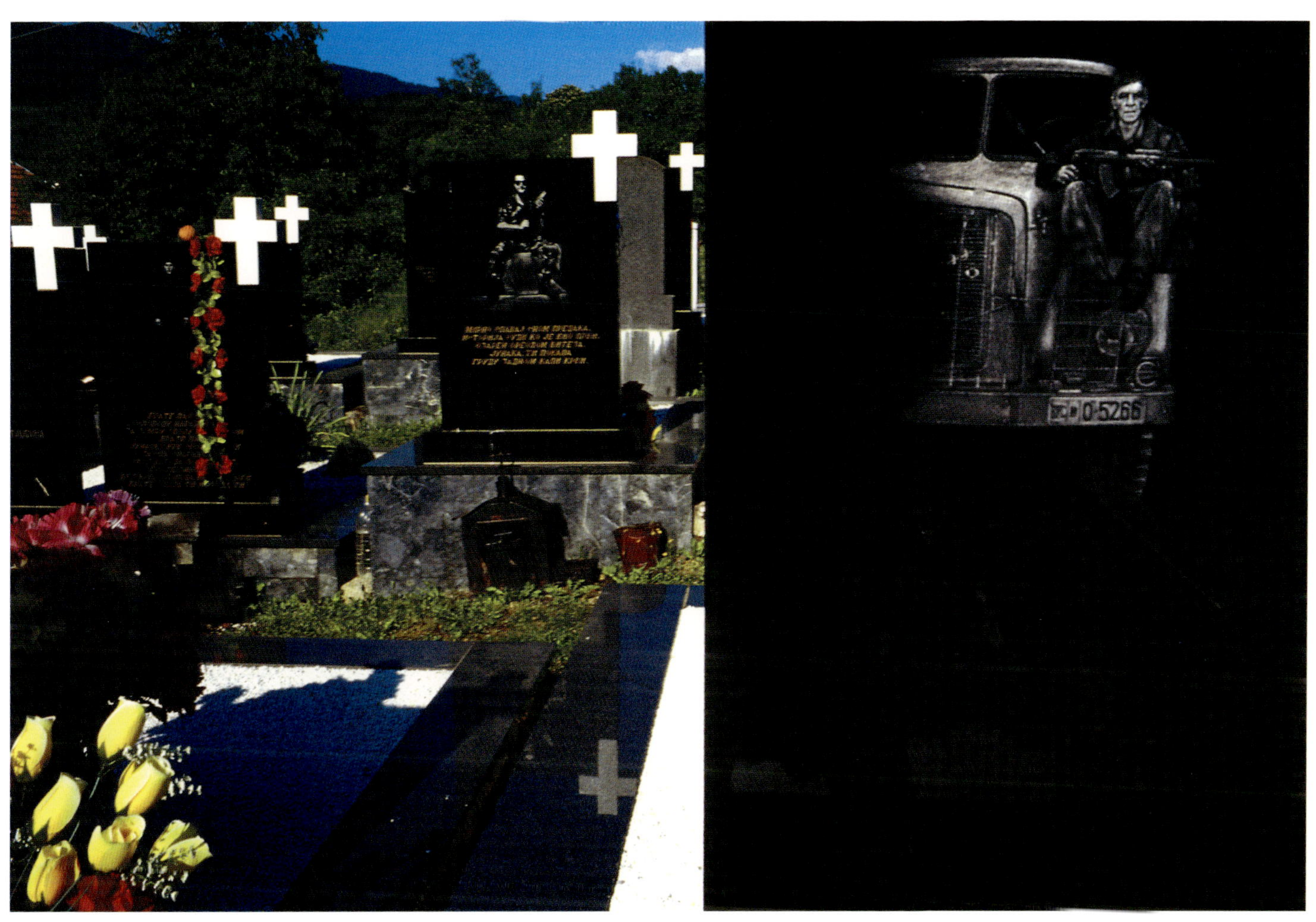

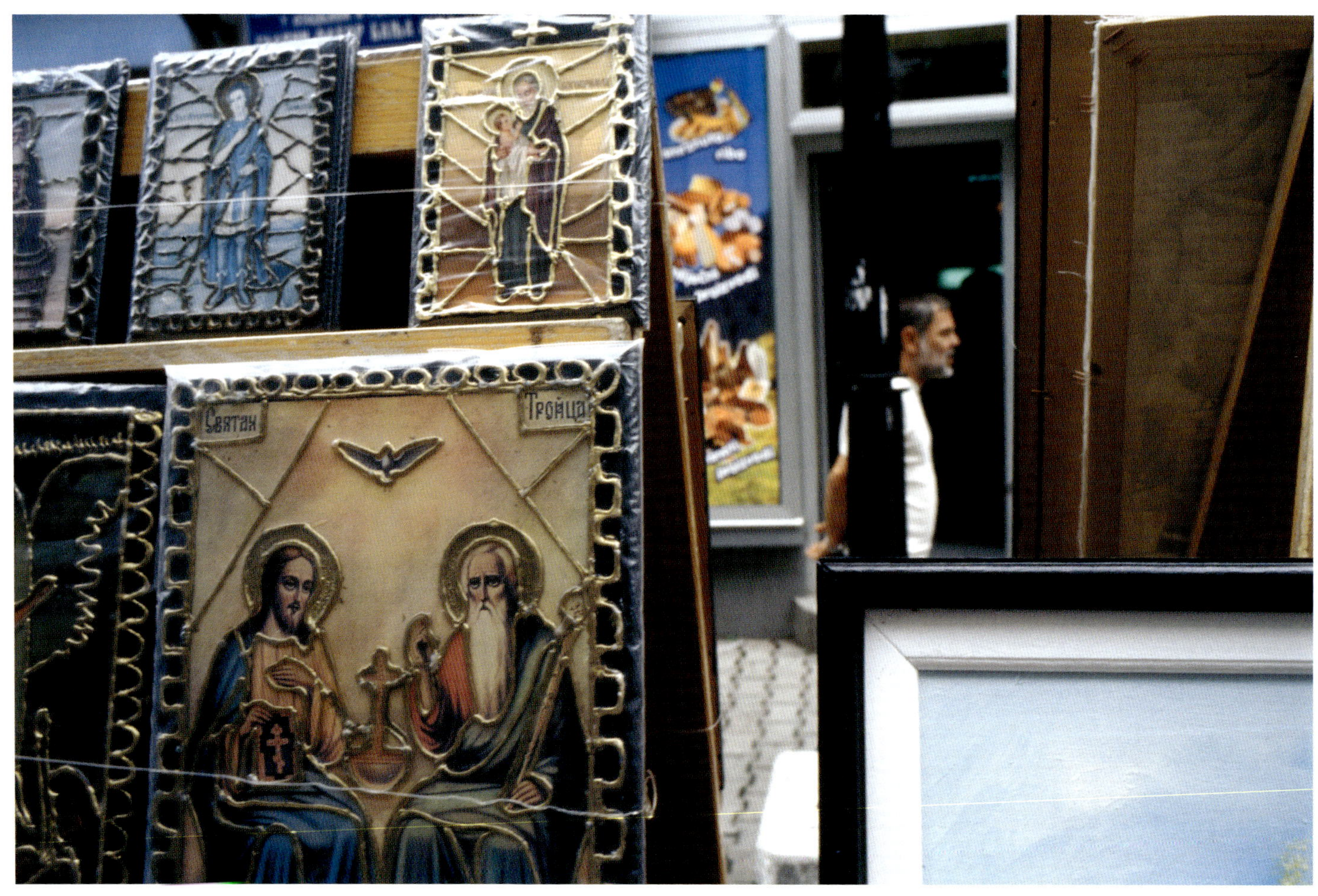
Святая
Троица

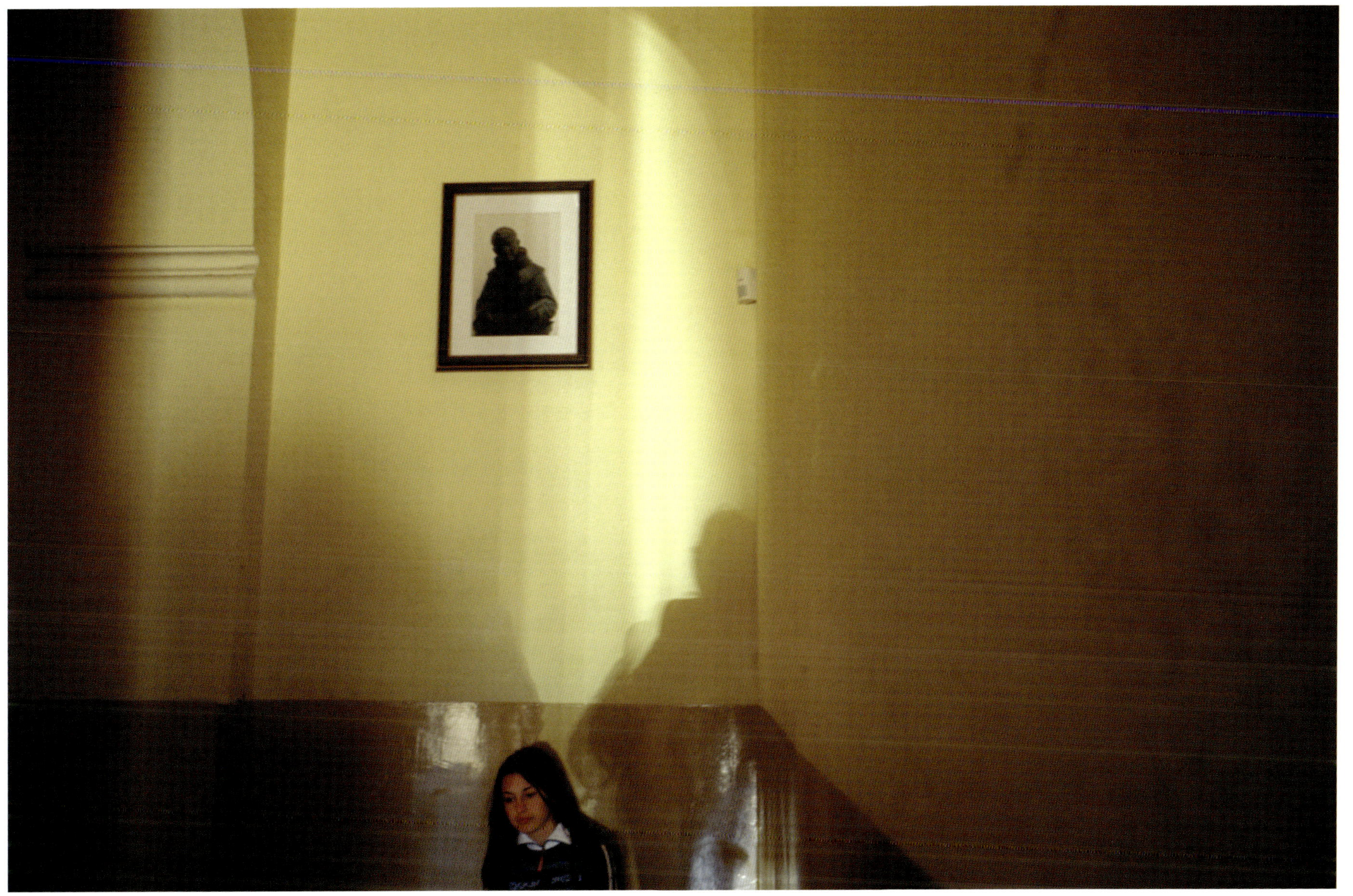

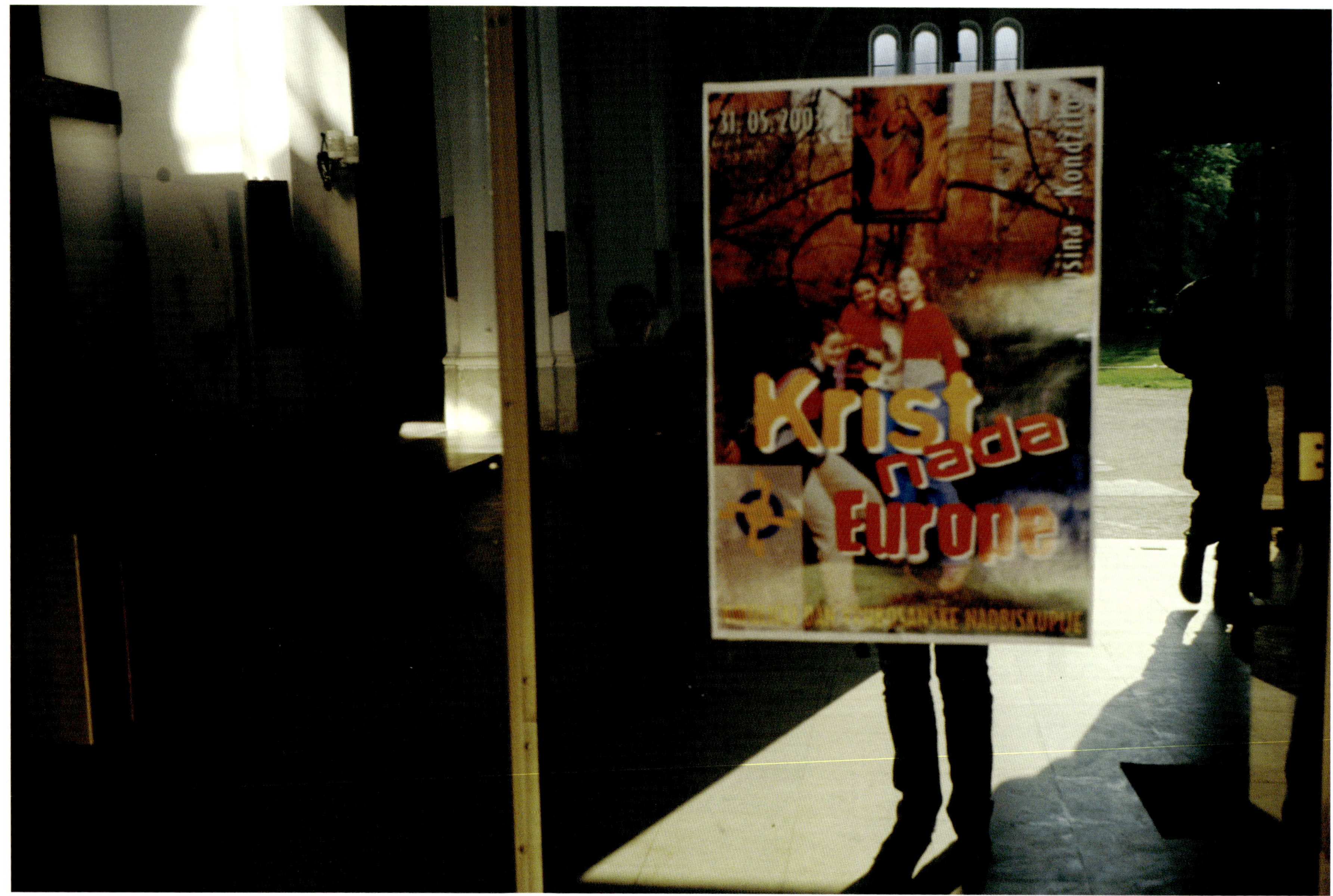
Krist
nada
Europe

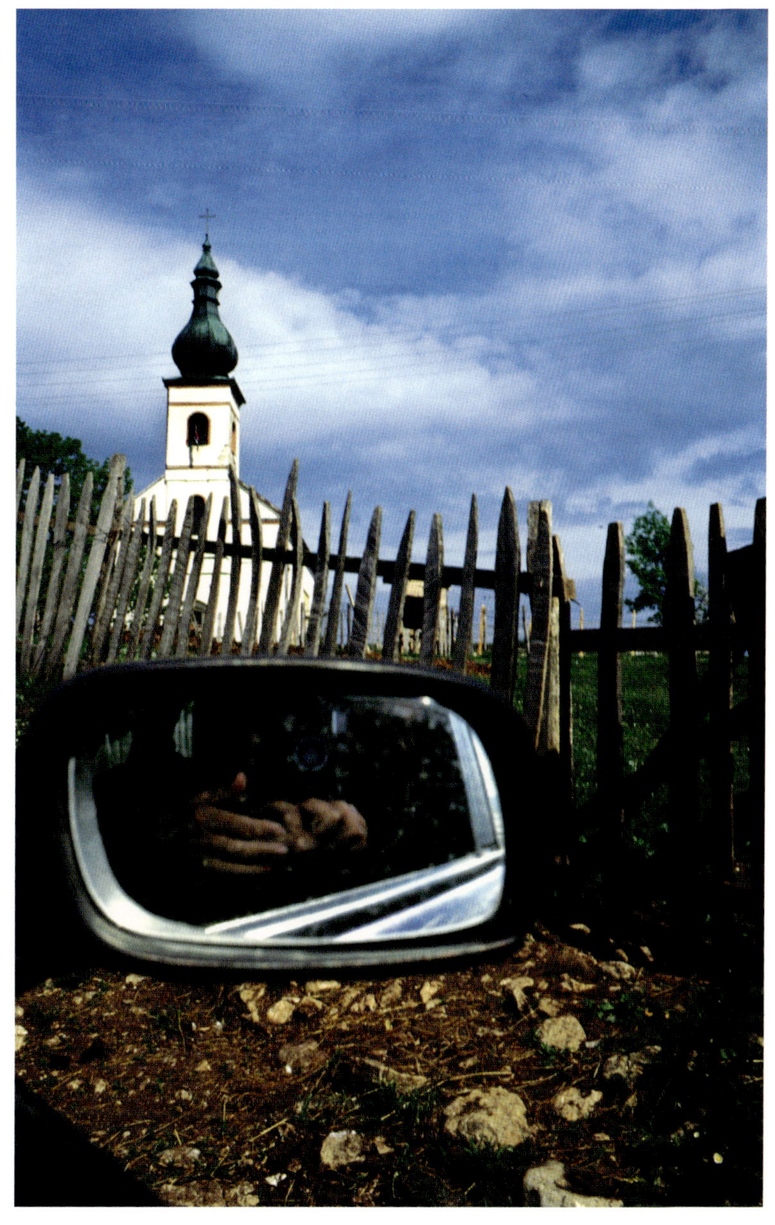

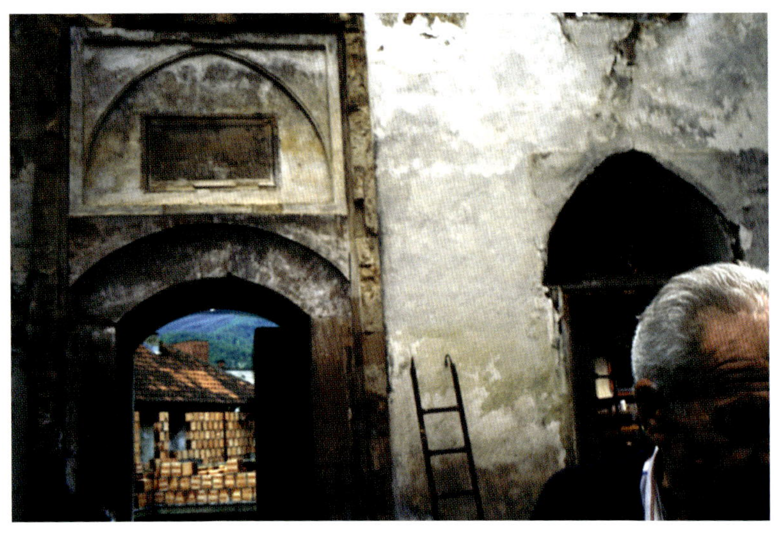

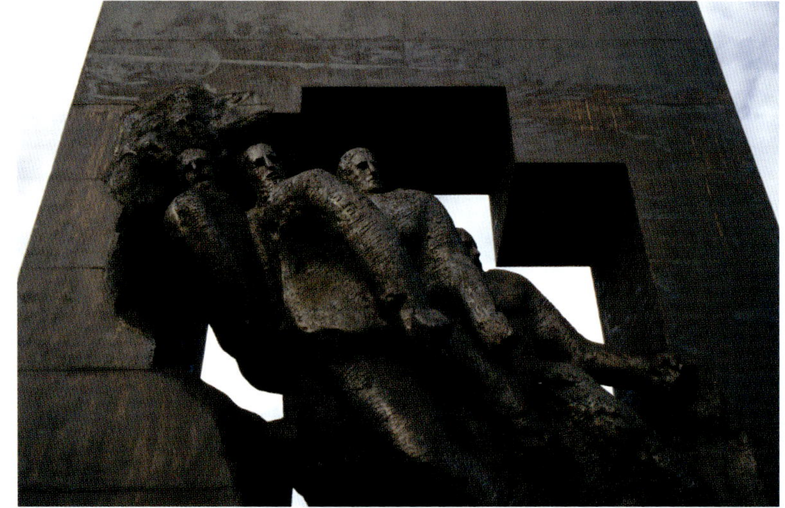

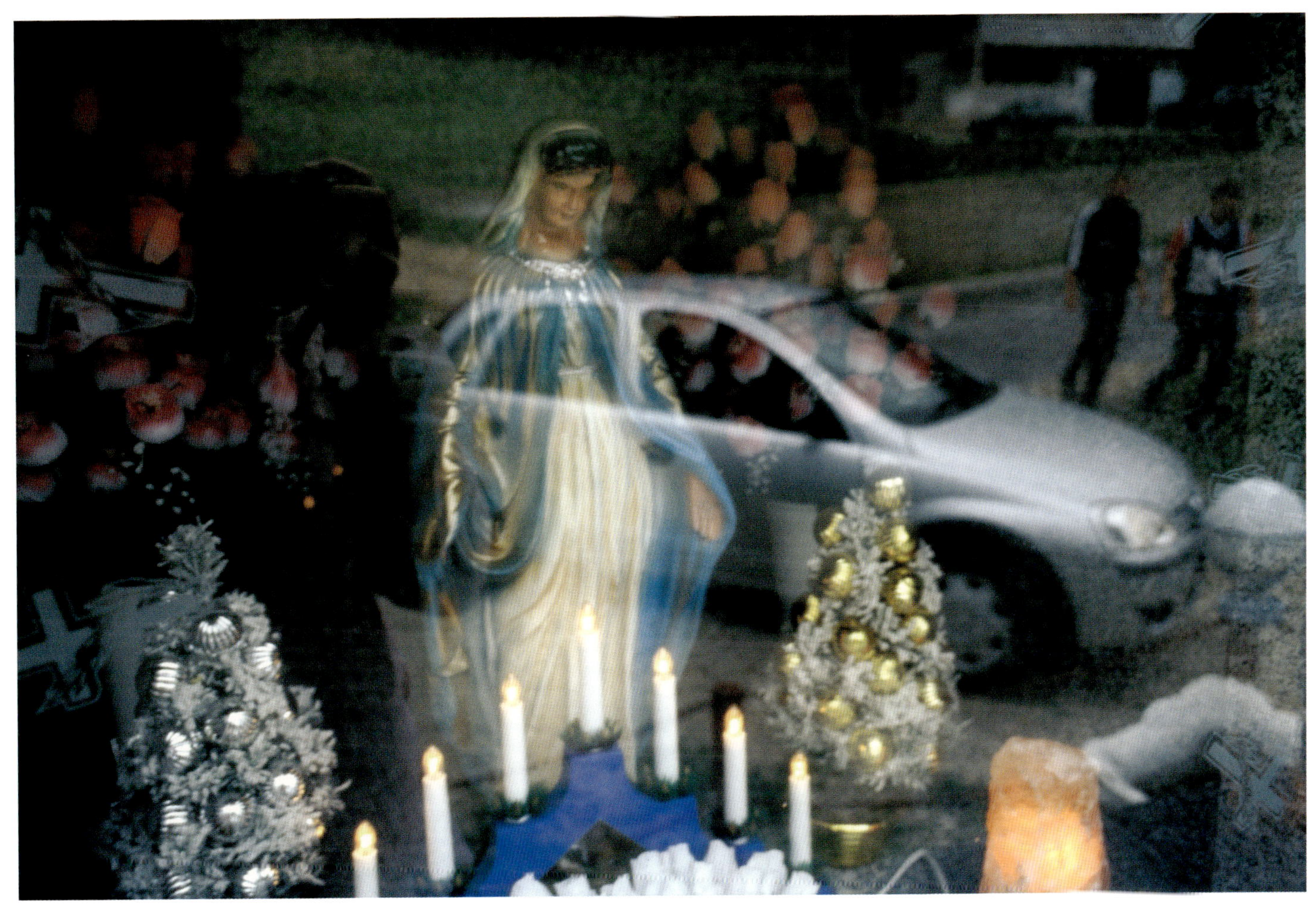

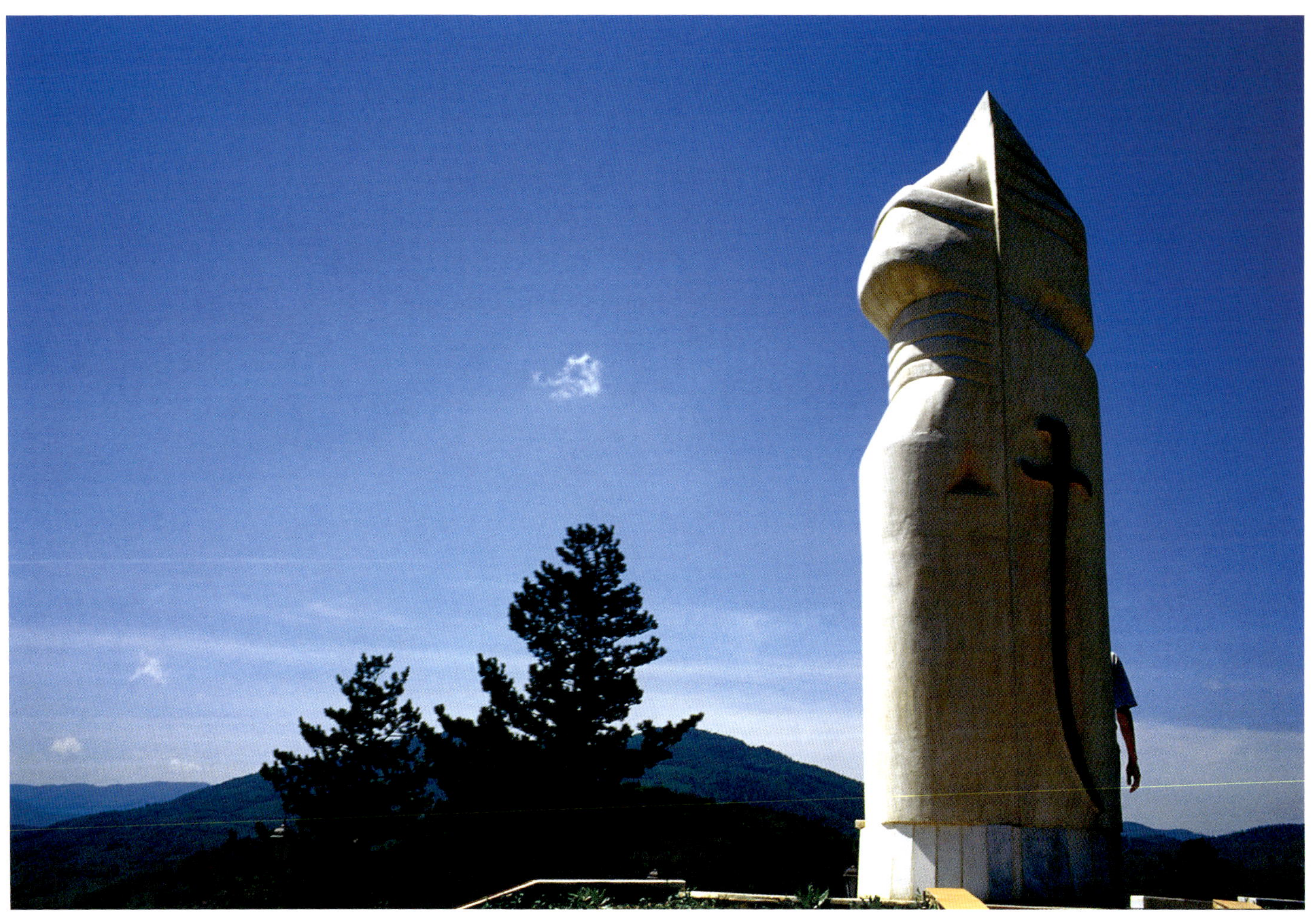

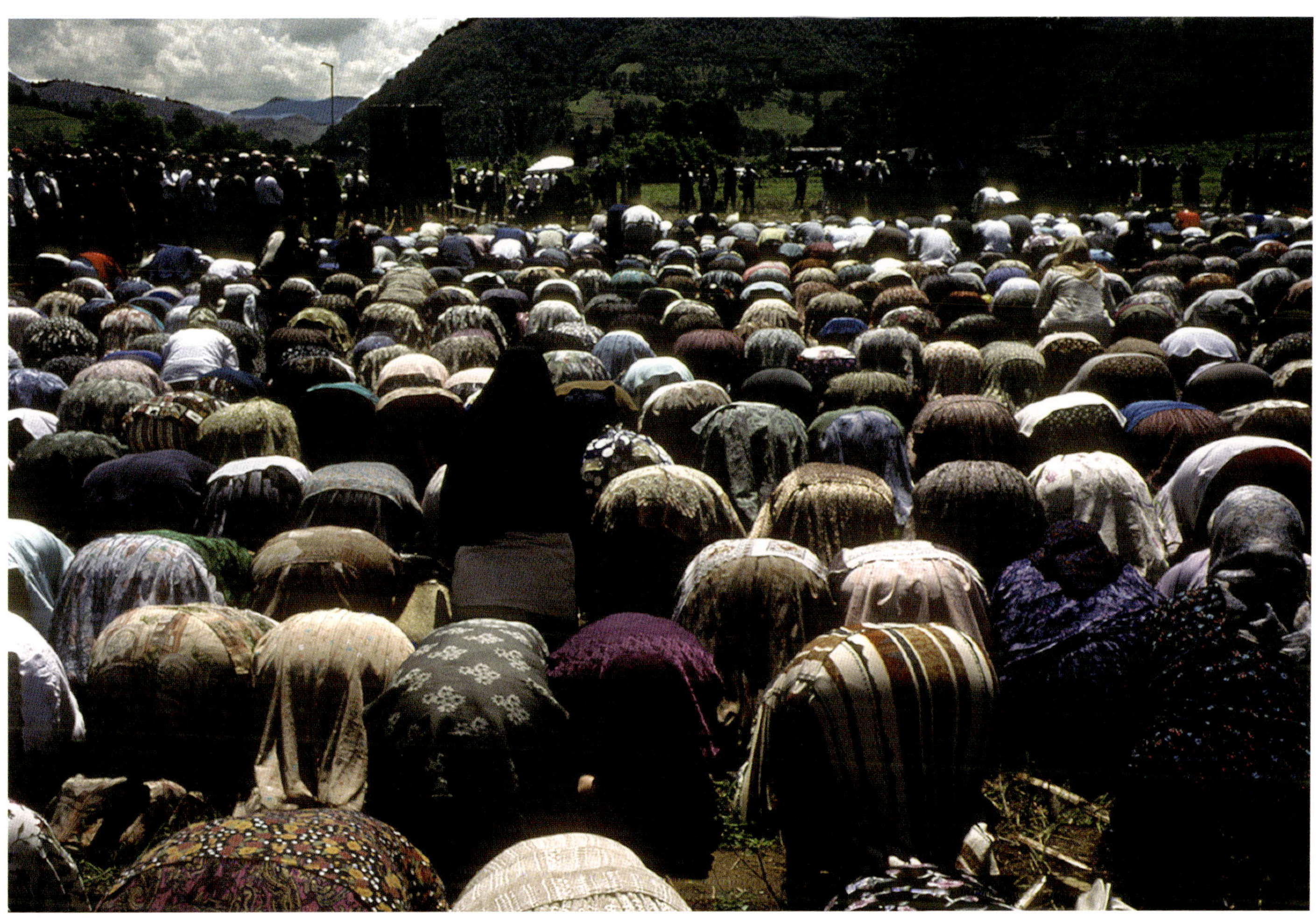

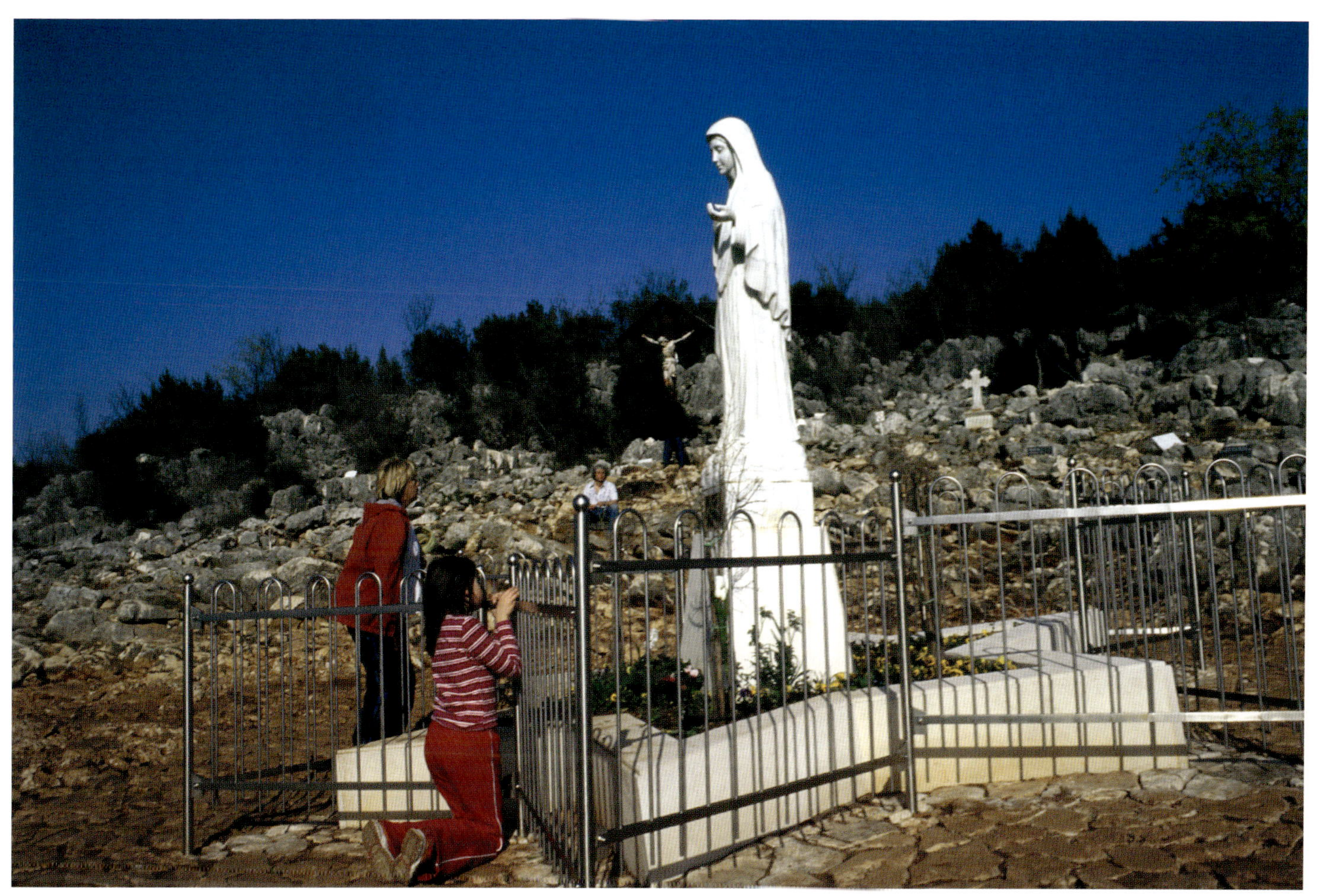

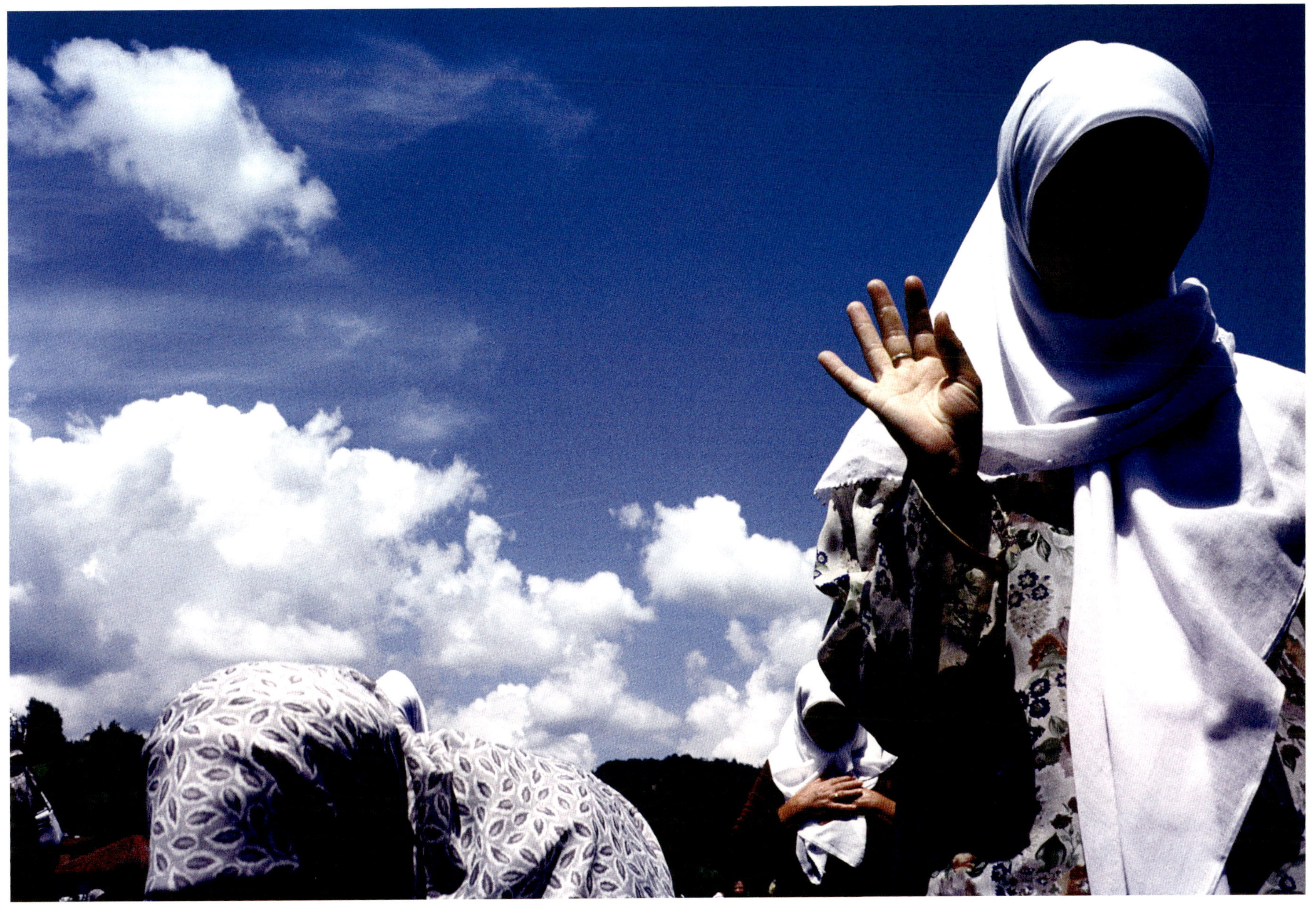

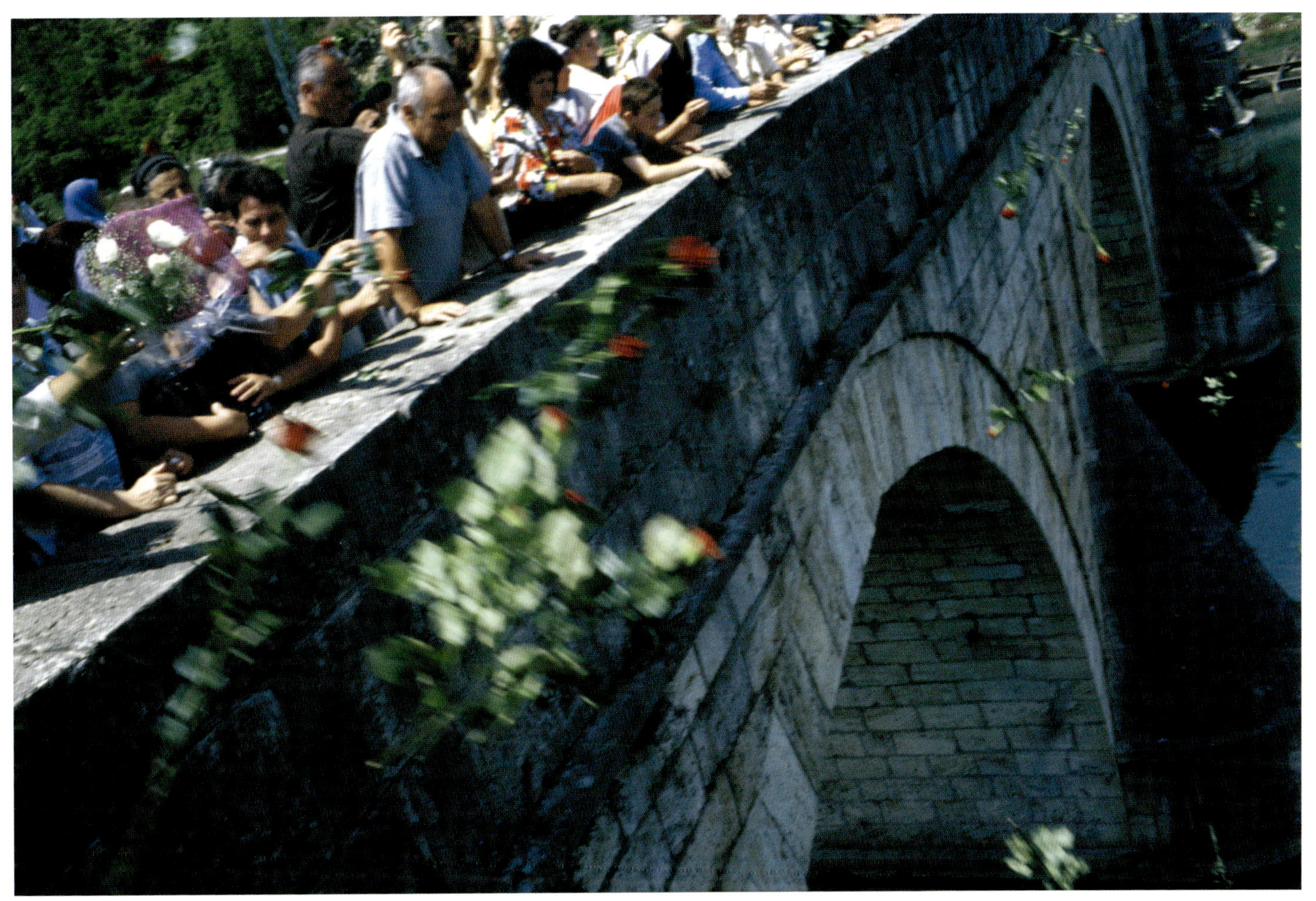

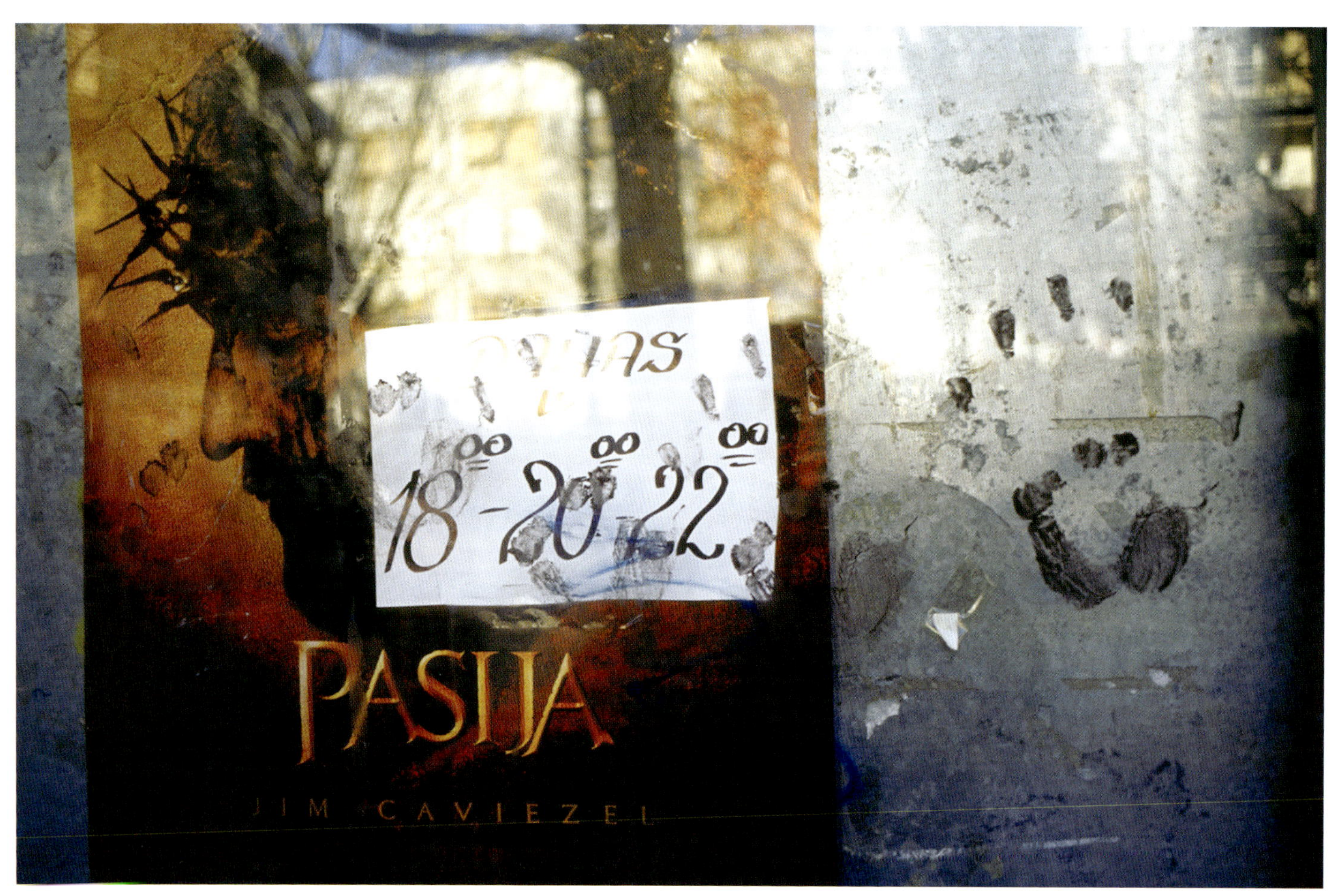
18^{00}-20^{00}-22^{00}
PASIJA
JIM CAVIEZEL

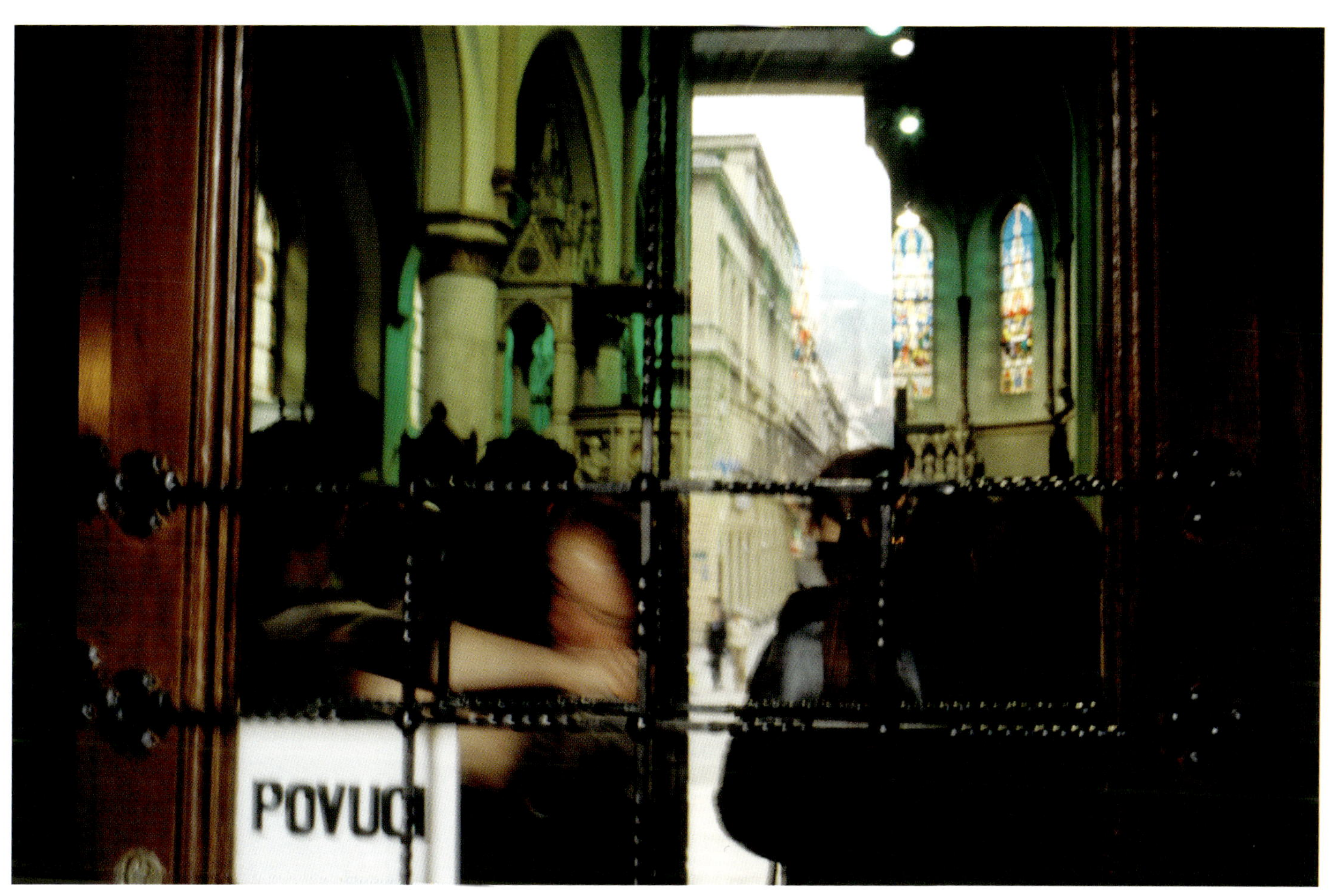
POVUCI

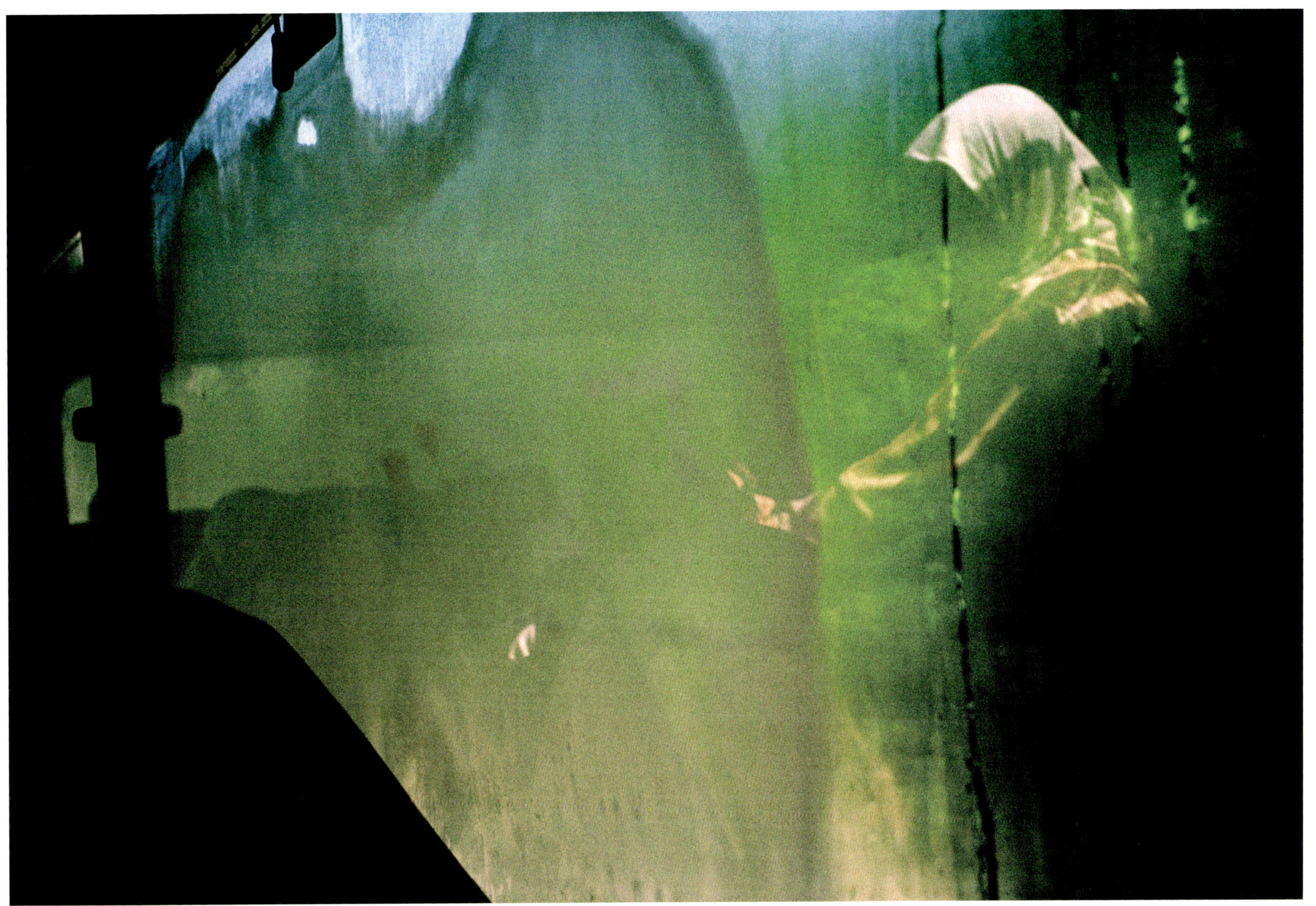

137 An Orthodox priest kisses an icon in Tvrdos monastery, near Trebinje, one of the many towns which Muslims were forced to flee when the war began in 1992. According to locals, this monastery has been one of the hiding places for Radovan Karadzic, who was the Bosnian Serb political leader during the war. Karadzic has been indicted for war crimes by the International Criminal Tribunal for the Former Yugoslavia, but has remained at large for years. May 15, 2003.

139 Laser-engraved headstones of Bosnian Serb soldiers who were killed during the war. The cemetery is in Visegrad, in eastern Bosnia, a town where some 2,000 Muslim men and boys were killed by Serbs in the spring of 1992. Eight years after the end of the war, the formerly Muslim-majority town remains overwhelmingly Serb. May 17, 2003.

140 Orthodox art work for sale on the streets of Banja Luka, which is the capital of the Serb Republic entity that makes up 49 percent of Bosnia. Muslims were viciously "cleansed" during the war, and few have returned since that time. Banja Luka, July 28, 2004.

141 A high school student sits in the hallway of Mostar's main high school, or gymnasium. Before the war, the school had a multi-religious student body, but after the war local Croats renamed the school after a Catholic priest and incorporated religious teachings in to the curriculum. Re-integrating the school, and re-naming it the Mostar Gymnasium, took years of effort. By 2004, Muslim students had returned to the school, but were taught in separate classrooms. Education—particularly curriculum for history and religion remains one of the most difficult post-conflict issues in the country. March 29, 2004.

142 A poster on an entrance to the Catholic church in Bugojno reads, "Christ, savior of Europe." May 24, 2003.

143 The Orthodox church in Bozinovici, the village where Ratko Mladic, the Bosnian Serb military leader during the war, grew up. Like Radovan Karadzic, Mladic has been indicted for his role in the war, but he, too, remains at large. The two men have become folk heroes for many Bosnian Serbs. May 18, 2003.

144a In Foca, workers are rebuilding a five-hundred-year-old mosque, one of a dozen that used to stand in the city. The other eleven mosques were completely destroyed by local Serbs when the war began in 1992, and Muslims were either killed or forced to leave. The contractor overseeing this project has hired a crew that includes both Serbs and Muslims. May 18, 2003.

144b A huge monument, featuring an Orthodox cross, stands in the center of Bjeljina, the town where "ethnic cleansing" began in April 1992. The sculpture is dedicated to the Bosnian Serb soldiers who lost their lives fighting the "patriot's war" of 1992-95. April 5, 2004.

145 A Catholic roadside shrine. Near Travnik, July 27, 2004.

146 A massive sculpture—a stylized version of an old Muslim headstone—stands above the town of Gorazde, on the spot where Serb artillery positions threatened Muslim civilians during the war. Along with the town of Srebrenica, Gorazde was designated as a United Nations "safe haven" for Muslims, but was virtually surrounded by and often attacked by Serb forces during the war. May 17, 2003.

147 Muslim widows pray during ceremonies marking the groundbreaking of a memorial site for the 7,000 to 8,000 Muslim men and boys who were slaughtered when Srebrenica was overrun by Serb forces in July 1995. Potocari, July 11, 2001.

149 This statue of the Virgin Mary marks the spot on "Apparition Hill" where six teenagers from the village of Medjugorje claim that the mother of Jesus came to them in a vision in 1981 and gave them a message of peace. Thousands of religious pilgrims from around the world visit the site each year; several of the teenagers, now grown, say they still have regular visions of Mary, who continues to give them messages to share with the world. March 30, 2004.

151 Muslim widows during the prayer for the dead offered at the groundbreaking of a memorial site for the 7,000 to 8,000 Muslim men and boys who were massacred by Bosnian Serb forces in 1995. Potocari, July 11, 2001.

153 Hundreds of Muslims gather on the old Turkish bridge on the river Drina in Visegrad to commemorate the approximately 2,000 men and boys who were killed during the beginning of the war in 1992 by local Serbs. Visegrad has remained a notoriously nationalistic Serb town since the end of the war, a climate that has made it difficult for many Muslims to return to their homes. The situation in Visegrad was so tense that it wasn't until 2002, seven years after the end of the war, that Muslims were allowed to visit and hold their first commemoration ceremony. This was the second such event. May 25, 2003.

154 A poster for Mel Gibson's film, "The Passion of the Christ," in the Catholic section of Mostar. March 29, 2004.

155 During Easter week services, friends hug inside the Catholic cathedral. Sarajevo, April 8, 2004.

157 On the day groundbreaking ceremonies are held for a memorial to the 7,000 to 8,000 Muslim men and boys killed by Serbs in the 1995 Srebrenica massacre, a widow is seen reflected in a bus window, where condensation has marked the surface of the glass. Potocari, July 11, 2001.

ovo mjesto
THIS PLACE

"I had an opportunity to stay in America, but I said, Thanks, but no thanks. No thanks, because I want to try here. People say to me these days, Haven't you regretted that decison? But I want to try here, to try to do something about the place where I've found myself. Where does that will come from? Probably from something inside me that is stronger than any problems. Not exactly optimism, but maybe belief that it really will be better someday. But it can't be better if you just sit back and say it will be better. I have to do something about it."

> **daniela torbic,** member of the pontanima choir

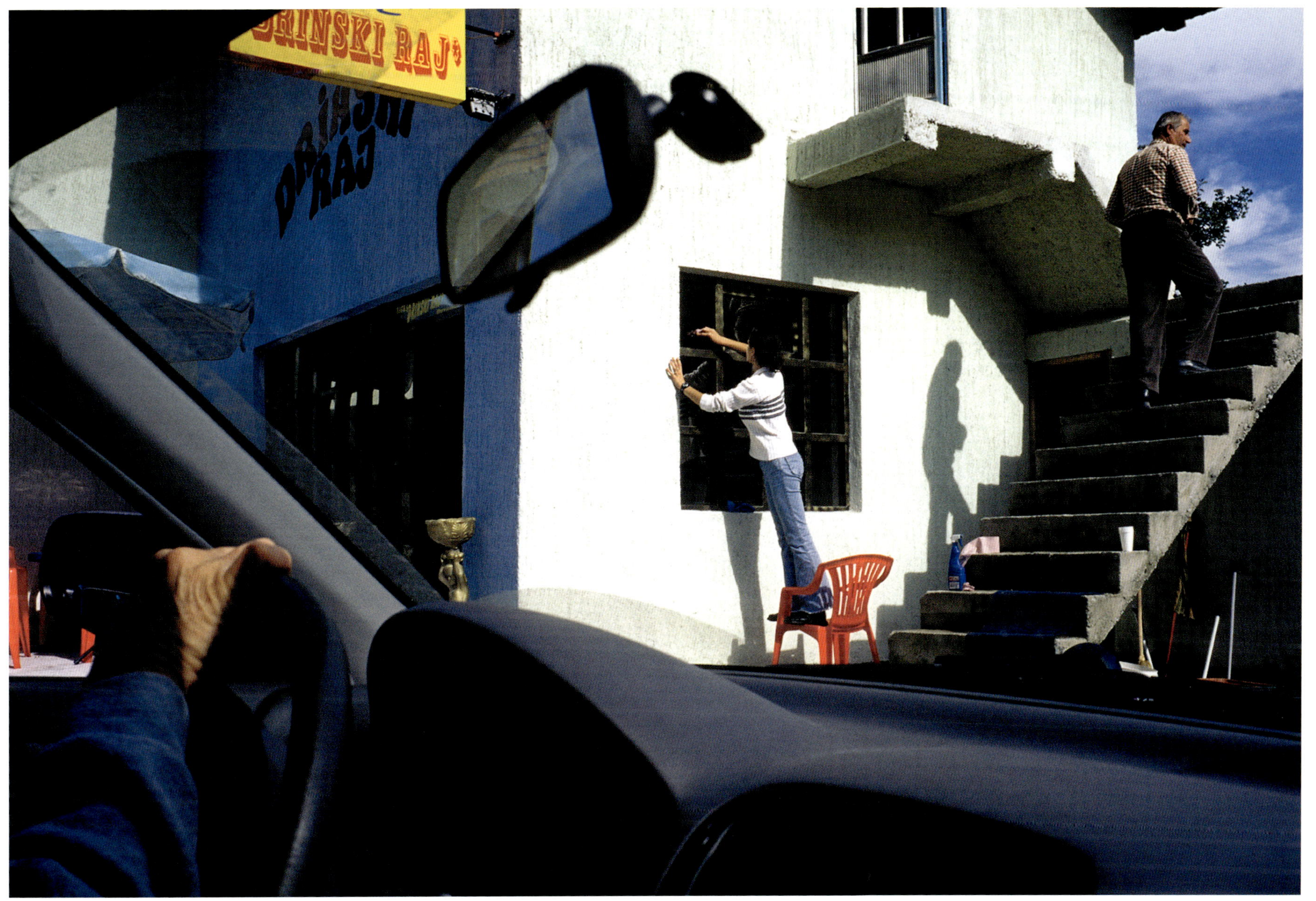
RINSKI RAJ

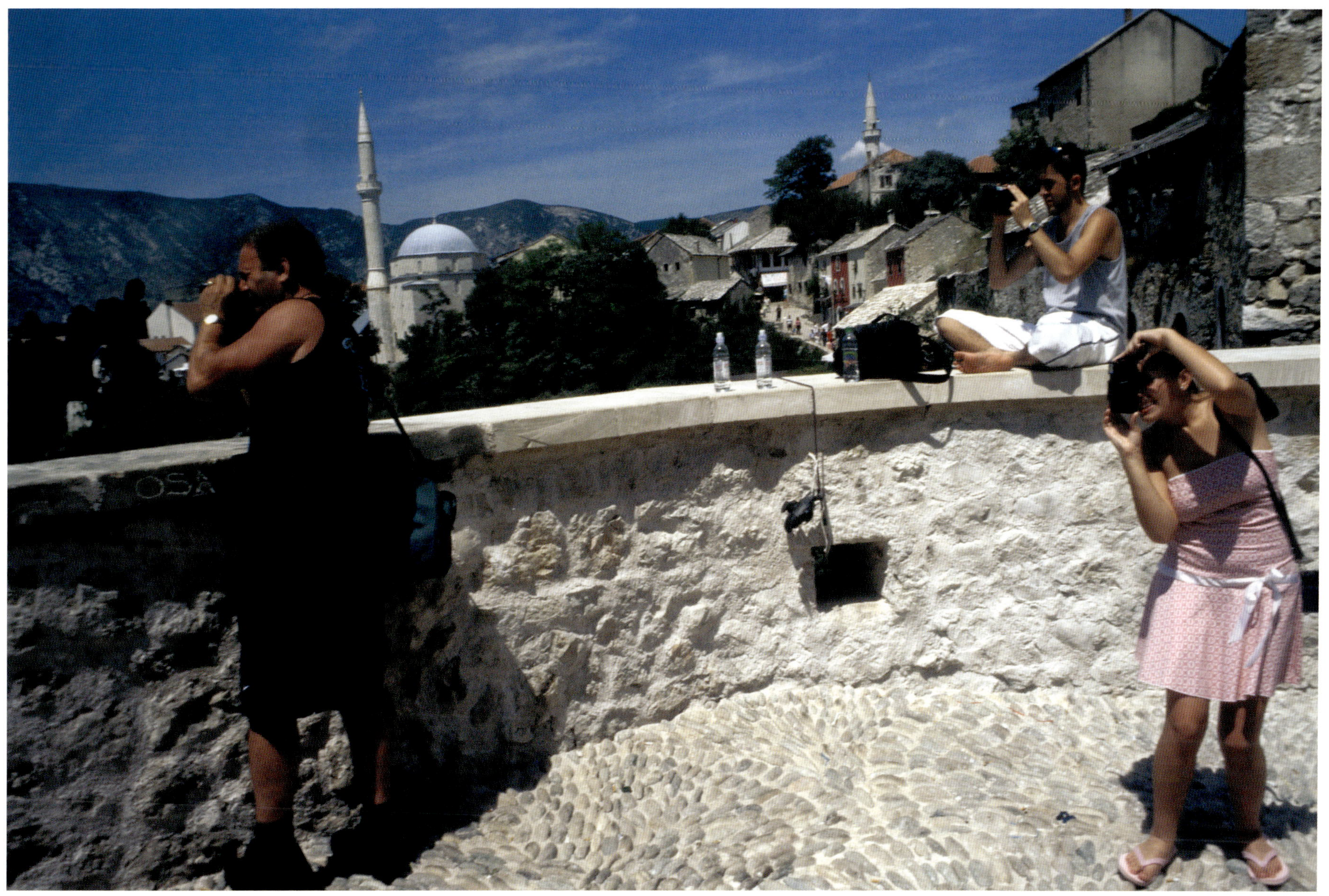

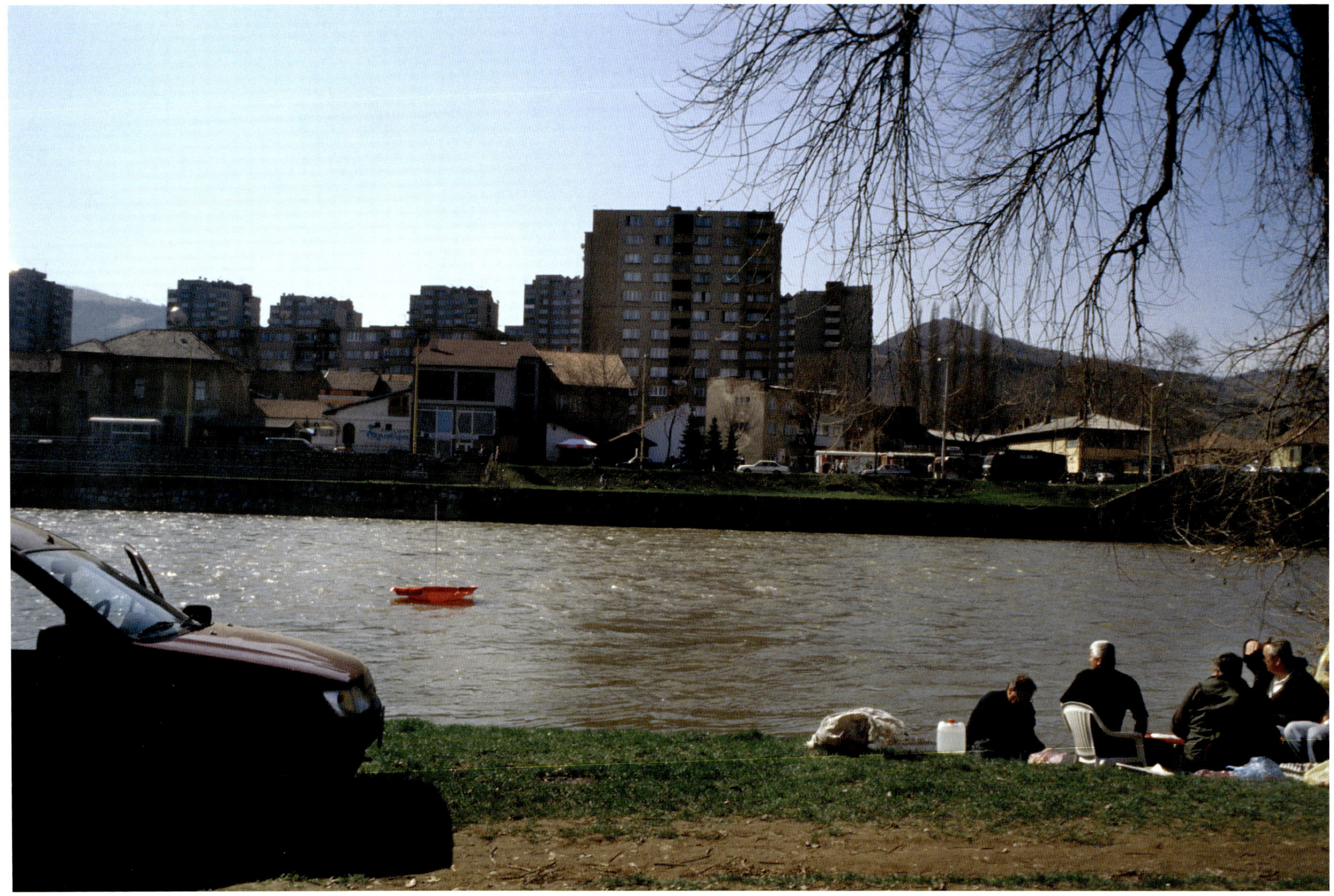

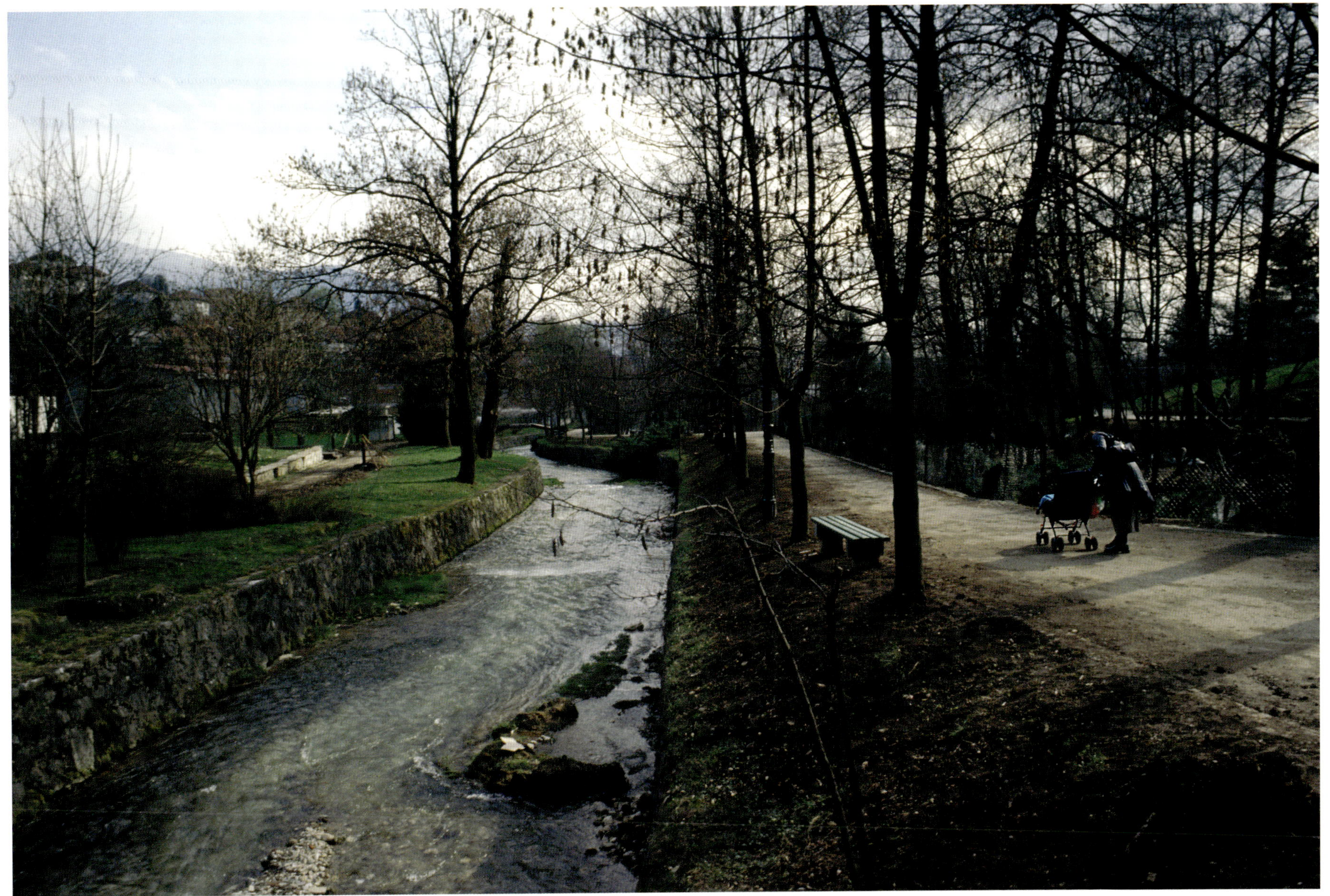

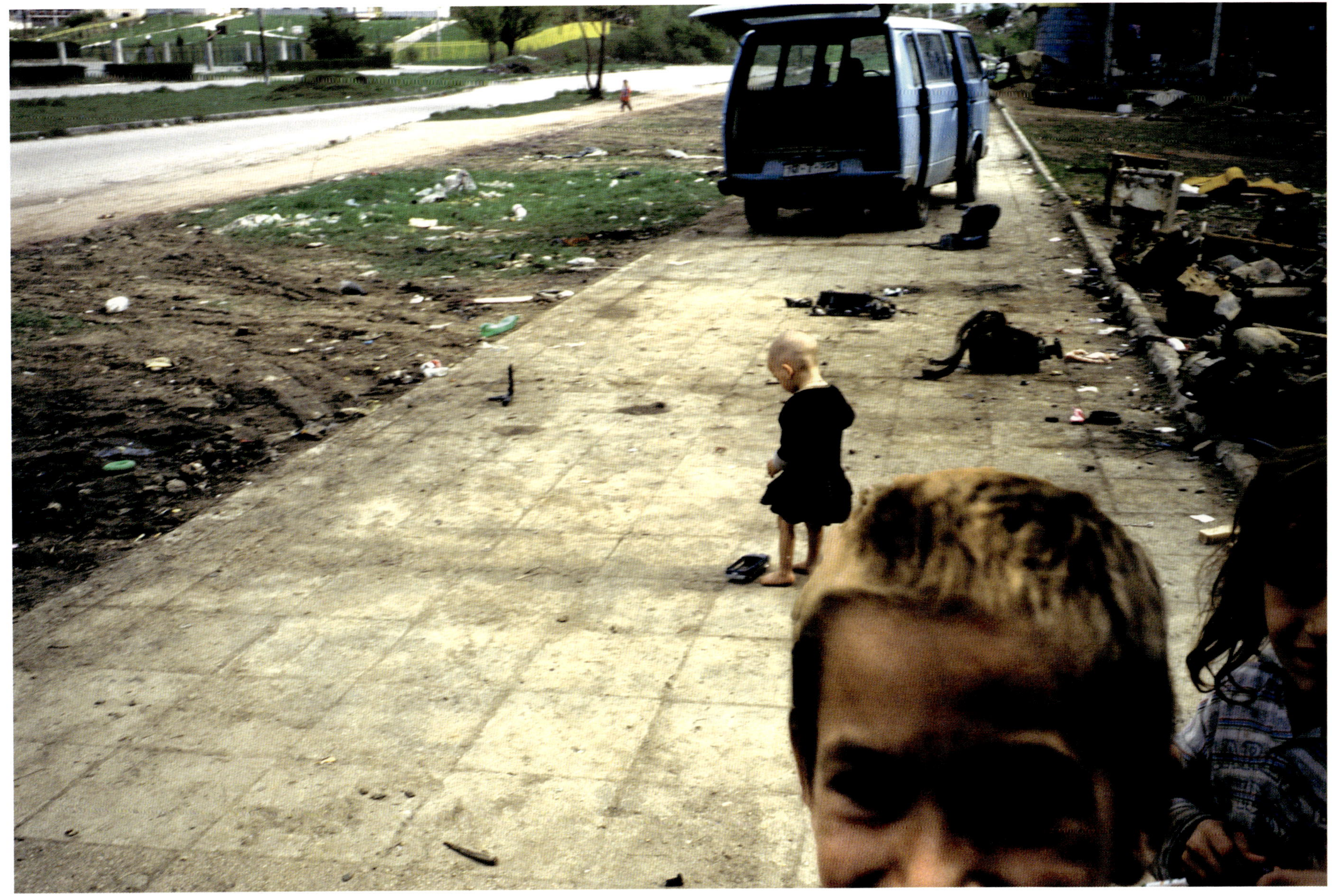

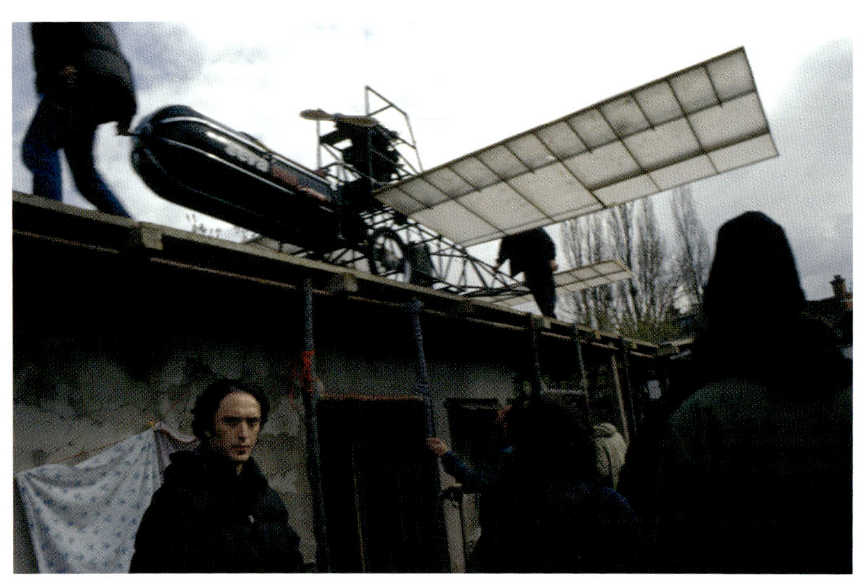

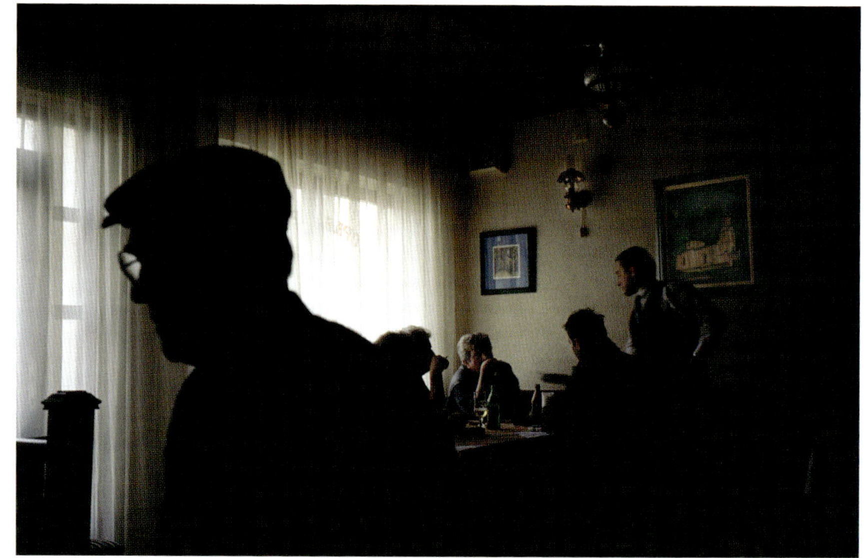

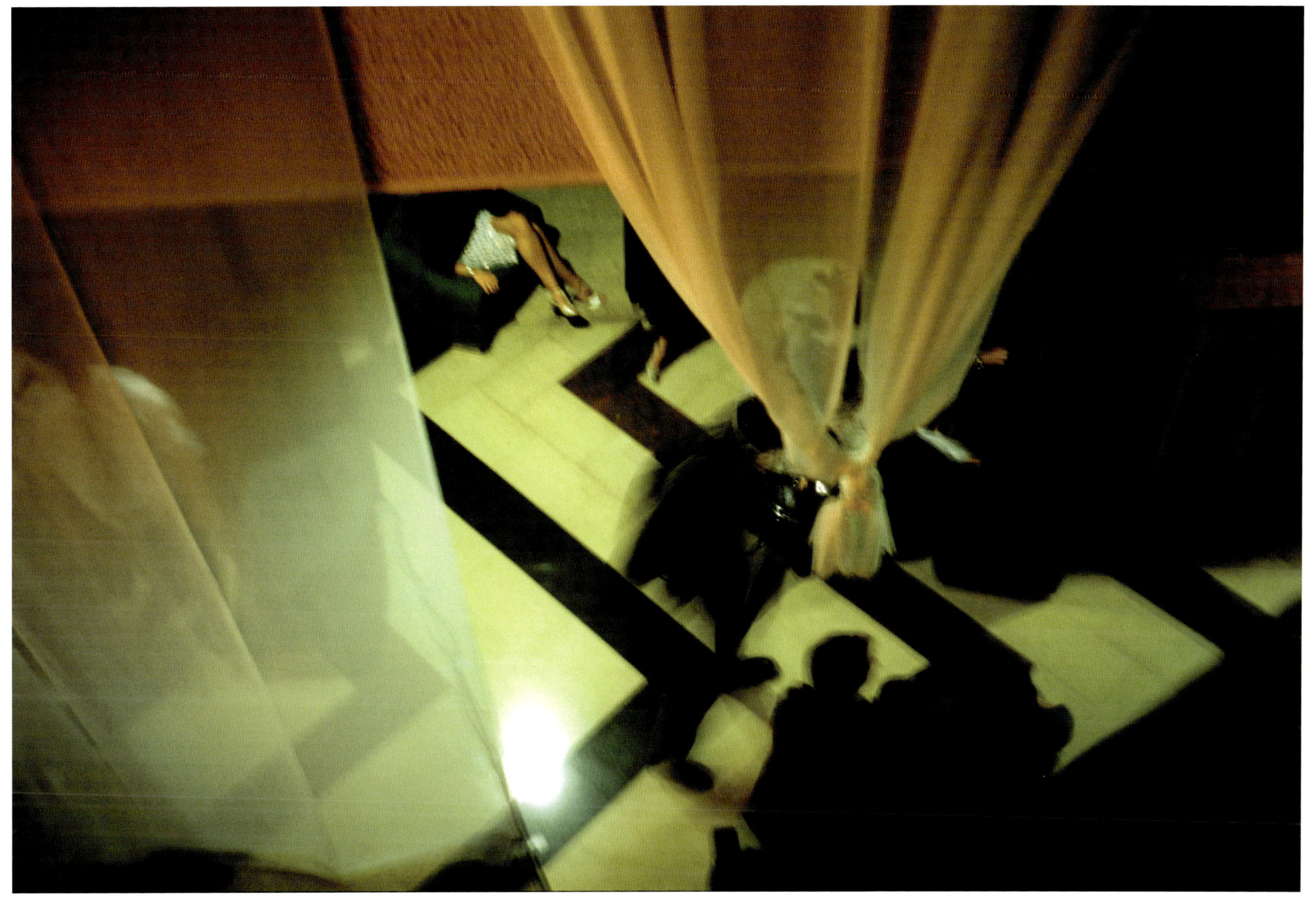

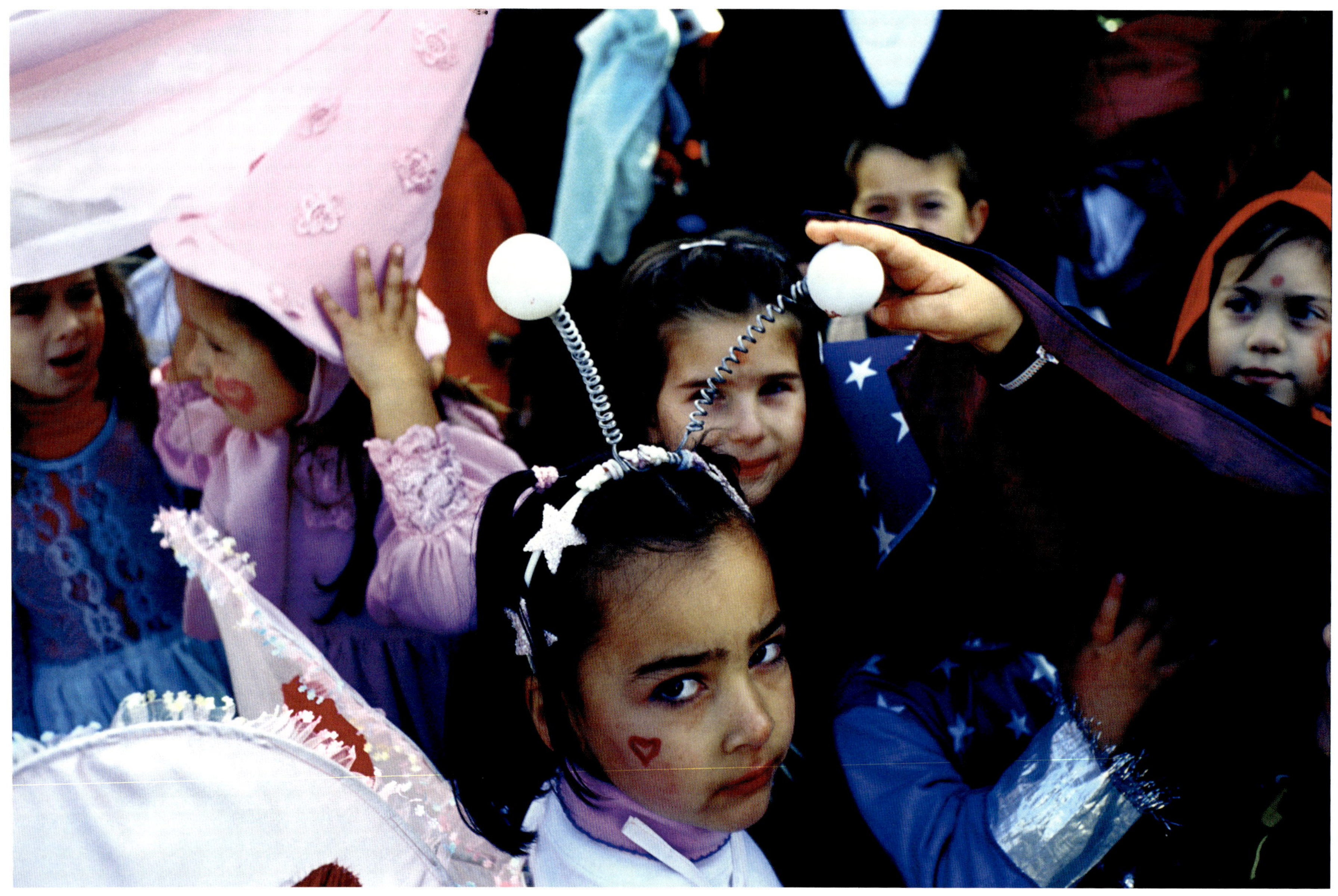

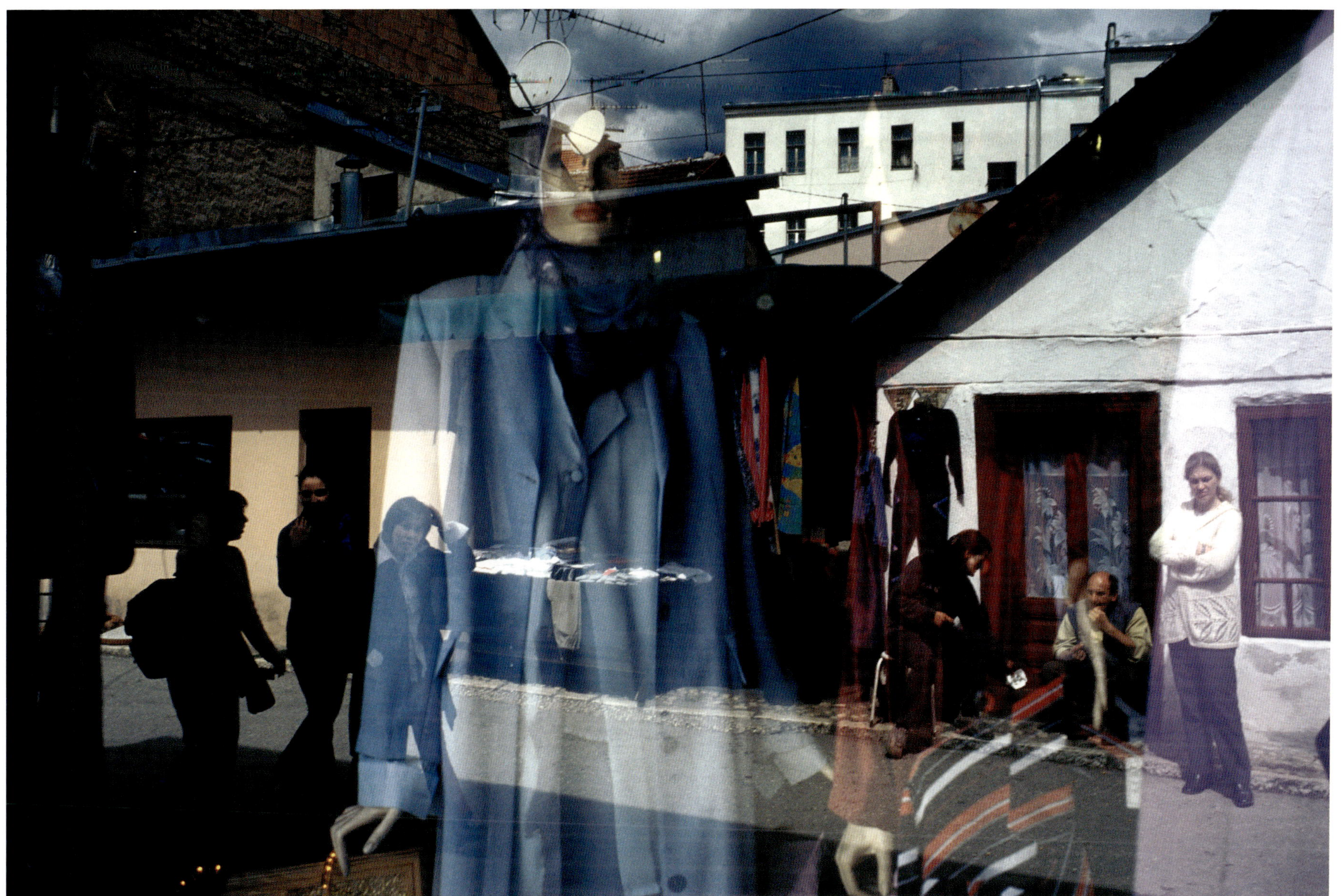

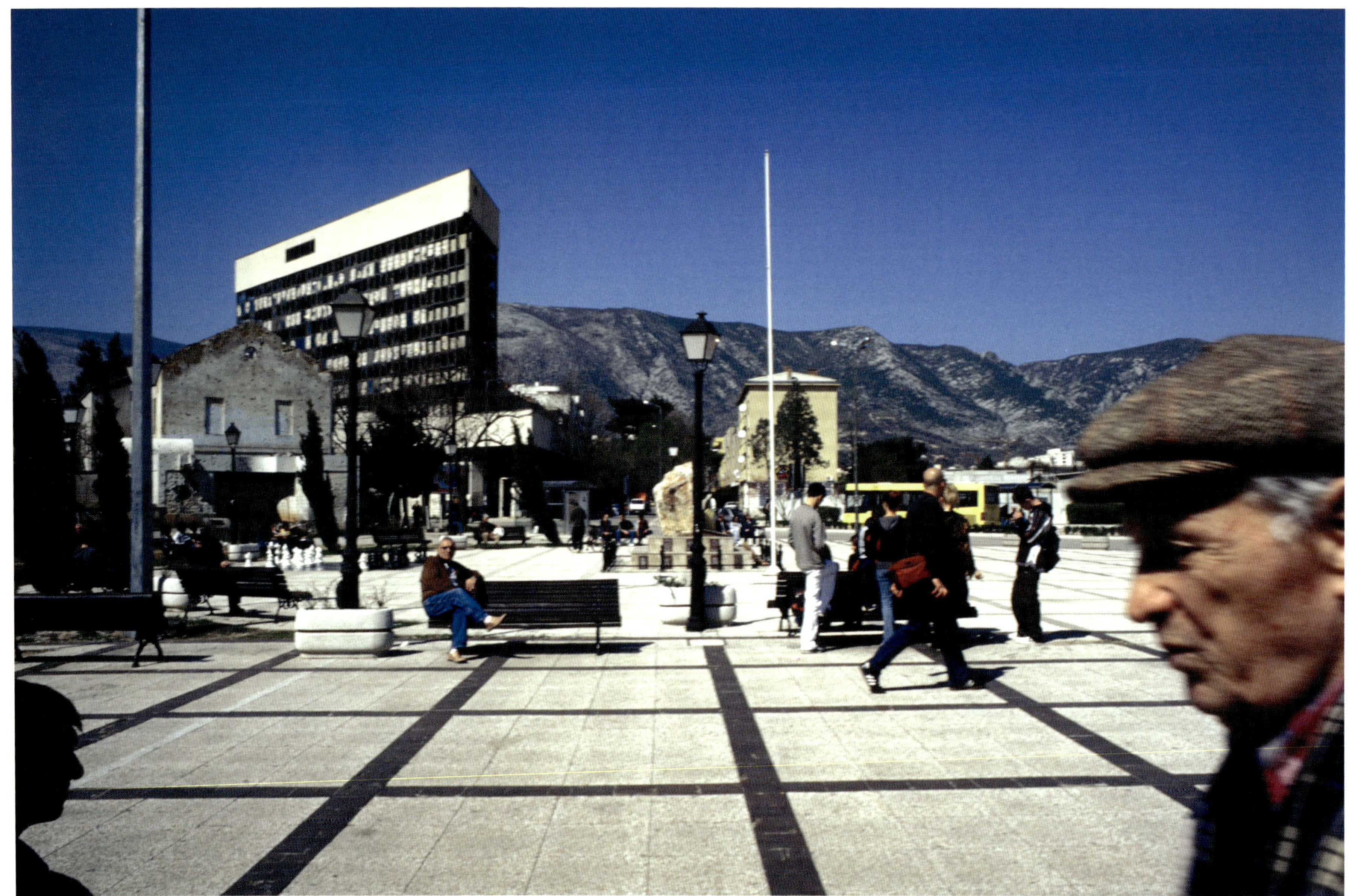

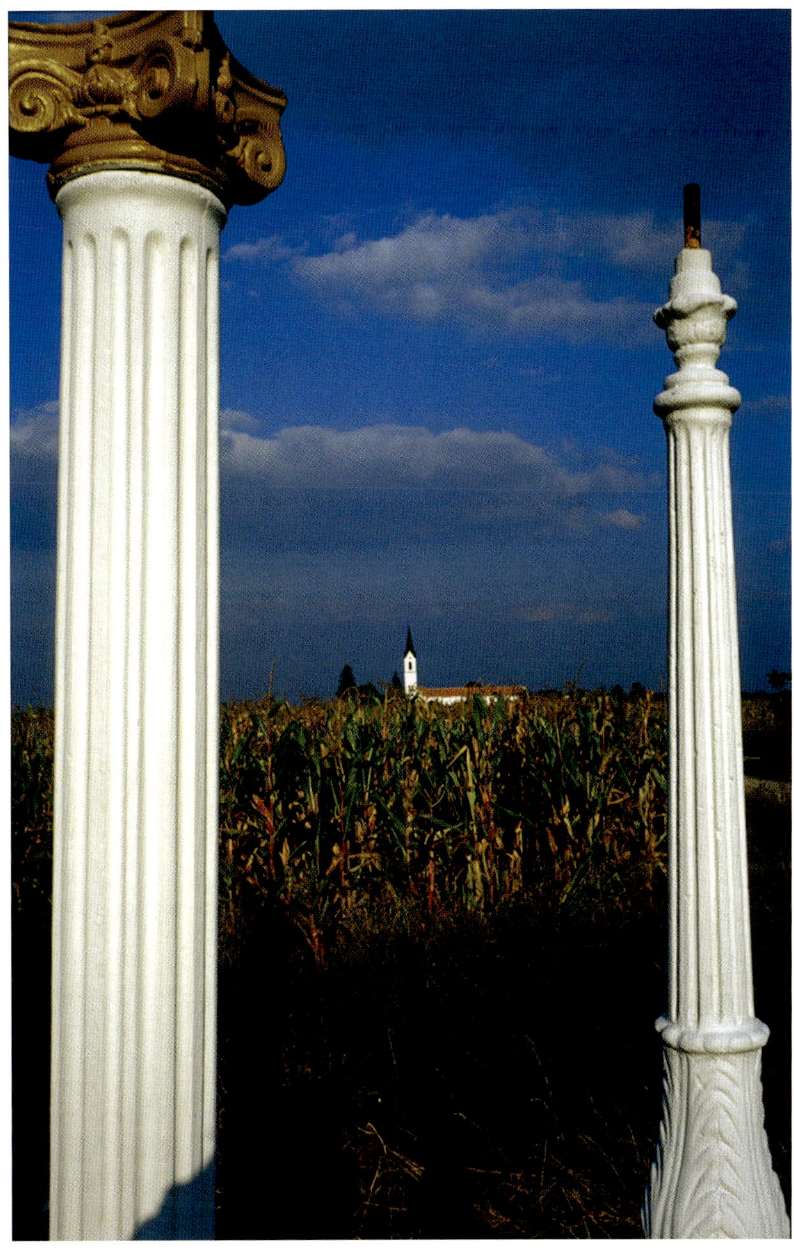

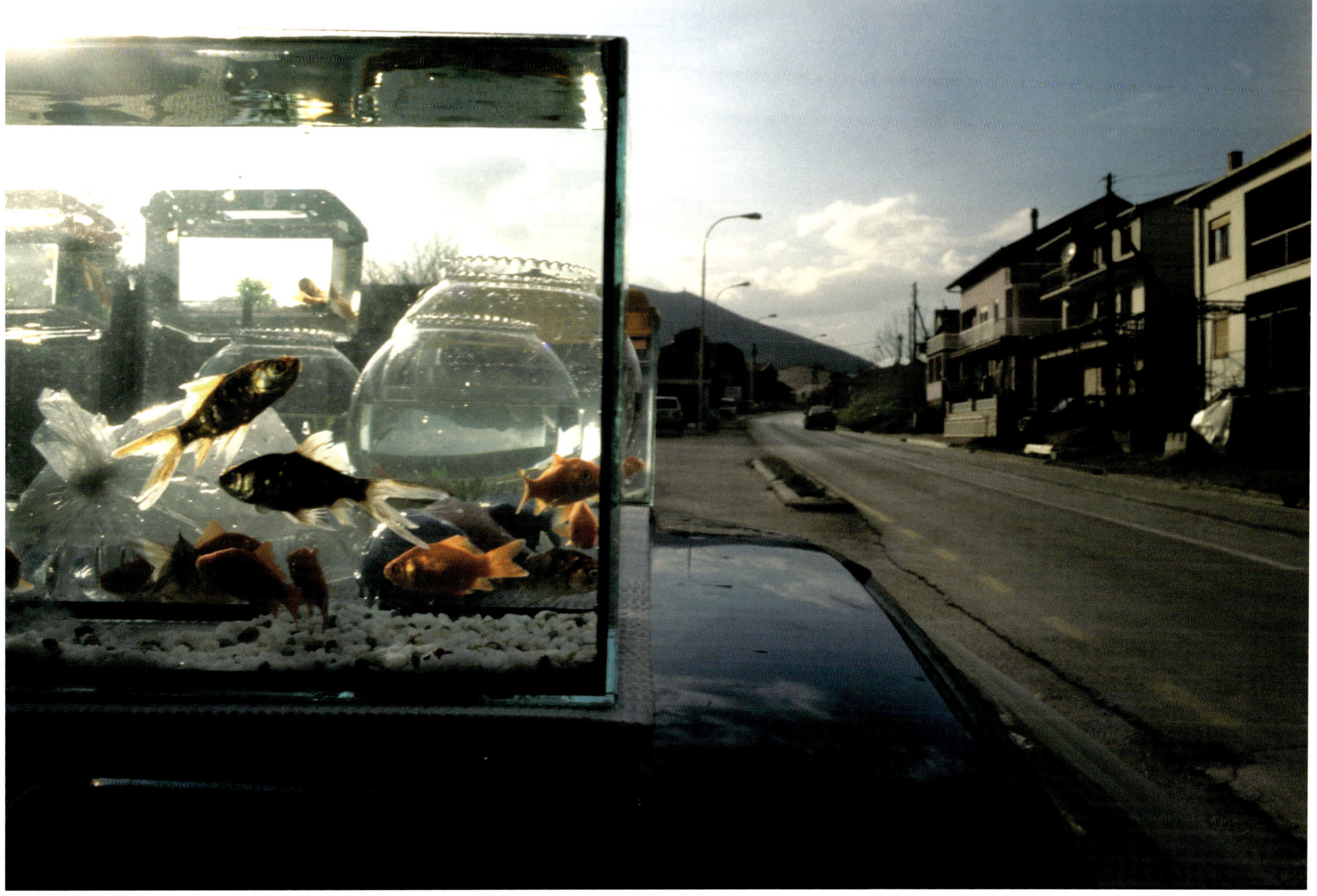

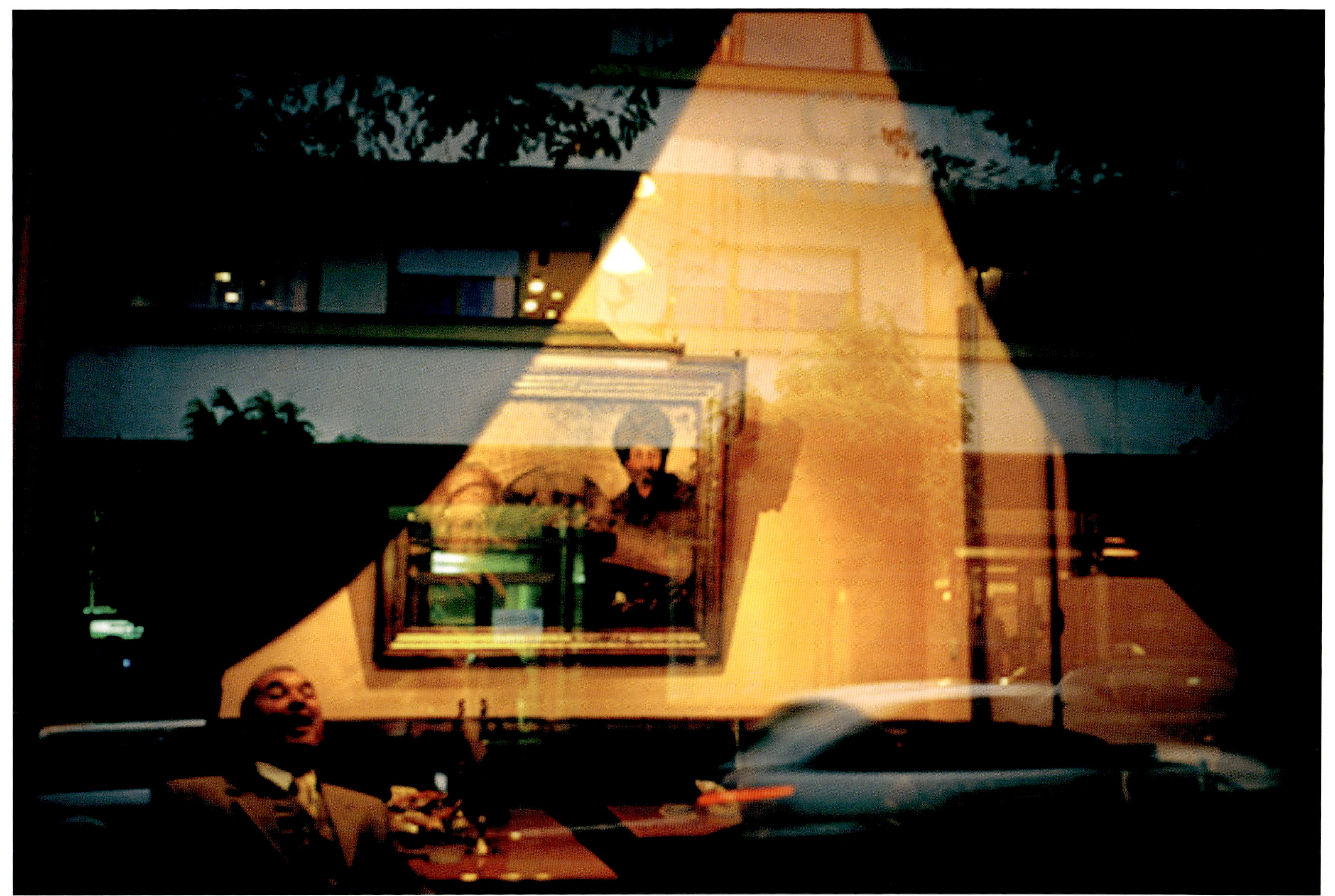

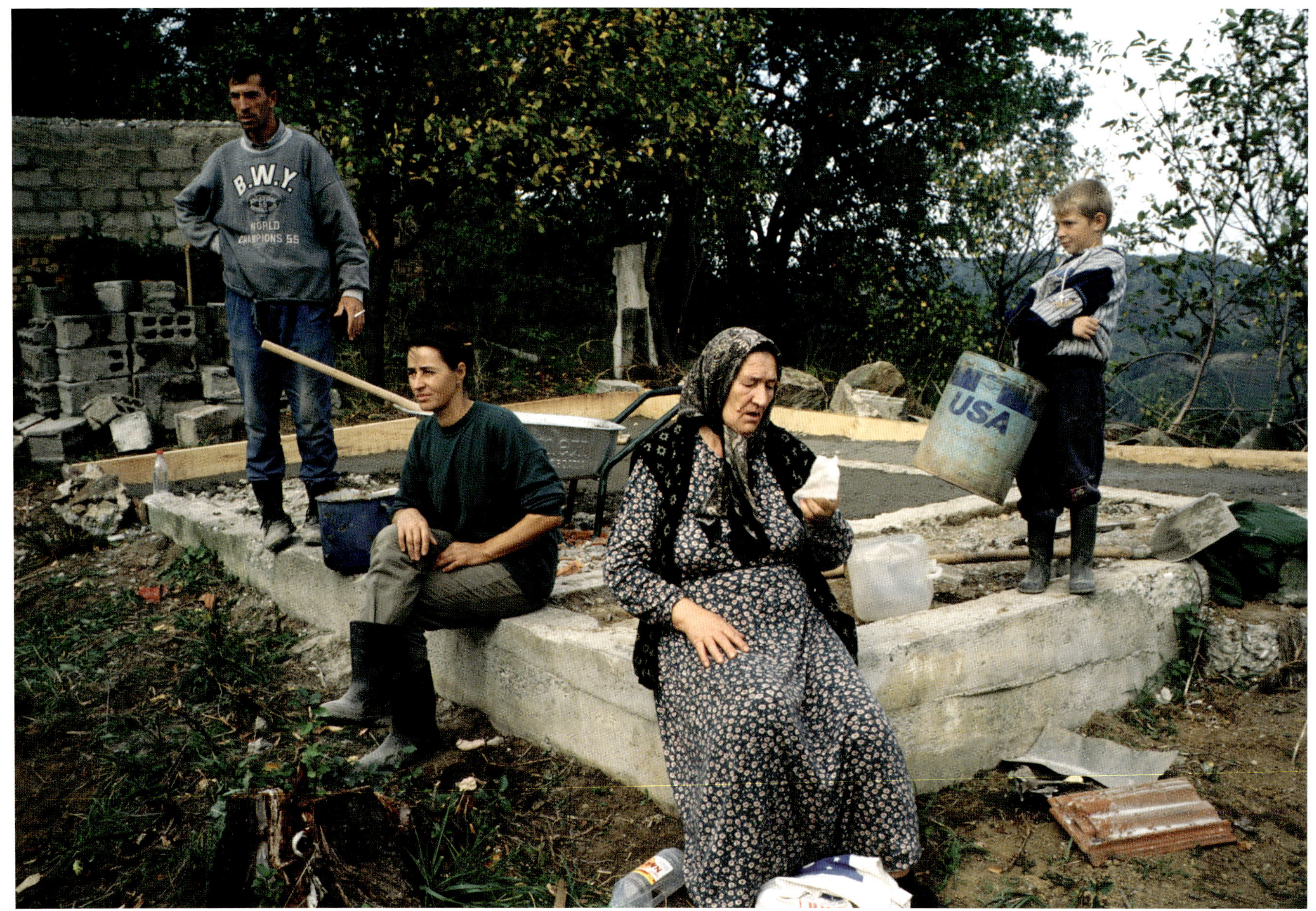
B.W.Y.
WORLD
CHAMPIONS 55
USA

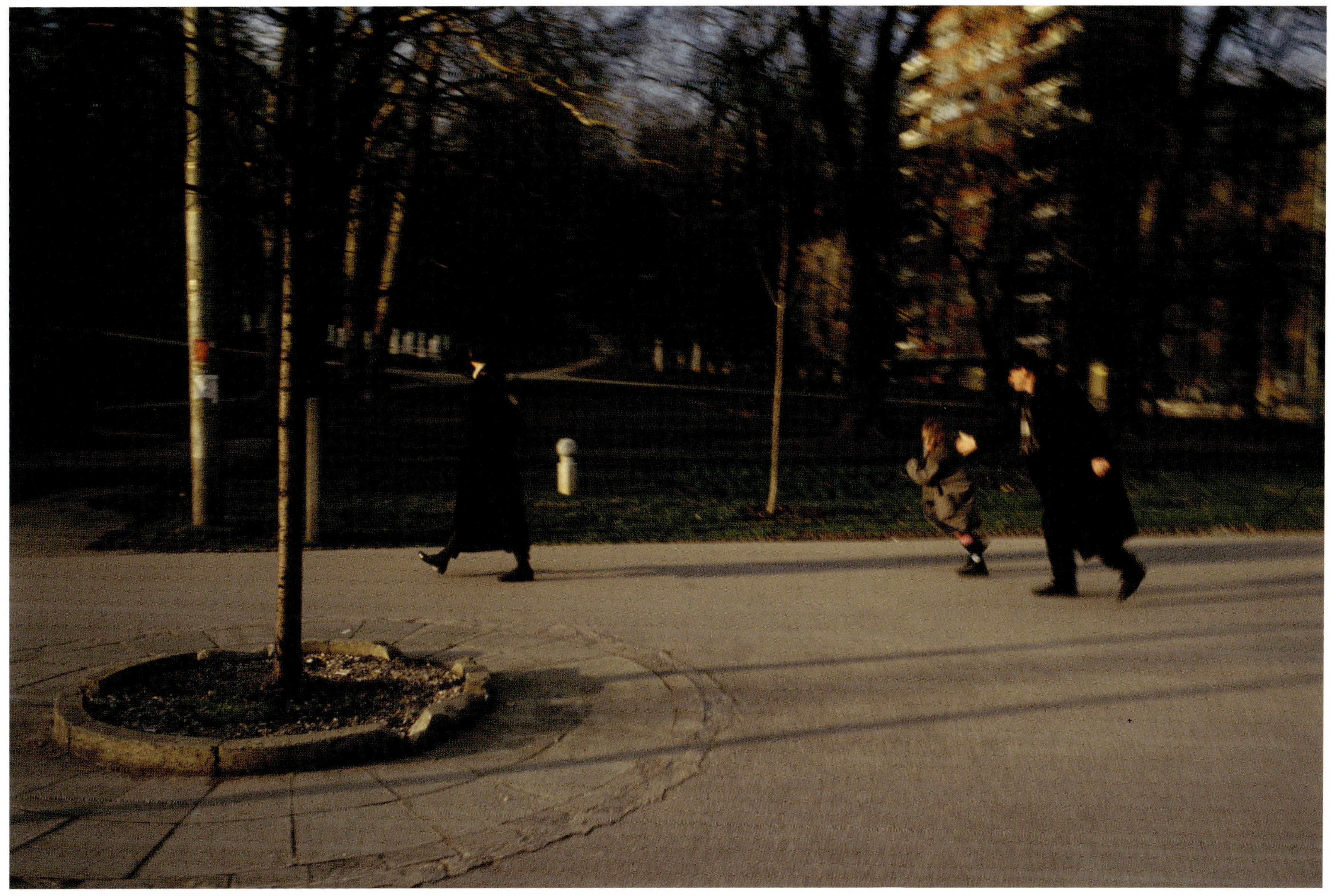

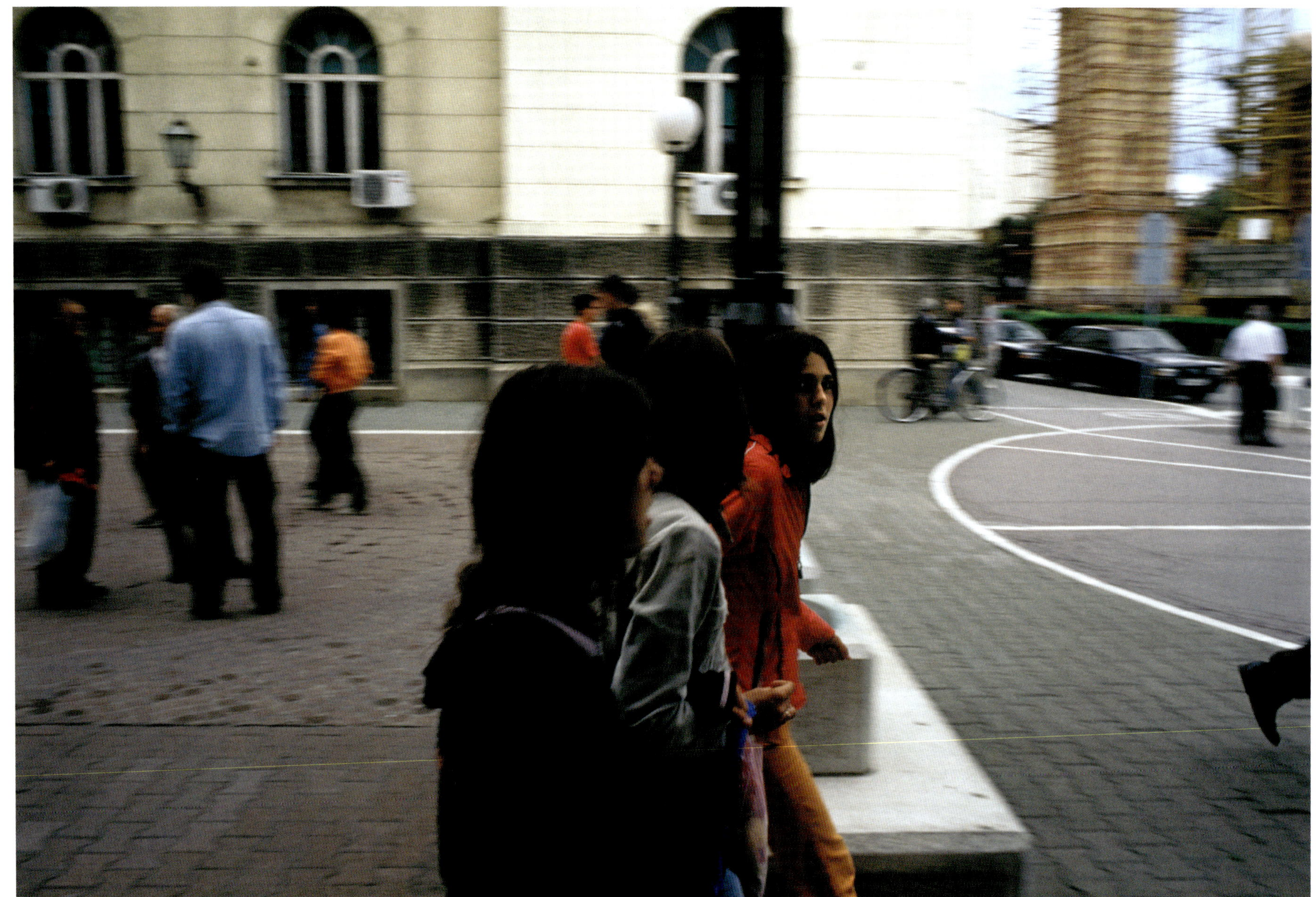

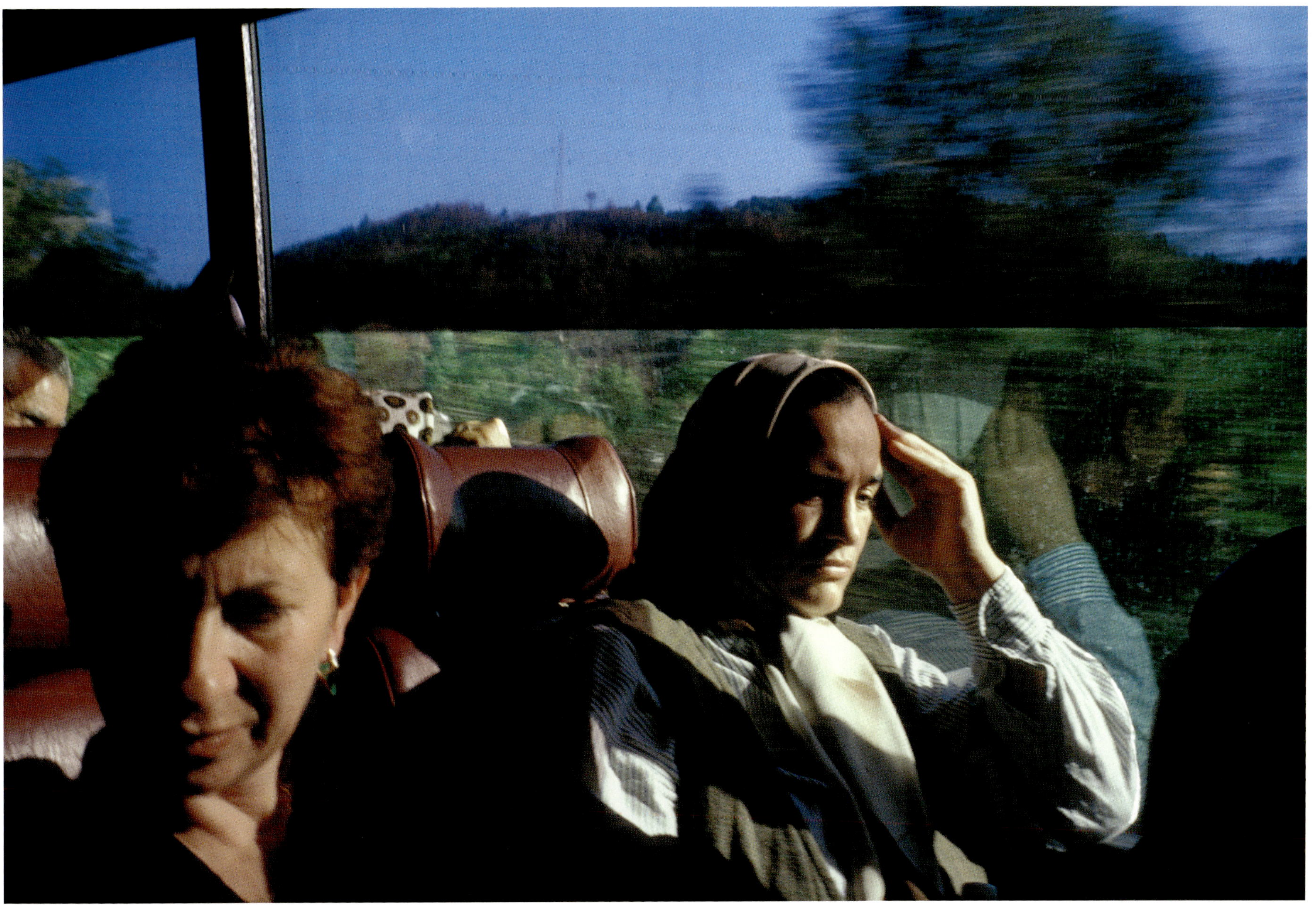

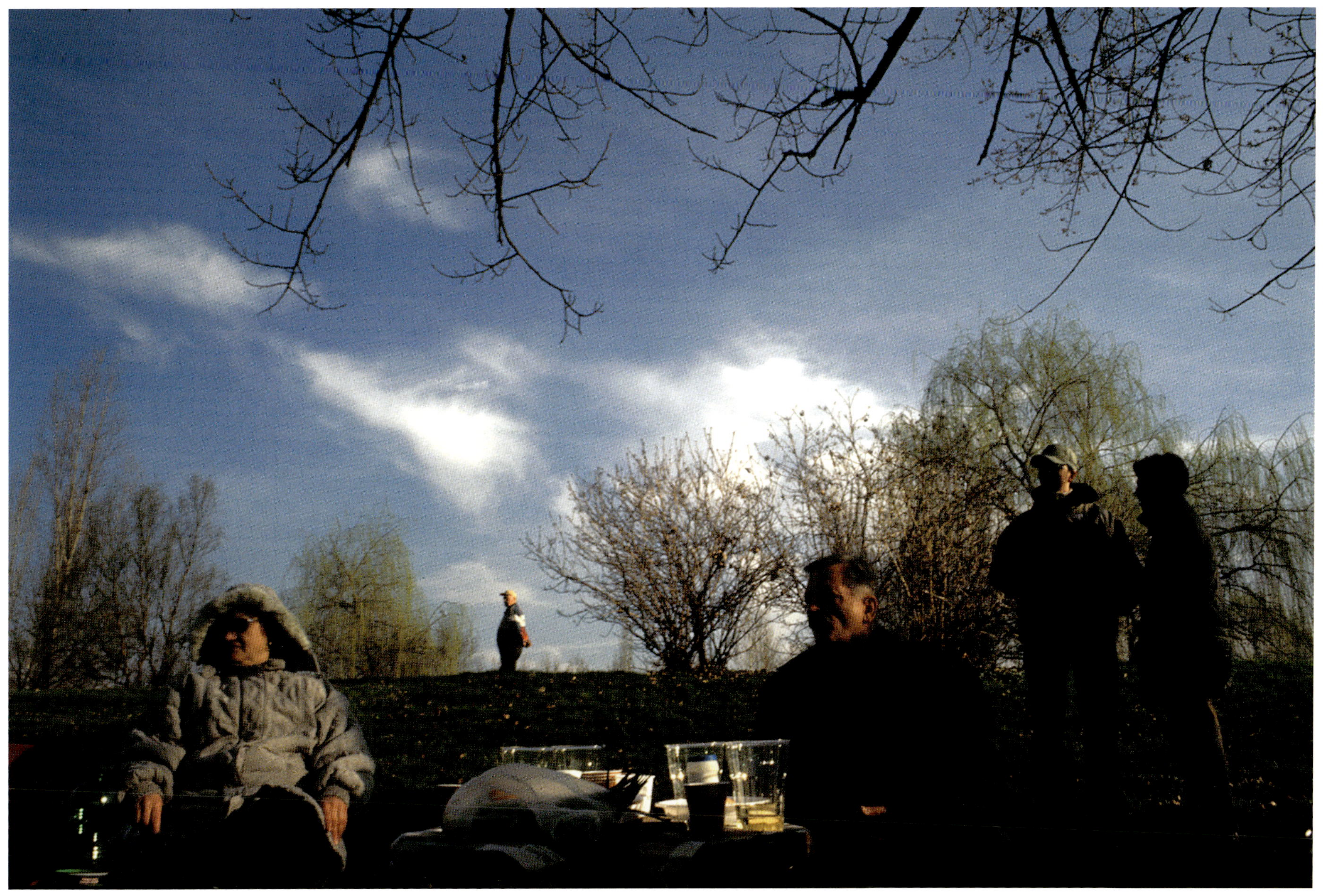

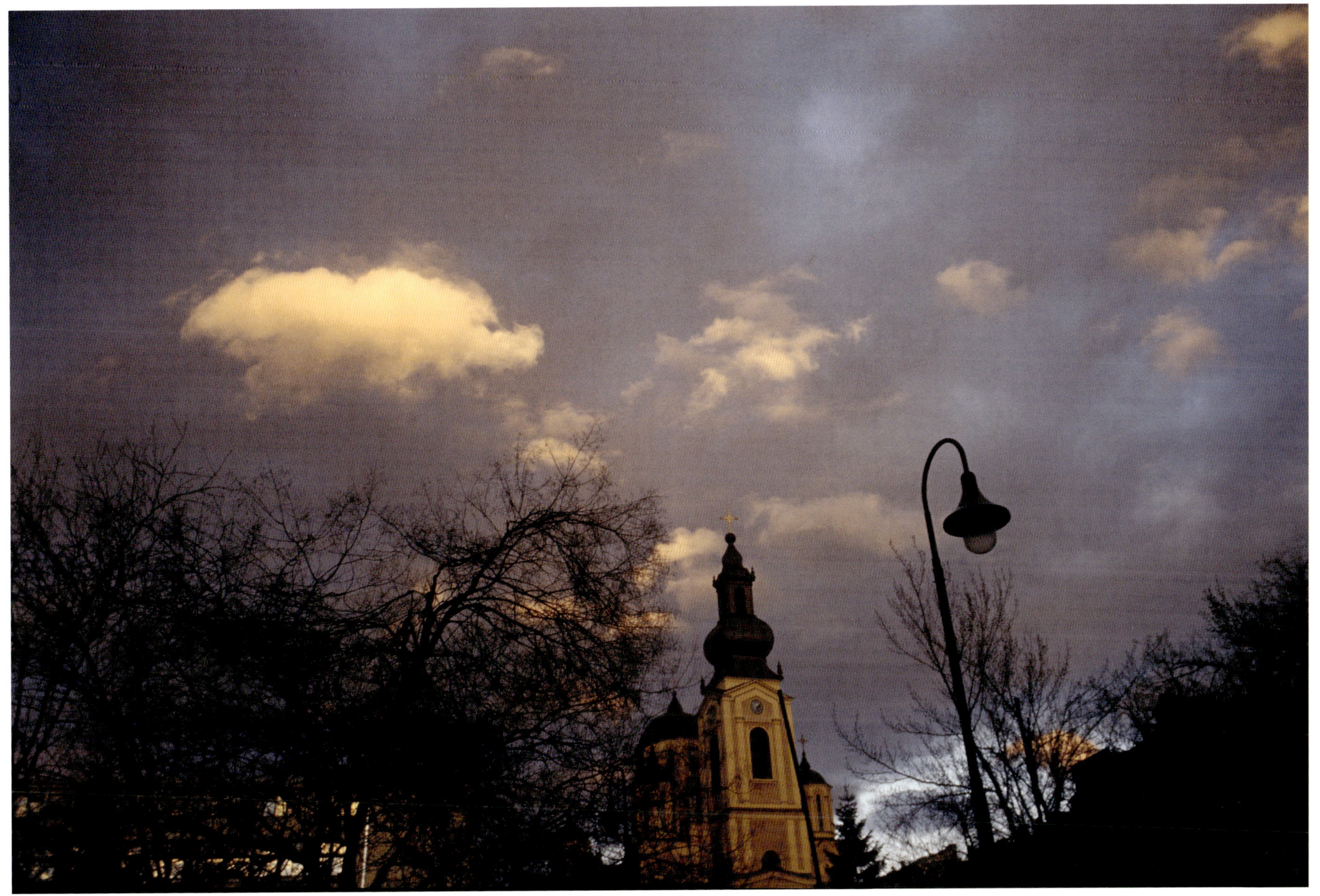

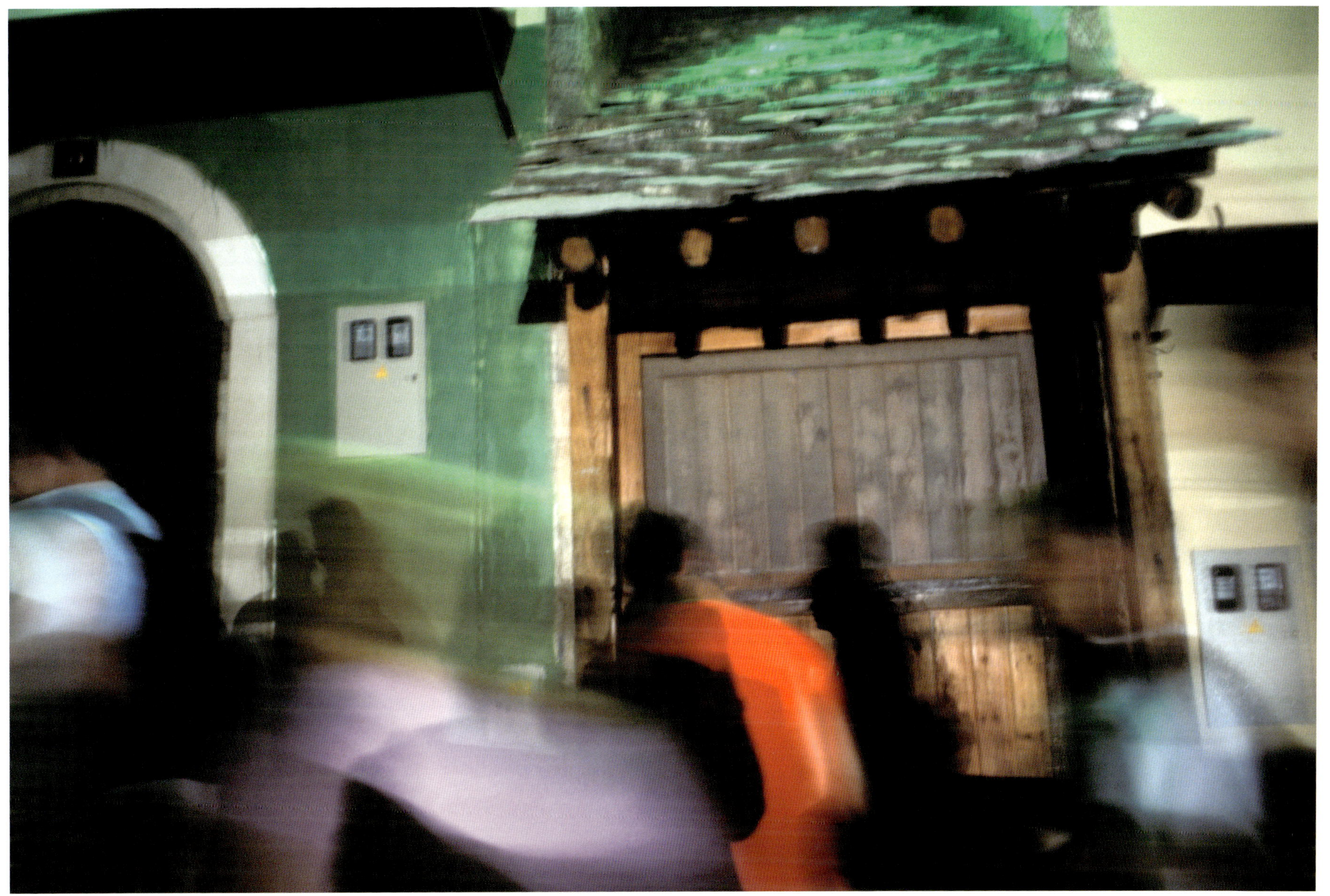

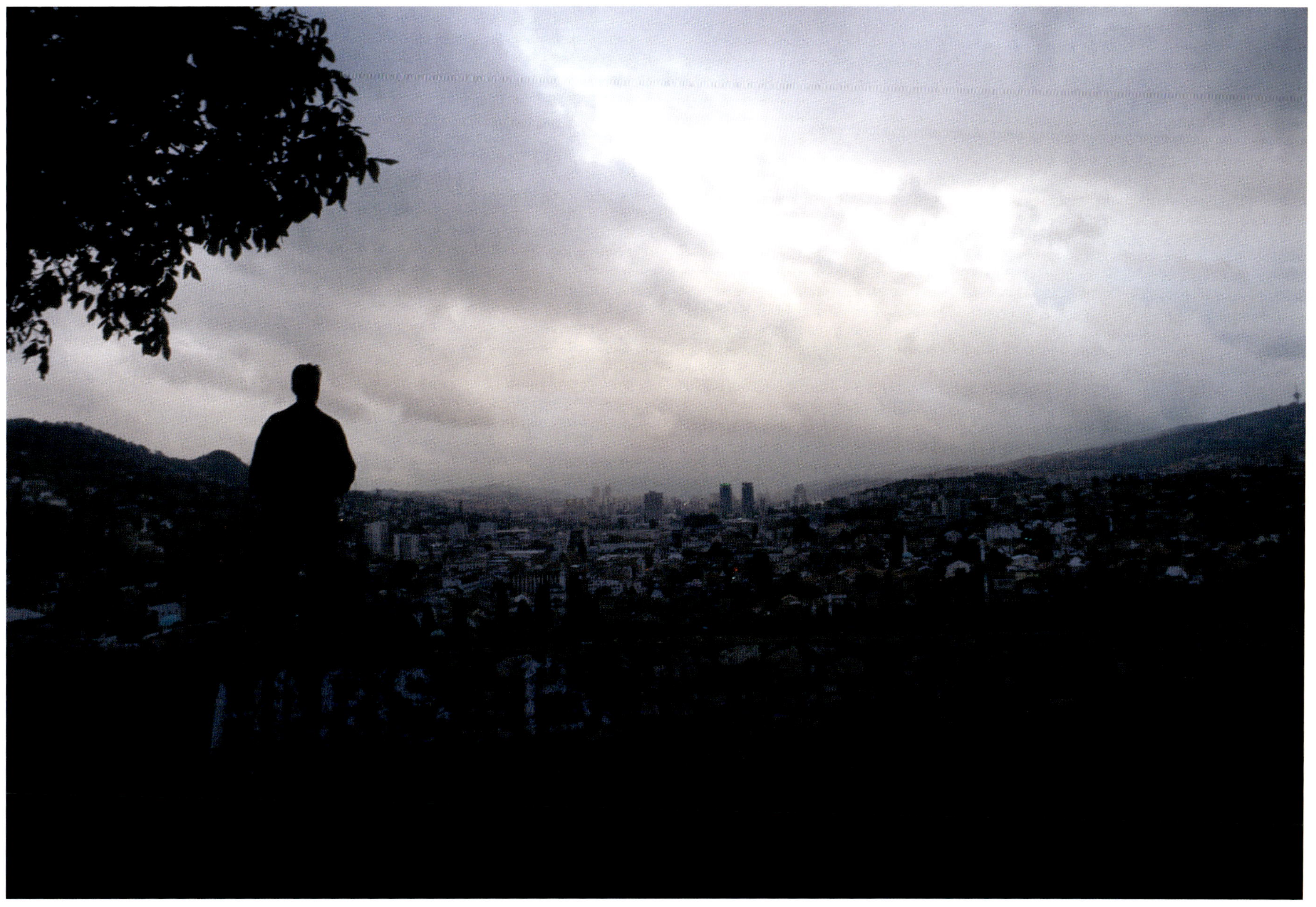

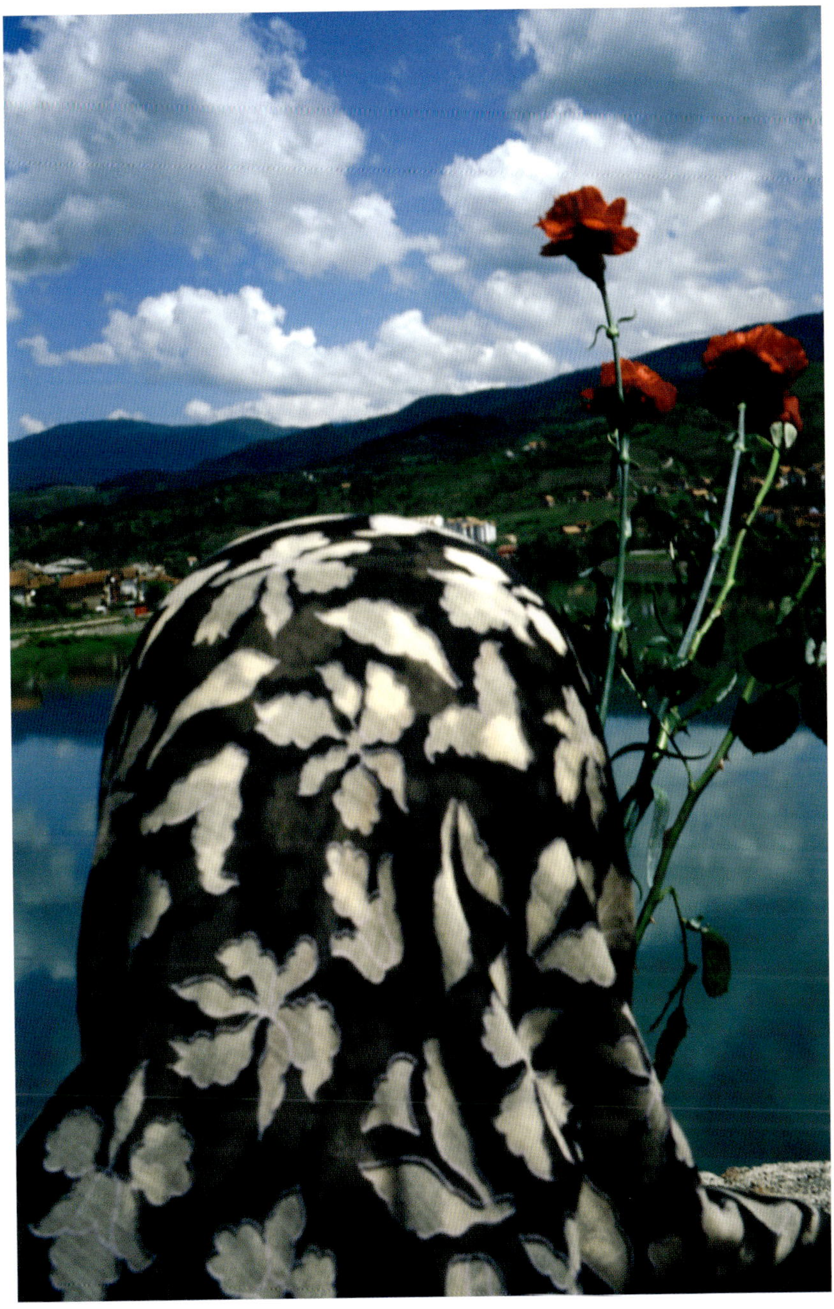

163 A rebuilt store open for business again; the second-floor living quarters remain partly finished, a common sight, even ten years after the end of the war. Many people rely on help from relatives living abroad to rebuild. Kamenica, September 24, 2002.

165 Tourists taking pictures of the rebuilt Mostar Bridge, the day after dedication ceremonies marking the completion of the work. July 24, 2004.

166 A red umbrella floats upside down past a group of picnickers. Zenica, March 21, 2004.

167 A mother pushes a stroller along one of the pathways of the Sarajevo Zoo. During the early months of the 1992-95 war, the international media covered the death of one of the last surviving animals—a bear—prompting an outcry from animal rights activists who demanded an end to the war. Sarajevans, who endured a three-and-a-half year siege of their city by Serb forces while the international community did little to intervene, still comment wryly about the fact that the deaths of the animals in the zoo seemed to create more protests against the war than the deaths of the 10,000 civilians who died during the siege. March 27, 2004.

169 Roma children, squatting with their families in one of the many buildings riddled by mortars during the siege of Sarajevo, play on a junk-littered sidewalk. April 19, 2002.

170a The film set of director Benjamin Filipovic's feature film, "Well-Tempered Corpses," a black comedy scheduled for 2005 release. Bosnia's film industry has been thriving in recent years, with many directors making films with war-related themes. Sarajevo, April 2004.

170b Dedo Fejzic, in shadow, was one of only a handful of Muslims to have returned to Visegrad by the spring of 2002, after being forced out ten years earlier in an "ethnic cleansing" campaign by Serbs, which took the lives of some 2,000 Muslim men and boys in the town, including Fejzic's brother. Fejzic had filed the legal paperwork necessary to reclaim his two homes, which had been occupied by refugee Serbs. He had known the Serb owner of this restaurant before the war, and liked him, but he was uncomfortable eating here the day I met him. He and his wife were also afraid to go out at night, and were uncertain about whether they would remain in Visegrad. A year later, when I returned to look for him, I learned that Fejzic had sold his property to a local Serb and moved to Sarajevo to be closer to his daughter. April 10, 2002.

171 Backstage at the 2002 Miss Bosnia and Hercegovina beauty contest, held at the Holiday Inn. Sarajevo, September 21, 2002.

172 Schoolchildren on a special dress-up day walk through the town of Prijedor. October 3, 2002.

173 A scarved mannequin in old-town Sarajevo is a reflection of the increased interest in Islam among many Bosnian Muslims after the war. Sarajevo, April 2002.

174 Street scene, Mostar. The building in the background was badly damaged during the war and still had not been restored nine years later. March 29, 2004.

175 Roadside scene, north of the city of Banja Luka. Non-Traditional architectural decorations such as painted columns and swans have become popular am ong many returning refugees who lived elsewhere during the war. More than 40 percent of the country's housing stock was destroyed during the 1992-95 war. October 3, 2002.

177 Goldfish for sale along the side of the road in Capljina. March 30, 2004.

179 Coffeehouse scene, with a modern painting on the wall of the old Mostar Bridge and the Turkish architects responsible for building it. The laughing man is Iza Lampa, who often sings with the popular Bosnian group, Mostar Sevdah Reunion. Mostar, September 25, 2002.

180 In the hills above Srebrenica, a Muslim family returns to rebuild a house destroyed during the war. By the year 2000, when record numbers of Bosnians finally felt safe enough to begin returning home, the international community began to suffer "Bosnia fatigue," withdrawing resources and moving to other parts of the world. The result was that only 22 percent of those wanting to return home in 2000 received aid to do so, despite the fact that the right to return home was recognized as one of the founding principles of the Dayton Peace accords, which ended the war in late 1995. October 2000.

181 Street scene, Sarajevo. March 2004.

182 Street scene, Banja Luka. July 28, 2004.

183 Srebrenica widows head back to Sarajevo after a day spent in Srebrenica, where they had gone to see the homes they were forced to leave in 1995, when Serb forces overran their town and massacred 7,000 to 8,000 men and boys. Most of their homes were occupied by Serb refugees after the end of the war, and the women were beginning the legal process of reclaiming their property—and deciding whether they wanted to return to their homes. October 2000.

185 These picnickers arrived at dawn to stake out the site where they will spend the day eating and drinking as part of Zenica's "cimburijada" festival, celebrating the first day of spring. March 21, 2004.

187 The main Serb Orthodox church in Sarajevo is lit by the setting sun. During the 1992-95 siege, Sarajevans respected all the religious and cultural monuments in their city, despite the fact that Serb forces were responsible for the siege. March 2004.

189 Floodlights illumine part of the old town of Mostar, turning passerbys into a colorful blur, during rehearsals for the dedication ceremony of the rebuilt bridge. July 22, 2004.

191 View of Sarajevo. July 2004.

193 A Muslim widow gets ready to throw red carnations into the Drina river, marking the spot where some 2,000 Muslim men and boys were executed during the "ethnic cleansing" campaign waged by Serbs against their neighbors in the early months of the 1992-95 war. The bridge, built during the Ottoman Empire, was made famous by the Nobel-Prize-winning author Ivo Andric in his book, "Bridge on the River Drina." Visegrad, May 25, 2003.

"We are not dying anymore, but Bosnia is on its knees. I just hope you journalists and the rest of the world will pay more attention to Bosnia. It deserves your attention in war; it deserves your attention in peace."

> **danis tanovic,** film director, speaking to the press after winning an Oscar in 2002 for his film about the war, "No Man's Land"

pogovor
AFTERWORD

> LAWRENCE WESCHLER

During my first few months covering the ongoing Yugoslav war-crimes tribunal in The Hague, faced day after day with the appalling sorts of testimony that have become that court's standard fare, I took to repairing as often as possible to the nearby Mauritshuis, so as to commune with the museum's three Vermeers. *Diana and Her Companions*, the *Girl With a Pearl Earring*, the *View of Delft*: astonishing, their capacity to lavish such a centered serenity upon any who come into their purview.

More recently, however, I've increasingly found myself being drawn toward the next room over, the one that houses Rembrandt's *The Anatomy Lesson of Dr. Nicholaes Tulp*. A work from the generation immediately prior to Vermeer's, it was painted in 1632, the very year of Vermeer's birth (the year, for that matter, of John Locke's birth, and Spinoza's as well), when Rembrandt, newly arrived in Amsterdam, was only twenty-six years old. With this astounding canvas, he was brashly hanging out his shingle as an accomplished portraitist. The year 1632 was likewise just about the midpoint of the Thirty Years' War, an incredibly vicious religious struggle that savaged Northern Europe with carnage every bit as harrowing as anything being described nowadays at the tribunal—mayhem that regularly slashed into the Netherlands, until the conflict was finally brought to a (provisional) end with the Treaty of Westphalia in 1648. The war had provided the occasion for the publication, in 1625, of the seminal work by an earlier son of Vermeer's Delft, Hugo Grotius, *On the Law of War and Peace*, a text often considered to be the foundation of all modern international law, and in particular that of these Hague tribunals. And that war's dark imperatives can likewise be seen impinging on Rembrandt's great painting.

The Anatomy Lesson is so famously overexposed, so crusted over with conventional regard, as to be almost impossible to see afresh. And yet, standing before the painting itself, I realized that for all my conventional acquaintance with its image, I'd never really seen it correctly—or, anyway, my memory was wrong in one crucial respect. The professor is poised in mid-lecture beside a cadaver, its left forearm splayed open to reveal all the sinewy musculature just beneath the skin. There is a mountain of onlookers: some gaze out strangely toward us while the rest—and this is the part I remembered most vividly—lean forward, gawking (like us) at all that gore. (Come to think of it, maybe the ones gazing toward us are staring precisely at our own queasiness in the face of such morbidity.)

Only, as I now could plainly see, that's not what was actually happening in Rembrandt's canvas. Of course, the theme of mortality and morbidity is there—rendered all the more unsettling by the conspicuous resemblance between the cadaver's face and those of many of the onlookers. For that matter it cannot be coincidence that the cadaver's face—that, after all, of a common criminal, which is to say the kind of person whose corpse was regularly given over in those days for this sort of dissective display—bears a striking resemblance to the conventional iconography of Christ's own, as in Andrea Mantagna's 1490 depiction of *Lamentation over the Dead Christ*, a possible source for Rembrandt. But the thing is, that cadaver, his face or his arm, is not what the onlookers are focusing upon; death (their own or anybody else's) hardly seems to be on their minds at all. On the contrary, the innermost trio is gazing at the professor's living hand, the one with which he has been demonstrating the grips and gestures made possible by this, and this, and this other newly exposed muscle or tendon. They're looking at it wonderstruck, spellbound, as if they've never before seen anything like it.

For what a marvel of motility it is – with its capacity for compression and extension, for flex and repose, grip and rotation. The hand in itself is a veritable miracle. One is momentarily reminded by the living hand hovering over the recumbent, still lifeless body of that other great painterly trope of creative dexterity: God's own hand extended toward the recumbent Adam's in Michelangelo's Sistine Chapel (an image that was surely known to Rembrandt from the countless etchings then circulating throughout the Netherlands). More to the point, a flexing hand – the focus of all this awed attention – is a painter's own foremost implement, the one with which he wields his brush. You can just imagine Rembrandt painting the picture, his own actual hand burnishing the professor's painted one as the painted class gazes on in hushed astonishment. (Indeed, at the moment of painting, the ones now gazing out at us would, of course, have been gazing at him.) This is a painting, then, about looking at hands, about vision and malleability – about the fundamentals of painting itself.

Or, more generally, about living. It's not, as we are sometimes given to recalling, a morbid dwelling upon death but rather a celebration, a defiant affirmation of life and liveliness and vitality generated, as it happens, at a moment when the world was choking with death and dying.

All of which brought me back to the tribunal, and to those hours I'd been spending hunched in the visitors' gallery, taking in the endless tales of horror and grisly death. I thought about the judges and the lawyers, the investigators and the forensic anthropologists. And I realized how, appearances to the contrary, all their labors aren't about death at all but rather about life and the living. They are about the living witness owed to every one of the once-living victims. "In these matters," the Polish poet Zbigniew Herbert (writing in the shadow of his own country's genocide-saturated history) insisted, "we must not be wrong / even by a single one / we are despite everything / the guardians of our brothers." They are about securing the possibility of an ongoing life for the survivors (the widows of Srebrenica, for instance, still stranded in limbo, straining for justice, or at least for confirmation of the fate of their loved ones). They are about healing a community once ravaged by war, so that liveliness can come flowing back over an otherwise blighted terrain. They are about the lives of generations yet to come, about breaking that cycle of atrocity followed by impunity, which plays such a large role in provoking atrocious communal retribution decades down the line. And, finally, they are about restoring the equilibrium of the living world itself, the world we all share. For, as Herbert concluded in his history-laden poem, "ignorance about those who have disappeared / undermines the reality of the world." It's a lesson that Rembrandt, too, was busy teaching.

And so you will doubtless understand what first drew me to this marvelous collection of Sara Terry's photographs on the aftermath of war in Bosnia. Indeed, you won't have much trouble guessing which was the very image that first grabbed my attention. That remarkable photograph of her friend Ewa, the white-haired Polish forensic anthropologist, reaching down (Tulp-like, Sistine-like) to grasp the almost-as-if-it-could-still-be-alive hand of that only-just-now-exhumed cadaver, further evidence of a terrible massacre coming on a decade ago – reaching down tenderly to cusp it in an act overbrimming with living witness.

The thing is, though: that's not what held me with this collection. Or rather, there turned out to be so much more. Many of us who have been following Bosnia and the former Yugoslavia over the past decade have been somewhat fixated on those issues of precise accounting, steadfast accountability, transitional justice, and the like. And while the ongoing playing out of all those processes will indeed prove vital to the return of life and the lively in those war-ravaged lands, Sara Terry is on to the fact that there is both more and less involved: that life goes on no matter what, for better or for worse, and as agonizing as it is to acknowledge, more often than not for the better. Because the world – the world in color (particularly one so splendidly captured as this) – is just so ravishingly beautiful. And the people in it so endlessly resourceful and given over to surprise.

My own master in all of this is another Pole, the poet Wislawa Szymborska, who has been plumbing some of these same themes in her recent poems. "Reality demands," she notes in one poem (of that title), "that we mention this: / Life goes on. / It continues at Cannae and Borodino / at Kosovo Polje and Guernica." Letters, she notes, "fly back and forth / between Pearl Harbor and Hastings..." And, indeed, "There is so much of Everything / that Nothing is hidden quite nicely." How "Where not a stone still stands, / you can see the Ice Cream Man / besieged by children." This terrifying world, she points out, "is not devoid of charms / of the mornings / that make waking up worthwhile." And in concluding, she highlights the way that "On tragic mountain passes / the wind rips hats from unwitting heads / and we can't help / laughing at that."

If you want to see what she means, just browse through these pages, rediscovering reality through Sara Terry's wise and gleaming vantage.

Szymborska titles another poem "The End and the Beginning," and she begins it by noting that "After every war, / someone has to tidy up. / Things won't pick / themselves up after all." Around the middle of the poem she acknowledges that "Someone, broom in hand, / still remembers how it was. / Someone else listens, nodding / his unshattered head." But in the very next stanza she further acknowledges how "others are bound to be bustling nearby / who'll find all that / a little boring." And she ends the poem by asserting, as does Sara Terry, as does Sara Terry in her own way again and again, that "Someone has to lie there / in the grass that covers up / the causes and the effects / with a cornstalk in his teeth / gawking at clouds."

So that perhaps now you will understand how I intend what I mean when I say that for all its capacious empathy and its lucid attentiveness in the face of near unspeakable pathos, what really captivates me in this collection is how blasted wide open Sara Terry is, time and again, to the possibility of being hijacked by gladness and light.

Lawrence Weschler is the director of the New York Institute for the Humanities at NYU. He is the author, most recently, of *Vermeer in Bosnia: Selected Essays*. His remarks on *Rembrandt's Anatomy Lesson* are excerpted from an article, which first appeared in *The Atlantic* and will be expanded upon in his forthcoming book, *Everything that Rises: A Book of Convergences*. The Szymborska translations are by Stanislaw Baranczak and Claire Cavanaugh and are included in the poet's *Poems New and Collected (1957-1997)*.

zahvalnice
ACKNOWLEDGMENTS

Those who deserve thanks beyond measure:

The dozens of Bosnians who have allowed me to enter their lives, some only for a moment, others for the unfoldment of friendships that continue to this day. This book would not exist without them.

Greg Auberry, Melinda Burrell, Nancy Shalala and the local staff of Catholic Relief Services in Bosnia for the many invaluable ways they supported this work and helped me explore the story of aftermath.

Keziah Conrad of the Pontanima Choir for allowing me to use part of her interview with Daniela Torbic, whose thoughtful words open the last chapter of this book.

Blue Earth Alliance, *www.blueearth.org*, and Malcolm Edwards for being the first to believe in this project and for supporting it so wholeheartedly through the years.

The scores of people – many of whom I have never met – who contributed financial support to this work, especially the following, who I also count as dear friends: Bonnie Bassett, Elisabeth Hoffman and The Catalyst Fund, Alan Webber and Frances Diemoz, Jackson Rappaport, Margaret Terry, Eda Roth, Jim and Carla Farrell, Cathy Karen, Molly Bingham, Gail Rothenberg and John Levy, Jim Henderson and Leonard Volk.

James Crump for his vision, patience, and partnership. Lawrence Weschler for his moving insight and eloquence.
Linda Johnson/Swell Design for bringing such grace to the design of this book.
Peter Ruyffelaere at Ludion for embracing this work and helping to bring it to a wider audience.

Diana Avakian-Stoneson, *www.aestheticsworldwide.com*, for so capably maintaining
and updating my project website, *www.bosniaftermath.com*. George Day for donating his time
and skill in designing and launching the site.

The many, many friends who offered a sharp eye and a kind word when I was in need, including:
Daniel Milnor, Rebecca Norris Webb, Nancy Foley, John Trotter, Darius Himes, Elizabeth Rappaport,
Frish Brandt, Timathea Workman, Denise Wolff, David Yoder, and Glenn Ruga.

Thanks, as well, to JP Pappis and Polaris Images for believing in and representing this work.

To Jeff Jacobson, Paolo Pellegrin, and Sam Abell – who each helped me answer the right question at the right time –
I owe more than they will ever know.

And finally, my heart's gratitude and love to Reeves,
who understood so well during the making of this work that they also serve who stand and wait.